Tony Urbina

S0-BCG-696

Also by SYLVESTER PETRO
The Labor Policy of the Free Society

A REPORT ON
THE McCLELLAN COMMITTEE HEARINGS

Power Unlimited

THE CORRUPTION OF
UNION LEADERSHIP

BY

Sylvester Petro

THE RONALD PRESS COMPANY

New York

Copyright, ©, 1959, by
The Ronald Press Company

All Rights Reserved

No part of this book may be reproduced
in any form without permission in writ-
ing from the publisher.

2

PRINTED IN THE UNITED STATES OF AMERICA

Library of Congress Catolog Card Number: 59–9560

To

HELEN

and

April and *David* and *Sam*

The greatest tyranny has the smallest beginnings. From precedents overlooked, from remonstrances despised, from grievances treated with ridicule, from powerless men oppressed with impunity and overbearing men tolerated with complacence, springs the tyrannical usage which generations of wise and good men may hereafter perceive and lament and resist in vain.

————*The London Times* (1845)

PREFACE

America is in danger—not so much from without as from within. The threat from Soviet Russia, serious as it is, need not panic us so long as our free institutions survive, for the freedom which has made us strong will, if preserved, make us stronger still. Our danger lies basically in the abandonment of our main strength—the principle of freedom under law. More immediately, it lies in the excessive power and special privileges of the big unions. Exploiting those privileges to form socially abusive industry-wide monopolies which they incorrectly call trade unions, the union leaders have brought about a state of affairs so menacing as to demand the immediate attention of all citizens and their representatives in Congress.

The Senate Select Committee headed by Senator John L. McClellan has gathered a great many facts about labor relations and pinned them down where they can be scrutinized. It has provided a long, connected view of events of which the public at large has had only sporadic glimpses, as of lightning flashes in the night, fearful when seen but soon forgotten. Workers and businessmen have long been buffers between the large unions and the public, absorbing shocks which were then passed on in muffled tremors, neither sharply felt nor clearly understood. In recording the multiple injuries which businessmen and workers have been receiving and for which the public has been paying in a thousand ways, all grievous, the McClellan Committee has performed a service of the first order. And I, as both a citizen and a student of labor relations, herewith express my appreciation.

This book could not have been written without the facts recorded by the Committee. Yet a book such as this has had to be written. The public does not read records which run to forty volumes. Furthermore, the McClellan Record does not interpret itself. The facts are there, but what they mean, and, above all, what they call for—these are something else again.

I have concluded from careful study of the whole Record that the failures of government, and the unlimited trade-union power and corruption there revealed, if permitted to run their course, can destroy us. I believe, moreover, that any person who reads this book from beginning to end, without prejudice, will come to the same conclusion.

The McClellan Record demonstrates that governments at all levels in this country have failed to apply the law of the land faithfully and vigorously to abusive union conduct, conduct which would not be permitted to other persons or organizations. It further demonstrates that unions have taken great advantage of this special privilege to defy the laws, precepts, and principles of the good society. Working men have been beaten and robbed. Businessmen have been the victims of extortion. Consumers have been exploited. Political figures and governmental officers and agencies have been corrupted. Few significant areas of society have been left uncontaminated. Out of unlimited power, unlimited corruption is breeding.

Let there be no mistake about it. The failure of government to perform its duty to the people is the fundamental cause of the evils disclosed by the McClellan Record. With government become as vast as it is, and with the laws become as proliferated as they are, we yet have in labor relations little government and less *law*. We have, instead, a series of special privileges for abusive and destructive trade-union conduct. The super-state has enmeshed honest and productive citizens in a debilitating tangle of contradictory rules and regulations, while nourishing the lust of the vicious and the unscrupulous, and tolerating their abuses with complacency, till now they threaten, not only the society which produces for them, but also the governmental officials who have been feeding them. In labor relations, freedom has become a fugitive, trapped, its arms held by a giant state while giant unions slug it.

Out of the wilderness of conflicting rules and the jungle of special privilege, the looters and destroyers who figure so largely in the McClellan Hearings have emerged with unlimited econ-

omic power and fearful political power. They have made the
most of an environment cut to their qualities.

*   *   *

This book has been written in order to provide an accurate
summary of the McClellan Committee disclosures and to alert
the public to the deficiencies and the positive evils of some of
the "reforms" proposed in Congress. Much of such legislation
deals only with superficialities, leaving basic causes untouched.
Worse than that, not only would such proposals confirm the
existing special privileges which have drawn to trade unions a
great many vicious and unscrupulous men—they would add
even more, and thus make worse the shocking conditions which
now exist. The sponsors of such legislation must be made to
learn that it is unacceptable.

Part I of this book describes the pattern of conduct and the
undesirable social consequences which the McClellan Record
reveals. Part II explains the governmental deficiencies which
give rise to the untoward conduct and consequences disclosed
by the Record. Part III is an attempt to show that the abuses
disclosed in the McClellan Record are basic and that unless
removed they must go on and on till they destroy us, or reduce
us to something less than the good and free society which we
wish to be and can be.

This book reflects the McClellan Record faithfully, although
it no more equals the Record's fullness and detail than the Record
itself duplicates the fullness and detail of life. Violence, coercion,
shakedowns, racketeering, regimentation of industry, abuse of
workers, employers, and the public, and the failure of government to protect the law-abiding from the lawless—all so much
a part of labor relations in this country—are only selectively
presented in the Record. For every corrupting and abusive
incident carried there, thousands have occurred in life.

Consider but one of the fundamental evils disclosed in the
Record: the imposition of union membership upon unwilling
employees by violence, coercive picketing, secondary boycotts,
and compulsory-unionism "contracts." Against the instances
found in the Record, and they are numerous and brutal enough,

hundreds are to be found in law cases outside the Record, though even more carefully documented there. Many, many more have never reached either the law courts or the McClellan Committee. It is not true, as some have said, that the McClellan Record exaggerates the existing evils among the large unions. No printed text could do so, and the McClellan Record does not.

The remedies set forth in the concluding chapter of this book are based upon the social, economic, and legal principles which I have set forth at length in a previous book, *The Labor Policy of the Free Society* (Ronald, 1957). In that book I tried to reason out, first, the aims and operating principles of the free society which all Americans desire; and second, measures designed to secure in labor relations the state of affairs required for a free, productive, and strong society. That book was based upon the factual assumption that conditions in labor relations were bad. The McClellan Record confirms that assumption in every respect.

The proposals offered here are basically the same ones offered there. They are few in number and unspectacular in character, but I am confident that they are sound and solid. They do not involve billions of dollars in additional taxes; on the contrary, they will cost less than we are spending now in the production of more and more commotion with less and less law. They do not require vast increases in the federal bureaucracy; on the contrary, they will reduce it materially, and thus remove the privileged sanctuary in which power and corruption are breeding. They will lessen the number of rules and regulations, but they will increase *law*. They will take away the unlimited power of some to abuse others, but they will in the process enlarge the freedom of all. They will slowly but surely remove the menace which now confronts us, while at the same time strengthening and defending the right of working men to have unions of their own choosing—unions which are their servants, not their masters.

* * *

The special privileges which trade unions possess are in the highest degree destructive—destructive of the individual rights of working men and businessmen, of our economic system, and ultimately of our legal, political, and moral framework. Un-

checked, the conduct growing out of these special privileges
would bring an end to law and order and subject all to the rule
of the arrogant, the racketeers, and the strong-arm men they both
employ. Seeing the pattern whole after almost two years of
unsurpassed service to the nation as Chairman of the Senate
Select Committee, Senator John L. McClellan said: "If followed
to its logical conclusion, it will lead eventually back to the
law of the jungle." (Transcript, 667) The problem, to echo
the Chairman again, is whether "the Congress will have courage
enough to enact some legislation to protect the working people
of the country against exploitation." (14509)

Our society is a good one, possibly the best that has ever
been. It is now in danger, and unless we are content to succumb
we must do what we can to study that danger, understand its
causes, and hit upon a true policy to meet and defeat it. These
are the objectives of this book.

Sylvester Petro

New York City
  February, 1959

CONTENTS

Part I

POWER UNLIMITED — CORRUPTION UNLIMITED

Power tends to corrupt and absolute power corrupts absolutely.

—Lord Acton

Chapter 1

THE PANORAMA OF
POWER AND CORRUPTION

Coercion marks the beginning and corruption the conclusion of the march of union power observable in the McClellan Record. The process begins with the use of compulsion
to secure members. Thereafter new and different coercive devices are used to bind the unwilling employees to the union.
After a union has learned the usefulness of coercion in increasing
membership, it falls into the habit of using even more in disputes with employers.

Some trade union leaders hold that any employer who
resists their demands is an "enemy of the labor movement"
who must be taught a lesson, and, if he continues to resist,
must be exterminated. If employees themselves refuse to
acquiesce in strikes, if, instead, they exercise their right
to continue working during strikes, they are considered traitors,
against whom brutal reprisals are not only permissible but
praiseworthy.

Law-enforcement officials sometimes stand in the way, however, and it therefore becomes necessary to take care of them,
too. Pure bribery is not always the appropriate method here,
and often a generous campaign contribution will do as well. If
the laws of the land pose an obstacle to the use of union power
against traitorous employers and employees, then the laws must
be changed, and full-scale political action, largely financed by
membership dues contributed in a substantial degree by workers
of differing political views, is the appropriate vehicle of change.
Candidates who support the unions' claims of special privileges

3

to coerce and compel get extensive, expensive, and enthusiastic political support; those who insist that the laws of the land should apply to trade unions are marked for extinction. Too often the unions have their way, although a startling exception here and there indicates that the black night has not yet fallen.

Meanwhile, alongside the structure of traditional unionism, there begins to grow in its shadow a murky pseudo-unionism. A two-stage process is at work. Frequent use of coercion and violence by traditional unions induces their leaders to include on their staffs—alongside college-trained economists—men with criminal records and backgrounds of brutality; if dirty work is to be done, it is just as well to have a person around who has had some experience with it. And the practical privilege to coerce, to extort, to shake down, to compel (such as has accrued to the unions) is precisely what the denizens of the underworld, the professionals of organized crime, have been searching for most avidly, ever since the rich pickings under Prohibition dried up.

If a single picket will harm a business badly enough to make the owner sign up with the union, maybe it will also serve to shake loose some immediate money. In either case the picket line is coercive, and if it is a specially privileged form of coercion in the one case, why not in the other? Thus the professional extortionist discovers a new tool for his trade, and thus too are born "racket-picketing" and its associated shake-down techniques.

Convicted criminals are in the unions then with both feet—as adjuncts to traditional unions, and on their own, cynically using the form of unionism as a cover for their age-old methods of getting ahead in the world. The one thing they have never learned is how to work for a living. As union agents and leaders they live very well off the product of those who have learned how to make a living through socially useful work—the businessmen and workingmen of the country.

Although society at large may know very little about all this, it pays the bill—an overwhelming, extortionate, and destructive bill. A shakedown induced by "stranger-picketing" has to be made up by the businessman somehow. It results in higher prices. But that is by no means the only kind of unnecessary and unjustified price increase which the customer has to pay. It is not even, relatively speaking, very important. When a traditional union gets higher wages by violently preventing employers from operating with workers who are willing to take less money, the public as a whole is the victim of unlawful extortion. The cost of living goes up. Fewer people can afford to buy the goods at the higher prices. Therefore there is less demand for those goods, and soon some of the workers must be laid off. Unemployment is the necessary result when unions insist on higher wages than the market will bear. They, not businessmen, have thrown people—their own members at that—out of work.

The situation is not made any better by the shrill accusations of the union leaders against businessmen about the high cost of living and unemployment. The plain fact is that no businessman ever *likes* to cut back production. He does so only when he has to. More often than not the union leader has been responsible for pricing union members out of the market. For that he ought to be fired, or law and law enforcement ought to be rigorous enough to keep him from abusing workers, union members, businessmen, and the public.

The point cannot be emphasized enough. The harm done by criminals masquerading as union officials is enormous and filled with the most ominous signs for the future of society. But it is still less than that produced by the power of the traditional unions. They daily coerce and brutally attack workers who decline to join or refuse to participate in strikes. They throw out of work hundreds of thousands of men because of their artificially inflated wage costs. They create irresistible inflationary pressures and compound the evil by encouraging costly and destructive deficit-spending by governments. Through the use of legal and political special privileges, they tie up entire industries into tight monopolies and cartels which abuse the public and threaten the destruction of the free and competitive economy which has always been the American ideal.

This is the panorama of union power. Traditional unions have secured for themselves special privileges which vest in them unlimited power. This power, like any other unlimited power, can only be abused, and it is abused. Violence and economic coercion by themselves create socially harmful conditions, the consequences of which are infinite and unpredictable. Besides, they exert a magnetic force, drawing to the trade unions some of the worst types of criminals, who find there an environment which suits them. The combination is a destructive force which no society can long survive: on the one hand, abuse of the citizenry and impairment of peaceful, progressive, productive activity; on the other hand, dissolution of the moral and political structure. In the special privileges of coercion and compulsion which unions have gained, there breeds a rotten growth which corrupts the whole moral and political structure of society.

Chapter 2

ORGANIZING FROM THE TOP

I own you. No matter where you . . . move, you are mine.

* * *

. . . finally we agreed that we were much too small, and . . . we signed recognition papers without a vote, and without a show of cards, and simply organization from the top.

* * *

The ultimate goal of the large affiliated unions is control of all American workers. They intend to secure such power in one way or another. If workers will not yield voluntarily, unions will exercise compulsion through employers, even though they must regiment all industry in order to do so and violate the fundamental principles of national labor policy as well. But violating fundamental principle tends to produce unforeseen and unwanted results. In labor relations it is becoming increasingly difficult to tell the difference between racketeering and traditional unionism.

The fundamental principle of modern labor relations law is free employee choice. Whenever employees want a union to represent them, they are entitled to have the one of their choice. Their employer may not refuse to deal with it; he may not fire them for joining it; he may not even threaten them with reprisals. That is the law. The other side of the story is that workers are equally entitled to reject union representation, and unless they freely choose union membership, their employer is required by law to refrain from dealing with any union. In fact, an employer who recognizes a union which his employees have not chosen commits a wrong—an unfair labor practice.

7

Yet, one union after another has used coercive methods to compel recognition against the wishes of employees. The types of coercion have been many, ranging from powerful boycotts of various kinds to outright violence, vandalism, and sabotage.

It is often simpler to compel an employer to force his employees into a union than it is to persuade the employees themselves that a union best serves their interests. Sometimes stubborn employees can be "organized" only through such compulsion. For the shadow union there is another advantage. If the employees have thus been regimented, the union does not need to be very solicitous about them, for they have nowhere to go.

It becomes a travesty. Racketeers work out a mode of conduct which leaves collective bargaining, labor relations, even the employees, except as a source of revenue, completely out of the scheme of things. The picketing and boycotting and violence which can compel an employer to recognize a union are useful to compel him to do many other things. They can make him use one product rather than another—a juke box provided by a friend of the union leader, rather than one distributed by some outsider. They can make the employer quit dealing with anyone who has in one way or another antagonized the union leader.

The besieged employer is mainly interested in getting back into business. If destruction of his business is the only alternative, it takes an extraordinarily stiff-backed employer to resist a shakedown. The picketing and boycotting "union" may have no interest in the employees as such; its leader, when he is really nothing more than a racketeer, will agree, if the price is right, not to bother the employer with any wage or welfare demands. And this is the origin of the "sweetheart" contract: a contract which does nothing more than confirm existing wage rates and other conditions of employment. Its real function is to smooth the way for a payoff, but it also serves often to keep other unions away from the employees.

The pattern is clear. It begins with a special privilege to coerce, vested in traditional unions on the false but popular conception that unions are public servants, rather than pure self-interest minority groups which can gain benefits for their members only at the expense of the most defenseless persons in society (see Chapters 8–11). They use this privilege to regiment all the employers and employees they can reach. The abuses which special privileges make possible are an invitation to the predators; here is a way to easy money. Thugs and racketeers invade the true unions and set up their own pseudo-unions. Soon it becomes difficult to distinguish between the two; for if it is true that "by their acts they shall be known," there is no solid basis of distinction. Their acts are the same.

Stranger-Picketing

"Stranger-picketing" means patrolling by a union which does not represent the employees of the picketed business. It is used for many purposes, ranging from forcing an employer to recognize a union as exclusive bargaining representative, to compelling the employer to quit dealing with some other employer (usually because that other employer's employees have rejected the union), monopolizing an industry, forcing union membership upon unwilling employees, shaking down the employer, and making him buy or use a product in which the picketing union has a financial interest. The objectives may vary, but the method is always the same.

Donald Skaff demonstrated to the McClellan Committee how stranger-picketing works. Employing forty-five workers, the Skaff Company was approached by Teamsters Local 332 in Flint, Michigan. The union presented for the company's signature a collective agreement. As Mr. Skaff, Secretary of the Company, put it: "The overriding theme in the entire incident is that we were prepared to have a vote of the employees involved from the very first day that we were approached by the teamsters. They were unwilling to have a vote. They wanted to organize from the top, and have us sign, and not have a vote of the employees." (6428)

The union resisted an election, Mr. Skaff's testimony disclosed, because the employees did not wish it to represent them

(6429). What was Mr. Skaff to do? The National Labor Relations Board would not take the case and order an election; the business was too small. On the other hand, the Michigan State Mediation Board offered no assistance. It could order an election only if the union agreed to it. Its advice, according to Mr. Skaff, was to yield: "the mediation board recommended that we join the union, since it was simply a case of who is the strongest." (6429)

Mr. Skaff decided to fight it out, and he continued to fight, even after the union set up its stranger picket line and engaged in the various forms of violence described in the following chapter. But the union's blockade ultimately proved irresistible. According to Mr. Skaff, the union's economic power could hold "our merchandise away from us, so we could not do business." (6431) Three months after Mr. Skaff had refused to sign, because "we still had a little fight left in us," the firm had reached its limit of endurance: "finally we agreed that we were much too small, and . . . we signed recognition papers without a vote, and without a show of cards, and simply organization from the top." (6433)

Some may consider Skaff at fault for saddling his employees with a union which they were never allowed to express their own opinion upon. The fact is, however, that a great many employers have been coerced in the same way, and many have felt that destruction of their businesses, with consequent unemployment, was the greater evil. The Record itself, newspaper stories, and court decisions demonstrate the frequency with which stranger-picketing has been a successful method of organizing from the top.

The employees do not really count in these cases. As a matter of fact there do not need to be any employees as of the time of the picketing. Far from it being a matter of employees as free men choosing a union, unions frequently make arrangements among themselves as to which employees will "belong" to them, as the Teamsters and Upholsterers did in connection with a new plant established by the Englander Company in San Leandro, California. Joseph M. Dillon, director of the warehouse division of the Western Conference of Teamsters, explained to the Committee:

> I was instructed by one of my superiors to assist in a picket line in connection with the upholsterers union, whereby after the plant was organized they were to take the production workers and we were to take the warehousemen and shipping clerks.

Chief Counsel Kennedy asked: "Did the Englander Co. have any employees at the time?" Mr. Dillon replied:

> I thought at first . . . that they did not. But I have since checked my office and I find out that they did have 4 or 5 people in the plant at the time.

Apparently wishing to get the point entirely clear, Counsel Kennedy then said: "And you were going to split the employees up with the upholsterers union?" Mr. Dillon said: "That is correct." (6209)

This case is a definitive example of organizing from the top. It reveals a common attitude among unions toward the principle of free employee choice. The national labor policy takes the position that employees have a right to unions of their own choosing; but unions insist upon the right to employees of their own choosing. Perhaps this is the kind of "virtual slavery" which Chairman McClellan was thinking of when he said, in connection with another phase of the investigation:

> If the Congress can meet its responsibility in passing legislation, and the members of these unions, where there is virtual slavery by the reason of this character of representation in official responsibility at the head of the union, maybe we can go a long way toward restoring integrity in these places where the poor working people now, the honest working people, are being imposed upon. (3964–65)

The Machinists joined with the Teamsters in another case revealed by the Committee investigators, this one involving automobile agencies in Philadelphia. Unlike the Englander Company, the Philadelphia agencies did have employees at the time of the "organizational" picketing. But the employees did not count, anyway. The unions made no attempt to persuade them, peacefully, to join; the employees had not asked the unions to represent them. The unions did not even, as they sometimes do, tell the owners to sign a contract. They simply picketed (and threw acid on some new cars). The usual blockade ensued, imperiling the business and hence the jobs of the employees, and costing thousands of dollars (10834 ff.).

The Journeymen Barbers (Barbers) also drew on the Teamsters' power to increase their membership substantially. A number of barbers had formed a union of their own choosing, the Barbers Guild. But the large, affiliated, Journeymen Barbers felt that the existence of such an independent union, no matter how well it operated and how much it represented the free choice of its members, was intolerable, an insufferable blow to their "prestige." (Tr. 57)

The Barbers accordingly set up stranger pickets at locations where members of the Guild were employed, including the Waldorf-Astoria Hotel, in New York City. Strangely enough, the Waldorf picket line at first had little or no effect, according to the testimony, before the Committee, of Robert Verdina, a former official of the Barbers (Tr. 104). Patrons and workers of the Waldorf continued to enter and to go peaceably about their business. Something more drastic obviously had to be done. The barbers working at the Waldorf did not want to change their union affiliation; the Waldorf customers were satisfied with their accommodations; even the other Waldorf workers could apparently see no reason to interrupt their employment.

At this point, the Barbers brought to bear a weapon so powerful that it humbled the Waldorf management almost instantly, and simply demolished the Guild. A call to Dave Beck, then president of the Teamsters, changed the Barbers' picket line into an instrument of such power. According to Mr. Verdina, after the call Teamster truckers refused to deliver food, milk, linens, and other items indispensable to the continued operation of the hotel (Tr. 105). A few days of this and, according to other testimony before the Committee, the hotel management indicated that it could not tolerate a shutdown of the hotel, and the consequent unemployment of 2,400 other employees, merely because the forty barbers insisted upon having their own union, in resistance to the Journeymen Barbers (Tr. 60–61). Faced with the prospect of such destruction at every location where they were employed, the Guild members gave in. They and their 300 Guild brothers employed elsewhere in New York City voted to affiliate with the Journeymen Barbers (Tr. 62).

Cases like this are sometimes said to demonstrate the "solidarity" of the "labor movement." But such remarks are usually as erroneous as they would be in connection with the absorption of the Guild by the Journeymen Barbers. Workingmen were the victims, not the moving spirits, in this case. Given a free choice in the matter, they would have had nothing to do with the annihilation of the Guild. The Guild members had what they wanted—a union of their own choosing. Other Waldorf employees had what they wanted—a job which no one had forced them to take and which was paying them wages they were satisfied to accept. The patrons of the Waldorf patronized and continued to patronize the hotel before and after the picketing began. Even the truck drivers who delivered supplies to the hotel did not voluntarily decline to continue to do the work for which they were paid; for they could not by the wildest stretch of the imagination have any interest in the destruction of the Guild. They interrupted deliveries only after they had received orders to do so from their superiors.

The Guild was destroyed because of the pure power desires of one set of union leaders and the established power of another set of union leaders. All relevant conduct in the case was dictated from on high. The plan was conceived in one power-hungry mind, and it was executed by order of the man who then held the position which commands the greatest unrestrained economic power in the country today, the president of the Teamsters Union. The working men were only pawns. Stranger-picketing is the name of the device by means of which so much existing union power is made to bring still more. The principle of its operation, since it underlies almost all the purely economic power of the trade unions, should be clearly understood.

Stranger-picketing can bring to bear on a single employer all the power of the unions. On the one hand, the unions have made crossing a picket line one of the worst crimes which a union member can commit, especially when he has been ordered to "respect" it. On the other hand, few businesses can long survive without outside services of one kind or another. This is a complicated and interrelated economy. Every firm needs pickups and deliveries. Raw materials have to be brought in, and finished products have to be transported to customers. Free movement of goods and services is thus a crucial necessity; without it businesses, and ultimately the economy, are choked. A single stranger picket is often in a position to do the choking, especially in strongly and pervasively unionized areas. But the Record shows that there are other economically coercive devices—usually called "secondary boycotts"—available to overcome resisting businessmen in areas where stranger-picketing will not do the job by itself.

Secondary Boycotts

The principle of the secondary boycott is exactly the same as the principle of stranger-picketing: both cut off the employers from vital markets and services. There is only a locational difference. In fact, many secondary boycotts are imposed by stranger-picketing, although other methods may be used to make customers and suppliers quit dealing with the employer who is the ultimate target of the union's demands. If a single stranger picket posted at that employer's place of business will serve to isolate him, nothing more need be done. But if the employer is substantially unaffected by such a blockade, the union must reach his vitals in some other way. The normal and frequent alternative—the secondary boycott—ranges away from his place of business, to attack his important suppliers, or customers, or distributors. If their activities can be brought to a halt, the business of the ultimate target will suffer, too, and it will have to capitulate in the same way that the Skaff Company did.

The McClellan Record demonstrates that these secondary boycotts are always used when ordinary strikes will not do the job, either because the union represents none of the employees or because it does not represent a sufficient number to shut down the employer. The most comprehensive secondary boycott to be found in the Record is the one the United Automobile Workers (UAW) exerted against the Kohler Company in the dispute described in Chapter 4. In the "clay-boat incident," the UAW took action which made it impossible for Kohler to secure the clay it vitally needed for continued operations. The UAW prevented unloading of clay boats at the docks of Sheboygan and Milwaukee, Wisconsin, or indeed anywhere else in the United States. After crossing the ocean to reach this country, on order from the Kohler Company, the clay boats had to leave the country, still loaded. The UAW's power does not reach foreign countries; the clay was finally unloaded in Montreal, Canada, and transshipped to Wisconsin by train—all at great and, needless to say, unnecessary expense (9750-9807).

The UAW's boycott reached out for Kohler customers and distributors, too. Symptomatic of the tendency of unions to corrupt elected officials, the UAW induced certain local governments to boycott Kohler products in their building projects. While disavowing any coercive action, the union also nevertheless did what it could to induce hospitals to refuse to use Kohler plumbing fixtures. It requested, and in some cases got, cooperation from plumbers, in the form of refusals to install Kohler fixtures. It successfully imposed boycotts against some of Kohler's retail distributors. A construction union fined workers who did some construction for Kohler during the strike. The Kohler Company survived the UAW's strike and boycotts, but a good many people were hurt in the course of the union's muscle-flexing (9753 ff.).

Not all employers emerge from a secondary boycott with only scars and losses. Some who resist are destroyed, and from the experience of such destruction, others learn that it is better to give in—to accept the union as bargaining representative of unwilling employees, even to concede it a closed shop.

Tom Coffey's employees voted against representation by the Teamsters. However, the Teamsters did not think that employees have a right not to have a union, at least if the union in question is the Teamsters. In spite of the election defeat, the union imposed a secondary boycott which eventually drove Mr. Coffey out of business, since he would not give in and accept it as overlord of his employees (Tr. 627). This and a number of other boycotts by the Teamsters induced Senator Ervin to say, while acting as Chairman of the Committee, that the conduct of Teamster leaders "makes Attila the Hun appear by comparison to be a very mild-mannered and benevolent individual." (Tr. 916) Senator Ervin felt pretty strongly about the Teamsters' boycotts. They were used, he said, "to coerce workers into joining unions which they did not want to join." (Tr. 913) Free trade is something which depends upon the Teamsters' permission, he concluded, observing that the power of the Teamsters to interfere with trade is greater than that of local, state, and federal governments:

> This super law which the Teamsters attempt to interpose over the Government of the United States and the arrogant implementation of their activities is something which continues to concern this Committee and, I believe, the entire country. (Tr. 916)

These statements, made late in 1958, echoed the remarks of Senator McClellan of a year and half earlier in the Committee's investigation of power and corruption. In July of 1957 the Chairman had said:

> Thus, with control of joint council No. 16 and the International Longshoremen's Association, Hoffa would have a stranglehold over the port of New York. The next step would be the entire eastern seaboard and the St. Lawrence Seaway. (3593)

At that earlier point, the Committee had seen only bits and pieces of the pattern of power; it saw only union control of areas, albeit large and important areas; only later was it to see the whole pattern of nationwide power. But Chief Counsel Kennedy also saw in July of 1957 that "there is no organization, union, or business, that has a greater effect on the community life in this country, a greater effect on our economy than the teamsters union." (3596) At the time he was preoccupied with spelling out the grip of the Teamsters on the New York metropolitan area. His demonstration was comprehensive and graphic:

> Now this is a map of New York City. These are the docks here in red, and these are the airports. Newark Airport and LaGuardia and the International Airport. All of the goods that come in here to the docks must be trucked out of the docks. They have to be trucked to their various localities wherever those goods are destined for.
>
> Into the port of New York, in 1955, came 191,551,291 tons of cargo. It is 20 percent of all of the cargo that comes into the United States . . .
>
> Once it gets to the ports it has to be trucked out. So once again the truckers have control of that.
>
> The goods that come into the various airports around New York City, Newark Airport, and LaGuardia Airport, and International Airport, once they arrive there, once again truckers have to pick it up, and take the goods where they are destined.
>
> The railroads for the most part, the main railroad that brings goods into New York City, comes in here to Hoboken, and the goods are then barged across into Manhattan, and from there once again the goods have to be taken by truck and shipped to the various areas, or if it stops here they have to be taken by truck and shipped north.
>
> So the truckers have an important and integral part, a key position in the New York area through the fact that they have control over the airport. If that gets into the wrong hands, of course, there can be a strangle hold over New York City. (3596–97)

The trouble is that such power is a strangle hold in any hands. To suggest that absolute power is acceptable, provided that it is in "good hands," is to neglect mankind's experience with dictatorial power, experience that teaches that absolute and unlimited power, once it exists, can only be abused.

Power to tie up businesses in secondary boycotts does not rest only in the Teamsters, although that union is undoubtedly the most powerful. We have already noted the nationwide boycott imposed by the UAW against the Kohler Company. Scarcely a union in this country has not done the same thing at one time or another in the industry over which it asserts control. The

Teamsters secondary boycott power is broader because its members service all industries, but within each industry the boycott power of the other unions works in the same way.

The Sheet Metal Workers' boycott of the Burt Manufacturing Company, a producer of ventilating equipment, has been imposed because Burt's employees are represented by a union of their own choosing, the United Steelworkers of America. The leaders of the Sheet Metal Workers (SMW) feel that they should control all the workers who produce ventilating equipment. The reason they give is that if some firms are allowed to use workers belonging to unions which accept wages less than those insisted upon by the SMW, the firms which employ members of the SMW will have higher labor costs and thus be at a competitive disadvantage. In the long run, the SMW officers believe, their own position will become untenable, and they will be compelled to reduce their wage demands, or yield their control of the workers to unions which will not insist upon wages so high that they drive the producers of ventilating equipment out of business (Tr. 184-85).

The solution conceived by the SMW leaders is to impose a secondary boycott against all firms, such as the Burt Company, which employ men who do not belong to the SMW (Tr. 185 ff.). Such a boycott can be exerted because SMW controls the installation of so much ventilating equipment. Its method is to order its members to refuse to install ventilating equipment fabricated by any firm which does not employ members of SMW. William O. Frost, an SMW official, testified before the Committee to that effect. He said that his union is not interested in representing the Burt employees (Tr. 196). Chief Counsel Kennedy observed that the only thing which would seem to satisfy SMW, then, would be for the Burt Company to go out of business (Tr. 209). When Mr. Frost denied this, the Chief Counsel asked him what the Burt Company might do to placate SMW and thus to induce it to ease the "terrifying" pressures which F. C. Sawyer, executive vice-president of the Burt Company, had described to the Committee. Mr. Frost's reply was a noncommittal, "I can't answer that." (Tr. 211)

Senator Curtis did not mince words in characterizing SMW's campaign against Burt. He called it a "brazen and cold-blooded" move to destroy the company (Tr. 230). SMW's practice of forcing installation firms to agree not to work with Burt Ventilating equipment is a variety of the secondary boycott known as the "hot-cargo" contract (Tr. 156). It involves control by a union of an essential management decision, the decision concerning the type of product or raw material which is to be used. The public expects businessmen to be as economical in their cost structures as they can, so that consumer prices and the cost of living can be kept down. Mr. Sawyer was expressing the consumer's point of view when he said of the SMW "hot-cargo" boycott:

> It is terrifying to me to think that in this country a business man can be so intimidated by a union that he will enter into a written agreement not to use a product which he thinks is best adapted for his business. (Tr. 139)

The Burt boycott demonstrates the dominant attitude of all trade unions toward the representation choices of employees, a point which is demonstrated, as we shall see, by the AFL-CIO "no-raiding" pact. The mistake of the Burt employees lay in their choice of the Steelworkers as their representative. Undoubtedly Burt could have avoided the boycott by replacing the members of the Steelworkers with members of the SMW. While Mr. Frost would deny that, there can be no genuine doubt on the matter, and the secondary boycott of the Burt Manufacturing Company is therefore properly characterized as another form of organizing from the top.

This boycott also reveals a union using its power to regiment an industry, to dictate who shall stay in business, who shall be employed, and what products shall be used. The direct and unavoidable result of such union dictation is a cartelized economy of high costs and high prices. Not only the working man but also the consumer and the general public are exploited by the union leader who insists upon such control of the economy.

Of the other examples of industry-regimenting boycotts investigated by the Committee, one in particular stands out. Ex-

amination of the collection of refuse in two of the largest
metropolitan areas in the country, Los Angeles and New York,
revealed to the Committee how union power can cartelize an
industry, and dictate to employers, employees, and the general
public. Safeway Stores ran into the boycott power when it
became dissatisfied with the Westchester Carting Co., the firm
which had been collecting its refuse in Yonkers, and attempted
to change to another scavenging firm. Mr. Wells, a public-
relations manager for Safeway, described his firm's experience:

> Shortly after that, we received calls in the office from
> the stores reporting that collectors were refusing to pick up
> refuse at various stores in the Bronx and Manhattan. Perhaps
> there were 12 or 15 stores involved. The reason given
> was that we had changed the collectors and unions in our
> store . . . in Yonkers. We tried to find a solution to this
> problem, some solution to get the collectors to pick up the
> refuse without going back to the Westchester Carting Co.
>
> After several days we had a rather serious problem with
> both the quantity of the refuse in the stores and the con-
> dition or the smell, and, therefore, the concern of whether
> the board of health might, possibly, close the stores.
>
> This, of course, meant that we had to make a decision
> rather promptly. After exploring all possibilities, it was
> decided that we had nothing to do but to try to make a deal
> with these people. We were told that the person who could
> make this deal for us to straighten us out was a gentleman
> by the name of Adelstein. So, a contact was made with
> Mr. Adelstein, who told us that if we would go back to his
> union . . . that our problems would be over. We requested,
> however, that we not use the same carting company, and
> he agreed to that request. Another carting company, I
> believe it was Rusco, came in and picked up the refuse, and
> immediately our problems were over and collections were
> made in all our stores. (6711)

It is not as though Safeway had attempted to substitute a nonunion scavenger for a unionized one. The employees of the firm
which Safeway had substituted for Westchester Carting Company were also unionized. But the union in control of Westchester Carting Company would not tolerate the change, and its
secondary boycott made Safeway replace employees who were
members of one union with employees who were members of
the boycotting union (6712).

The control was much more complete, and much more stringent, in the Los Angeles area. There, businesses, home-owners, and workers were thoroughly regimented by the boy-cott power of a syndicate composed of owners of dumps, operators of scavenging firms, and a union. Captain James E. Hamilton, commander of the intelligence division of the Los Angeles Police Department, was the key Committee witness (6672). The police became interested after receiving several complaints from home-owners concerning the poor service which they were receiving from the scavenging firms, and the substantial increases in the costs of that service. He found that no matter how dissatisfied the customer might be with the service, there was no possibility of changing to a new collection agency. Investigation revealed that a plan for parceling out exclusive territories in which no competition might enter was enforced by the union controlling the workers in the scavenging firms and at the dumps. As Cap-tain Hamilton put it,

> . . . if an independent went into an area to try and solicit accounts, he was cut off at the dump by a union business agent. So, in effect, it appeared that the business agent was the enforcer for the association. . . . The dumps are . . . under contract with the same local that the drivers belonged to. So that the contract . . . is such that only union drivers should dump there. (6675)

There is no basic difference between this power play and the one exerted by the Sheet Metal Workers against the Burt Man-ufacturing Company. In both, trade union power sparked a form of regimentation of business which, by destroying competi-tion, raised costs and prices, to the ultimate harm of the economic system and its principal beneficiary, the customer. The only difference is that the garbage-collection cartel came more im-mediately and more vividly to the attention of the public, so that people got for once an immediate taste of the diet unions have been forcing down the throats of businessmen for a genera-tion. That its fundamental principle of operation was the same is revealed by the way the union made it impossible for a new competitor to enter the field. Captain Hamilton tells of an army veteran who thought there was room in the scavenging industry for an enterpriser prepared to offer a service.

> . . . one ex-GI from World War II said he thought it was a
> good business to get into, and he got himself a truck and
> fixed up a bunch of barrels and he started to soliciting in
> a new residential tract, where there was no pickup service.
> He had built his route up to about 1,500 customers, all
> primarily home pickups, when he was stopped at the dump
> one day and told by the checker at the dump that he would
> have to see Matula. (6676)

The details of the ensuing runaround are too lengthy for
reproduction here. Chief Counsel Kennedy's summary will, however, suffice:

> So this was an example of an individual that tried to get
> into the union who was told by the head of the union . . .
> to see the association. The head of the association told him
> that he could only come into the association if he gave up
> two-thirds of his business. He refused to do that. He went
> back to the union and the union would not allow him to
> come in. (6677)

The Committee's Record on boycotts leaves little room for
doubt that the affiliated unions, out to control the entire labor
force, will do whatever seems necessary in order to achieve that
end. Having near-monopoly power already, they are in a position to apply bone-cracking pressures against any employer whose
employees resist unionization or who happen to belong to another union. They do not care about free employee choice.
In fact they reject that principle, for they feel that employees
belong to them, and that anybody who stands in their way must
be demolished. Encouraged by a society which has conceded
to them a special privilege to engage in cost-raising coercion,
the unions daily engage in price-raising monopolistic and preda-
tory practices permitted to no other person or entity in society.
If it is necessary to trample upon individual rights and to trans-
form the free-enterprise economy into their own cartelized image
in order to gain their ends, they will do so—so long as society
permits them the special privilege of monopolistic coercion.

Compulsory Unionism Agreements

The distinction between traditional and racketeering unionism
fades as one considers examples of compulsory unionism imposed

upon employees who have been organized from the top. Ordinarily the union which seeks recognition from an employer
by stranger-picketing will also insist upon a contract requiring
union membership and the payment of union dues by the employees as conditions of employment. However, the most vivid
example in the Record of a compulsory unionism agreement
imposed from the top did not involve any picketing at all, only
a threat.

The dimensions of union power take on a certain sharpness
when one realizes that the firm was the Atlantic & Pacific Tea
Company (A & P), one of the largest enterprises in the United
States. The employees involved were grocery clerks in A & P's
eastern division. The unions were, on the one hand, certain locals of the big Amalgamated Meat Cutters (Butchers), and on
the other, several smaller affiliated unions representing clerks.
There is some doubt that the grocery clerks wished representation by any union. There is very little doubt that, if they wished
union representation at all, it was not by the Butchers. Yet the
Butchers got them. It secured recognition from A & P as their
exclusive bargaining representative—which means that they could
not bargain for themselves or through any other union which
they might prefer to the Butchers. More than that, the Butchers
induced A & P to sign a contract requiring the grocery clerks
to join the Butchers and, with loss of their jobs as the alternative,
to pay dues to it (11187 ff.).

The Record is tortuous on this phase of the McClellan Hearings. At one time or another, each of the unions, as well as the
company, appeared in a pretty bad light. The Chief Counsel
of the Committee made no attempt to disguise his suspicion
of the good faith of the company (11374 ff.). However, the
worst to be said of the company is that it did not resist the
Butchers as vigorously as it had the clerks' unions—and as an
outsider might have wished. Yet it must always be remembered
that outsiders do not have payrolls to meet, customers to serve,
and nearby competitors, ready, willing, and able to supply customers with the goods which they cannot get from stores which
are shut down by a strike and a picket blockade.

A & P's position in the hearings was that it signed its clerks
over to the Butchers because the Butchers threatened to strike

and picket if it did not (11221). Complicated charges and countercharges concerning the legality of A & P's recognition of the Butchers under the circumstances were exchanged (11227, 11441–74). The fact remains that—no matter how questionable it was for A & P to recognize the Butchers when the clerks did not want that union—the Butchers could have shut down the stores with a strike and picket line, and no relief in federal or state courts would have been available. Under federal law such action would have been considered privileged and lawful; the federal Norris-LaGuardia Act specifically prohibits the federal courts from enjoining such conduct. No relief would have been available in the state courts, as we shall see in Chapter 10, because of the pre-emption doctrine—the theory that the jurisdiction of such courts has been pre-empted by the federal legislation.

One must keep in mind, however, that several thousand A & P grocery clerks were eventually saddled with a union which they did not want, and compelled to pay dues to it (11247). In one election, covering the Brooklyn clerks, they had voted overwhelmingly for no union (1,100 to 302). On charges that the company had interfered with their free choice, a new election was ordered in the Brooklyn unit. In that election, held early in 1953, Local 1500 of the Retail Clerks union won by a large majority (11277 ff.).

Meanwhile, however, the company had recognized the Butchers, for all eastern division units, on the basis of the strike and picketing threat, and on the basis of the large vote against representation by the Retail Clerks in the first election. The Butchers had also presented A & P with a large number of cards, ostensibly signed by grocery clerks, authorizing the Butchers to bargain for them. Under the law, an employer cannot reject such proof of majority standing. Employers have in many cases been held guilty of unfair practices for refusing to bargain with a union which bases its claim for recognition upon authorization cards. Convincing evidence in this case shows, however, that the cards were forgeries, produced by a mass-production signature line in the Butchers' offices, rather than by the employees involved (11485, 11593).

When asked by an officer of the clerks union how he had managed to sign up so many A & P clerks, in view of their repeated votes against representation by clerks unions, Max Block, president of the Butchers' local, replied: "Well, you are not a novice in the business. . . . They can be organized later." (11521)

The success of the Retail Clerks in the 1953 election did give it some leverage, in spite of the previous recognition of the Butchers. Local 1500 induced the Butchers to agree to permit it to "service" the contract which the Butchers had secured from A & P, with the further understanding that after two years the Butchers would "turn over" the clerks to Local 1500 (11242). This amounted to an abandonment by Local 1500 of its election victory and of the NLRB certification which had followed that victory (11284). However, the ultimate results were disastrous for Local 1500 and extremely favorable to the Butchers, which reneged on its understanding with Local 1500, induced it to participate in an all-unit election, despite the fact that 1500's voting strength was concentrated in only the Brooklyn unit, and in the all-unit election, beat it handily (11246, 11283).

There is a great deal more to the story of the Butchers Union president, Max Block. But at present we need only note the accuracy with which Senator McClellan used the term "pawn" in describing the plight of the grocery clerks, especially the clerks in the Brooklyn unit (11298). Although they obviously favored representation by the Retail Clerks, they were forced to subject themselves and pay dues to the Butchers. Senator Curtis, agreeing with the Chairman, thought the result shocking and anomalous (11247).

Later in the same hearing, when the conduct of the Butchers' officers was displayed, showing their callous abuse of the union members, Senator Curtis was confirmed in his conviction that the fundamental cause of the evils in labor relations is organizing from the top, buttressed by the still more rigorous control of compulsory unionism agreements (11371). Such agreements make employees pay dues to unions as a condition of continued employment. After being forced to accept a union which they do not want, they must finance its officers, even when all they get from them are abuses of trust, and a good many other types of abuse as well.

* * *

Compulsory unionism thus takes its place with stranger-picketing and secondary boycotts among the principal methods whereby unions assert control over unwilling employees. All have one essential feature in common: they make unions the masters of employees, not their servants; employees are selected by unions, and divided up according to the plans and dispositions of the union leadership. But the AFL-CIO's celebrated "no-raiding" pact, in spite of the nearly universal praise it has received, is the most comprehensive example in American history of organizing from the top. Choice of membership is made there at the highest level—AFL-CIO headquarters—not by employees. They are only pawns.

Employers too are pawns. Failing to secure representation rights through the free choice of employees, unions exert their coercive pressures against employers through stranger-picketing and other forms of the secondary boycott. In the process they pry from employers a control over employment which binds the employees ever more tightly to the unions. Under the law, employers are forbidden to fire a man who wishes to join a union. Through compulsory unionism agreements, however, unions may compel employers to fire employees who are dissatisfied enough with their unions to wish to discontinue contributing their financial support to it.

If, from all of this, there emerges a corruption which involves completely cynical disregard of employee interests, no one should really be surprised. The pattern of power and of action was bound to have such results.

Racket-picketing and Sweetheart Contracts

Horace A. Crouch had a gun behind the door when two investigators from the McClellan Committee called at his home in Portland, Oregon (182). It took a certain amount of probing by Chief Counsel Kennedy later, during the Hearings, to find out what Mr. Crouch feared. After interrogation, it turned out that he had crossed the Teamsters and, as he put it, "sometimes in Portland the teamsters get pretty rough." His offense against the Teamsters was that he had testified before an Oregon grand jury, presumably about the consequences of a business mistake he had made (183).

It seems that Mr. Crouch had made the mistake of leasing in his restaurant, the Mount Hood Cafe, pinball machines of which the Teamster leaders disapproved. Frank Malloy, a Teamster agent, allegedly told him that unless he took out those machines, supplied by one Stan Terry, and replaced them with Acme machines, of which the Teamsters approved, his restaurant would be picketed. Protesting that his employees were already signed up with the Culinary Workers, Mr. Crouch expected that he would thus escape the picketing. He had a great deal to learn.

One of the first things he learned was that Stan Terry had tried to get Teamster approval of his machines, but had failed. "I asked Stan Terry," said Crouch, " 'Why don't you join the union?' And he said, 'They won't let me.' " The second thing he learned was that Mr. Malloy was serious in threatening to picket, despite the fact that the restaurant was already organized by another union. And the third thing he learned was that he could not stay in business while his restaurant was picketed by the Teamsters (184). His description is short but definitive: "I couldn't get coffee, I couldn't get bread, I couldn't get meat deliveries." (185) After four days of the picketing, Mr. Crouch removed the offending Terry machines. He said he had to—the only alternative was bankruptcy. The picketing had brought his business to a standstill. Not only could he get no deliveries of supplies; he could not even get any customers to enter the restaurant. As it happened, he never did install the Acme machines. He waited for three months, till his original supplier, Stan Terry, finally got clearance from the Teamsters, and then he put back the Terry machines (186). Mr. Malloy, the next witness before the Committee, took the Fifth Amendment when questioned about the Crouch affair, and, for that matter, on most other subjects broached by the members of the Committee (187).

There are numerous instances of such picketing in the Record. Indeed, Wallace Turner, an Oregon journalist whose courage and enterprise had much to do with stimulating the McClellan investigation, and who was the first witness before the Committee, said that his interest, and that of his associate, William Lambert, had first been excited by the Teamsters' pinball picketing:

> It was another of the incidents that led us to believe all was not proper in the teamsters union in our community. This was the situation: A Portland tavern operator bought a shuffleboard machine from a Seattle company to replace one he had been operating on a commission basis with its owner, a Portland coin-machine dealer. Soon after the machine was installed, pickets from the teamsters union appeared and shut off the tavern's beer deliveries. All other coin machines in the place were removed by their owners. Customers quit coming in. The tavern was almost bankrupt.
>
> It developed that the trouble stemmed from a conspiracy between the union and an association of pinball dealers to monopolize the industry. No tavern owner was to be allowed to own his own machine. They had to rent them from particular persons, otherwise the union would step in and picket the offending tavern. And this is exactly what happened.
>
> THE CHAIRMAN. Are you . . . stating that in an effort to control these machines . . . a place of business would be picketed by the teamsters union members?
>
> MR. LAMBERT. That is right, sir.
>
> THE CHAIRMAN. In order to prevent the delivery of goods to that business?
>
> MR. LAMBERT. That is right, sir.
>
> THE CHAIRMAN. You said you did not think that was a legitimate union activity or interest.
>
> MR. LAMBERT. It most certainly is not; in my judgment.
>
> THE CHAIRMAN. In other words, it involved nothing with respect to labor, wages, or working conditions of the members but it was simply to undertake, and . . . to force a monopoly.
>
> MR. LAMBERT. That is exactly right, sir. (10)

The transition is thus made. If, as unions have learned from a great deal of extremely successful experience, their picketing blockades can force employers to recognize unions as bargaining representatives, they can serve a good many other purposes as well. The money to be derived solely from the dues of a forced membership is nothing to be sneered at; still, additional sources of revenue are not to be neglected. More efficient thinkers can see, however, that a certain amount of wastage is involved in securing additional income through the indirect method of a tie-up with a firm supplying slot machines. Besides, not all businesses subject to an immobilizing stranger picket line have any use for slot machines.

A short cut is then conceived: why not eliminate all waste motion by offering to withdraw the pickets—for a consideration? Solomon Joseph Freedman, the senior partner of a Philadelphia food purveying firm, reported to the Committee an extremely interesting conversation which he said he had had with a union official during the course of a violent and bloody organizing campaign by several unions against the Horn and Hardart restaurant chain. Chief Counsel Kennedy asked Mr. Freedman: "Was an approach in fact made to you that the strike [sic] could be settled?" (10732) The ensuing colloquy is interesting:

> Mr. FREEDMAN. Well, the approach was made to me regarding how well I was acquainted with the . . . official staff of Horn & Hardart . . .
>
> Mr. KENNEDY. Who did you have this conversation with?
>
> Mr. FREEDMAN. Shorty Feldman.
>
> Mr. KENNEDY. Who is Shorty Feldman?
>
> Mr. FREEDMAN. He is the agent for local 929.
>
> Mr. KENNEDY. Is he an important figure in the Teamsters Union in Philadelphia?
>
> Mr. FREEDMAN. Well, yes, he is. He is their business agent. He is the one that we have to look forward to at the terminals; that is, he is the one that we have to account to for any misdemeanors . . . He said, "Joe, how well do you know them?" and I said, "Well, I know them well." He said, "Do you know them well enough to talk to them and make a deal?"

I said, "What kind of a deal? You know, those people don't go for deals. If I know Daley or some of the other executives, they are pretty honorable people, and I don't think they will go for deals."

He said, "Well, do you want to talk to them?" I said, "I will talk to one of the men which I have contact with," which I referred to as Dan Hanlon. He said, "For $50,000, we can take care of this," and I said, "What do you mean take care of it?"

I said, "Do you mean you can settle the strike, that they will stop picketing?" and he said [here the transcript of the Record is garbled] . . . "Well, it would have to be divided three ways." I said, "Well, I don't know, Sam."

After a couple of days . . . elapsed, he again approached me, and I thought, "Well, I will mention it to Mr. Hanlon," which I did.

[Mr. Hanlon] said, "Mr. Freedman, if I were you, I wouldn't even mention it to Mr. Daley. He wouldn't go for any deals or any capitulations whatsoever. If you would mention it to him, I think he would order you out of the office."

I said, "Well, I figured it that way, but I felt it no more than proper for me to bring it to you anyway, and you take it from there."

At a later time, [Shorty Feldman] said, "Did you talk to them?" . . . I said, "I did, but they are not interested." (10732)

In the interests of accuracy, it ought to be said here that Mr. Freedman exonerated Mr. Morris Schurr, the president of Mr. Feldman's local, of any complicity in the affair. According to Mr. Freedman, when he told Mr. Schurr about the approaches which had been made, Mr. Schurr said: "No, I don't know anything of it, and he is crazy. He shouldn't have done it. I have nothing to do with it." (10733) In the further interests of accuracy, it ought also to be noted that when Chairman McClellan asked whether the union continued to employ Feldman as business agent, after "the president knew he was going around making such propositions," Mr. Freedman's answer was "yes." (10733)

Sometimes the victim, having at first cooperated with the Committee, has second thoughts when it comes to testifying for the Record. Such seems to have been the case with Julius Wolfson, a garage owner employing eight men. Chief Counsel Kennedy was taken by surprise when, having asked Mr. Wolfson whether an offer had been made to remove a picket line, for a consideration, Mr. Wolfson took the Fifth Amendment. Mr. Kennedy then asked:

> Isn't it correct that you were interviewed by an investigator of our committee, that the investigator went into this whole matter in detail, that you told him about the payments that you had to make to Benjamin Lapensohn? Isn't that correct? (10851)

Again, Mr. Wolfson pleaded the Fifth Amendment. Mr. Kennedy told Mr. Wolfson that he could be of great help to the Committee: "You have a great opportunity, a great chance, Mr. Wolfson, to help and assist the committee in its work." (10851) But even against such a plea, Mr. Wolfson remained silent. Perhaps Mr. Sawyer, of the Burt Manufacturing Company, used the correct adjective when he said that he thought the things the Committee was discovering were "terrifying."

In view of Mr. Wolfson's change of heart, Mr. Kennedy called as a witness George L. Nash, the investigator who had interviewed Mr. Wolfson. Mr. Nash testified that Mr. Wolfson had told him a story along these lines: a stranger picket line had been set up which left Wolfson no practical alternative to signing up with the union. As Wolfson was about to sign the union contract, however, according to the story he had told Nash:

> Ben Lapensohn came into the room, took Wolfson aside, and asked him, Wolfson, who he knew who could help him out of a situation. Wolfson mentioned many names, including that of a city official now deceased. . . . Lapensohn told Wolfson to see this city official and tell him what happened. Wolfson did so, and a few days later this official advised Wolfson he would have to make a payoff. Wolfson then gave this official $750 in cash. Wolfson claims that he borrowed the money from a friend. The friend was interviewed and he confirmed that from time to time he loaned Wolfson money in cash. In January 1955, a few months before the initial contract between Wolfson and local 596 was to expire, Lapensohn came to

> Wolfson's garage . . . and told him that he was to enter
> into a new contract with the local, and the new contract
> would have about the same provisions as the old one. At
> that time, Ben Lapensohn asked Mr. Wolfson for $1,500.
> A week or so later, Wolfson gave Lapensohn $750, again in
> cash. (10853)

There is more to the story; repeated attempts were made to reach
Wolfson for more and more. Wolfson is said to have balked,
finally, and in the end to have entered into a contract with someone else, at "more moderate terms." (10854)

The sweetheart contract is a natural outcome of the course
of conduct we have been observing. The picket line brings the
employer to heel. The employees do not count. Their wishes
concerning unionization have not been consulted; therefore the
union owes them nothing. In return for a payoff, the employer
gets a "labor" contract which will not hurt too much. In the pure
sweetheart contract, the employer merely agrees to pay his workers what he has already been paying them.

For all anyone knows, the Philadelphia story occurs in every
strongly unionized area in the United States. The Committee
focused its attention in this phase of the investigation, however,
only upon New York and Chicago. There it found a great deal
to ponder.

Chicago apparently has had a long history of hoodlum pene-
tration of the trade unions. Virgil W. Peterson, a director of the
Chicago Crime Commission, filled in the Committee on events
dating back to the 1920's (12510). Chicago racketeers who,
according to Mr. Peterson, "weren't interested in the welfare of
the employees, of course," infiltrated the building trades and held
up contractors who could tolerate no delays because of penalty
clauses in their building contracts (12512). How was the holdup
effectuated? The key, according to Mr. Peterson's testimony, was
the right to strike:

> Well, a racketeer would go to a contractor and say in
> substance, "Well, if you give me $20,000 or $30,000 or
> $50,000, we won't call a strike; and if you don't give me
> the $50,000 we will call a strike." (12513)

Senator Curtis, always interested in getting to the causes of the evident abuses, asked Mr. Peterson:

> Why do these hoodlums—some of them are gangsters and murderers and gamblers and extortionists and all sorts of bad actors—why did they select unions as the field of exploitation?

Mr. Peterson replied:

> Well, when they are able to dominate a particular union, it is, as I think will be shown in these hearings, a tremendously lucrative operation for the hoodlums themselves.

A little more of this colloquy is interesting:

> SENATOR CURTIS. By "lucrative," where do they get their money?
>
> MR. PETERSON. Well, with reference to the income of the union itself.
>
> SENATOR CURTIS. The checkoff of dues?
>
> MR. PETERSON. The dues from the employees. . . .
> (12512)

And, he added, the income from the strike and picketing threats recounted above.

The latter source of attraction has apparently continued. As the Committee learned, a good many restaurant owners in Chicago were compelled to pay off in order to avoid picket lines. The pay scale or working conditions of the employees did not count. The unions hit high-paying and low-paying restaurants indiscriminately. So long as the employer was willing to enroll his employees into the union and pay their dues, or compel them to pay dues, the union left him alone. If the employer resisted, as did Edward H. Reade, the union hit him with everything it had (12689). But if the employer played ball, as some did, the union would not insist upon his paying the union scale (12637ff.). The union could not do too much about employers who were paying union scales or above. It could still threaten to picket, as in the case of the London House in Chicago. But the picket line would be withdrawn, if the employer forced the employees to pay dues to the union. Naturally, they were given no choice in the matter (12672).

Some have thought that employers were equally to blame with the racketeering unions in these cases, and much has been made of the fact that employers and sometimes employer associations hired persons of suspect character to deal with unions for them. Such conclusions and contentions involve a lack of understanding of the situation facing employers threatened with a strike or picket line, especially when the threat comes from a racketeer. A colloquy between Senator Mundt and Edward H. Reade, a Chicago restaurateur, may promote understanding of the situation:

> SENATOR MUNDT. Is the basic reason that you have formed an organization called the Chicago Restaurant Association, and developed this collective resistance to unionism, the fact that in Chicago the Restaurant Union has fallen into the hands of thugs and people with whom you simply cannot deal at arm's length on a legitimate basis?
> MR. READE. I think the happenings at the Nantucket Restaurant for 2 years and 2 weeks perfectly demonstrate the fact that it is impossible for me to get any relief from anybody under any conditions, and the only help that I was able to get was the support of my fellow restaurant people who participated in this voluntary contribution. There is no other way to stop these people at the present time which has been explained to me as because we are in a no man's land. . . . We neither are protected by the local government or the Federal Government, or we are not given relief by the local government or the Federal Government. (12711)

The exploitation of workers and extortion from employers found in the Chicago restaurant industry is repeated in the sweetheart contracts in New York City (3591 ff.). The same causes and effects were disclosed to the Committee there. Among the employers who bore witness to the pressure exerted against them by racketeers posing as unionists, the experience of Paul Claude, the owner of a small machine shop in Brooklyn, was typical. He told the Committee that he had been visited repeatedly by a person, variously identified as Max Chester and Emanuel Kessler, who offered him a contract he could "live with" for $2,000 (3920). Chester made Claude nervous, especially when he referred, as he often did, to Claude's children,

their health, the peril of playing in the street, and other such
"pleasantries." When Senator Curtis asked Claude whether his
employees wanted Chester's union, Claude said: "They knew
nothing about unions one way or the other." (3934) Claude
went quickly to the police after Chester's first visit, but the local
captain, according to Claude's testimony, said, "You have to make
some kind of a deal with them because they are legitimate."
(3923) It cost Claude $1,400 and his eight employees $3 a
month each, in compulsory union dues, to get rid of Chester.
Chester himself was the next witness. He took the Fifth Amendment on every question, including the Chairman's request for
his address, and another as to whether or not he had been in the
hearing room, as of course he was, during Claude's testimony
(3935, 3939). When the Chairman asked, "Did you ever do
an honest thing to help honest laboring union people in your
life?" Chester's response was: "I respectfully decline to answer
on the ground that to do so may tend to incriminate me."

It was Chester, according to Claude, who said:

> You have got to pay us off because you are mine . . . and
> I own you. No matter where you are going to move, you are
> mine. (3924)

Chapter 3

VIOLENCE IN ORGANIZING

We parked [the truck] at a different location every night. We finally resorted to parking it in back of the police squad, thinking that there they wouldn't molest it.

But they towed it away from that location several times. The last time that they towed it away, that was the end of it. . . . They dumped it in the river.

* * *

[The waitresses] became very incensed about the tactics. One of them said that if we joined up with the union for them, they would all quit. Believe me, she would stick by it.

* * *

When economic pressures fail to impose unionization or to secure for unions the "bargaining" victories which they consider their right, the Committee learned, unions will frequently resort to violence. The Record shows, moreover, that violence is an instrument of policy, not only of the racketeering pseudo-unions, but of the old-line traditional unions as well. Some "legitimate" union leaders take a pious attitude. They deplore and condemn violence. Yet they consider it their right to block access to the premises of employers against whom they have called strikes. They feel that no worker has a right to continue working during a strike, not a "moral" right, anyway; and that it is the duty of every employer to shut down his business when a strike is called —or when the place is picketed for "organizational" purposes. If he does not, and violence ensues, then it is the employer's fault; and the "scabs" have only got what they deserved. The duty of the police, these union leaders seem to feel, is to protect the "human rights" of the strikers and picketers, not the "property rights" of the employers, the nonstrikers, and the nonunion men. Violent obstruction would not occur if employers shut down their plants and if workers did not try to enter struck plants or cross picket lines. The fault therefore rests with those who do not cooperate with the union. Thus goes the thinking of the union leaders, or thus at least do they argue.

The theories and arguments we shall consider in later chapters. Our concern in this and the next chapter is with the facts. Is it true that violence, intimidation, and property destruction are deliberately chosen instruments of policy in union "organizing" and "bargaining" campaigns? The answer indicated by the Record is "yes."

Organizing Rights, and Wrongs

It is not as though unions have no right to use peaceful persuasion in increasing their membership. Quite the contrary, the law gives union organizers special privileges available to no other group in society. In certain circumstances employers are even compelled to make their private property available to union organizers. Always the employees are protected by law against any form of employer reprisal, should they voluntarily choose union membership.

These special privileges are apparently not enough, from the point of view of the unions. They still leave the job of inducing employees to join, and they leave with employees at least the bare legal right not to join. It is much simpler, as we have seen, to organize from the top. But if the economic coercion of stranger-picketing and other secondary boycotts fails to do the job, then violence, intimidation, vandalism, and large-scale property destruction will often be called into play. For these purposes, it is always well to have on the union payroll men who have had plenty of experience. Pondering the question "why certain labor leaders want racketeers as local union heads," Senator McClellan thought that a part of the answer was that "racketeers, because of their ruthlessness, toughness, et cetera, are good organizers, [and] can gain an increase in member-ship. . . ." (3592)

The Teamsters wanted no part of any election among the Skaff employees, it will be remembered, and they did not intend to bother with any attempt to persuade voluntary membership. They preferred to set up a stranger picket line. When that failed, because, as Donald Skaff put it, "we still had a little fight left in us," the union took off the gloves (6433). Physical assaults, breaking of windows, stink bombs, interference with both employees and customers—all these "organizing" methods were tried on Skaff. Since regular deliveries were blocked by the union, Skaff tried to make pickups with his own employees. Here, in his words, is what happened:

> On April 4 we had two men out, one by the name of Bill Moore, and he was standing beside his truck awaiting direction as to where to pick up his merchandise, and there was a vicious attack by four or five men who hit him with a sharp object, as the doctor called it at the hospital, and knocked him to the ground. They spun around the railroad station attempting to run over him and he rolled under his truck, and when we took him up to the hospital he had twenty stitches in his head. . . . (6432)

The same kind of story is encountered repeatedly in the Record. When an Indianapolis restaurateur refused to recognize a Bartenders union, some of his employees were beaten, a fire broke out on his roof (phosphorous crystals found by the police indicated arson), and four sticks of dynamite were thrown against the front of his home. His suppliers got similar treatment. One had his garage burned and a truck destroyed in the fire. A second truck stalled like a rock; shellac had been poured into its motor. A substitute who volunteered to take the place of this immobilized supplier had fire bombs thrown at his home three weeks later (13831–37).

Edward Reade, the restaurant owner whom we met briefly in the preceding chapter, ran into a great deal more than a picket line. He found his alley blocked by union autos so that he could not have garbage removed. A privately engaged garbage collector waited while Mr. Reade called the police. Two officers came and, according to Mr. Reade, "talked to these union officials for quite a long time." About two hours later, Mr. Reade continues, "Frank Trungale, who is known to me as the top man in this union, . . . went over and very graciously gave the sergeant on duty permission to let our garbage truck come in and remove the garbage." (12696) By then, however, "The man that was driving the garbage truck got so upset over the whole thing that he left." According to Mr. Reade another driver had had his life threatened:

> . . . James O'Connor threatened to kill the man that was operating this truck, in my presence and in the presence of these policemen that were stationed in the alley.
>
> I went over to the police officers and asked them to please make a notation of the fact that "this gentleman threatened this gentleman's life," and at a later date when I tried to get someone to come into court and testify to this fact I was never able to find any policeman that knew anything about that affair. (12696)

Donald W. Strang's employees had never been approached by Local 450 of the Bartenders and Waiters Miscellaneous Union; Mr. Strang himself resisted to the bitter end a full-scale attempt to organize them from the top; and yet after all was said and done their names turned up on the union's membership rolls and dues were paid in their name for a full year (12572–83). Such in brief is the over-all story of Mr. Strang's experience with an "organizing" drive at his Niles, Illinois, restaurant.

Our concern here is with only one phase of the story—the methods used by the union when Mr. Strang resisted the attempt to organize his workers from the top. The first thing Strang knew about it all, he saw a group of stranger pickets around his restaurant. Shortly thereafter he had a visit from two union officials:

> They said they wanted to talk over the matter of me joining the union for my employees, and I told them that in my opinion they were going about this thing all wrong, that if they could come in and say that my employees wish to be represented by them, that was another story, but I said, "As far as I know, none of our employees want you to represent them," and I said "For me to join for them against

their will, or to force them to join in order to keep their
jobs was just the same as telling them what church they
had to belong to if they wanted to work for me."
    I considered it un-American, unconstitutional, and I
would not do it.
    I said I would close the store first. (12574)

From that point on, things got pretty rough. Customers and
employees were harassed: tacks were spread over the parking
lot, tires slashed, the motor of a car ruined because sugar had
been put into the gasoline tank. There was also a virtual blockade which Strang described to the Committee:

The teamsters union cooperated with them so that we were
unable to get any deliveries of food. We were unable to
have our garbage taken out. We were unable to have our
money removed by armored express, so we had to do that
ourselves. We brought in food with my automobile and
in the automobiles of other employees, such as the manager's
and supervisor's. We had to go to the source of the food or
to other restaurants where food was delivered and we would
try to lose the people following us, which they usually did
when we started out, so that they wouldn't know to what
restaurants we got the food given to us. (12575)

Garbage dumps would not accept refuse from Strang, and when
the health department got after him he finally had to go to another town to get rid of the garbage which was piling up (12576).
    The union went after the waitresses, according to Mr. Strang:

Then there was intimidation. Our employees were intimidated, they were followed home, run off the road. They
drove cars, followed right to their homes. Girls going
home late at night were followed and were fearful.

And here of course the real nature of the unions' "organizing"
problem emerges: often employees simply do not wish to belong,
and take most unkindly to harassment. Continuing with Strang's
account,

[The waitresses who were followed] became very incensed
. . . about the tactics. I remember one time one of them
said that if we joined up with the union for them, they
would all quit. Believe me, she would stick by it.
    But the next day she came back and said her husband

was afraid for her. She was crying. But he was afraid
she might get hurt. And that happened with other employees. (12576)

Some authorities tried to be helpful, others did not. The state
authorities, according to Strang, were oddly reluctant:

> I called the State police for protection of the Howard
> Johnson truck coming from Cleveland, Ohio. . . .
>   I had a hard time getting them. I even went down to
> the office, but they didn't seem to be around. Finally I got
> him on the telephone, and he said, "Well, I am sorry, but
> my hands are tied. I have been called off by the Governor's
> office, it is a local proposition, and we cannot do anything.
> I am so mad, and our men are so mad, that they are hot
> under the collar. All of those hoodlums, we would like to
> put them in jail. But I can't do anything about it."
>   I said, "This is interstate. They are coming through
> the State. They are not in the State. It is not local."
>   He said, "I can't do anything about it now. But I will
> tell you now, you are getting a raw deal." (12577)

Spotty, half-hearted, reluctant police protection seems to be
all that beleaguered employers and nonunion employees can
expect in many "organizing" campaigns. Such certainly was the
experience of nonunion truckers and barbers in what several witnesses described as a "reign of terror" campaign of union "organization" in Tennessee. According to Chairman McClellan, Committee investigators uncovered 173 separate acts of violence
occurring there between 1953 and 1957, law enforcement was
highly inadequate, and, as he put it, "only eight of the 173
acts of violence have been solved." (7053-65)

No useful purpose would be served by a duplication here of
the Record. A couple of examples of the violent "organizing"
which has gone on in Tennessee will suffice, and the more curious reader may refer for the complete picture to Part 18 of
the Record.

As usual, the unions involved showed no interest in personal
solicitation of memberships, and they avoided like the plague
participating in any secret-ballot elections for determination of
whether or not the employees wished union representation. On
this, the experience of J. R. Pemberton, part-owner of the New-

man-Pemberton Trucking Company, is typical. He testified that a Teamsters local at first attempted to avoid an election by filing unfair-practice charges against the company—a procedure often utilized by unions to avoid elections, it might be added. After the NLRB found the unfair-practice charges unfounded, the union disclaimed any interest in the organization of the New-man-Pemberton employees—another common method of avoiding elections. Meanwhile, however, the union had been picketing and committing assorted acts of violence and vandalism (7071).

Mr. Pemberton testified that his company's trucks had had seventy-six tires cut and punctured in a Cincinnati terminal; his wife was awakened several times by a ringing phone during the night, to be told that "if she didn't stop me from trying to operate they would dynamite, she was liable to get blown out of bed, or different things like that"; trucks were run off the road; one truck was fired on, and though the driver was unharmed that time, two tires were punctured; the same driver was shot through the shoulder on another trip; some of his trucks were dynamited, with damages of $25,000; and the total damage and loss of business to his firm, as a result of the violent action, amounted to $210,000. In each instance, Pemberton indicated, police investigations came to little or nothing (7069–79).

A barber having trouble with the Barbers union suffered two broken windows, and had to do his own investigating. Curiously enough, a police officer swore in an affidavit filed with the Committee that he failed to follow up a most promising lead given him by several eyewitnesses to the shattering of the windows (7161–62). He swore, furthermore, that he received no reprimand from his superiors for his handling of the case, even after the barber solved it himself and secured a conviction when he went to the district attorney with his evidence. The district attorney, in another affidavit filed with the Committee, made this general remark: "Every so often police officers and deputy sheriffs, in an effort to explain inaction, advance some false reason for a failure to do their duty." As to the window-breaking affair, the district attorney said:

> The barbershop incidents came to my attention, as I now recall, other than by State's warrant. Some young men

had witnessed the damage to these barbershops and had called it to the attention of two deputy sheriffs. The officers accosted Canaday and Peters shortly after the incident and released them without even searching their vehicle. Had they done their full duty at that moment they undoubtedly would have found much incriminating evidence on Peters and Canaday since they were using Smith's car. I picked up this case, indicted them, and tried it with the aforesaid results [i.e., convictions]. (7499)

Donald Skaff had the same kind of experience with the police in Flint, Michigan. He said that a three-hour session with the Flint chief of police was unproductive:

> . . . we requested help from the police, who told us that they could not get involved in a labor incident. If we could furnish proof of who started the fire in our building, or of who threw the stinkbomb in my mother's home, they would be glad to prosecute them.

Was it usually necessary, Senator Mundt asked, for a complainant to perform investigations and find proof for the police: "If a bank is robbed in Michigan, do the police refuse to look for the bank robber unless you can tell them who did it?" Mr. Skaff could only reply: "That is not a labor incident, sir." (6431)

Are These "Labor Problems"?

There are those who contend that all these cases of union violence do not really involve labor relations or labor-management problems (12582). But such contentions, reflection will prove, involve a lack of understanding of the real nature of the problem. On the one hand, the special privileges of compulsion which trade unions enjoy have given them an appetite for greater immunity which they attempt to secure through political action and the corruption of public servants and elected officials. On the other hand, their special privileges have attracted thugs and racketeers. These matters will be dealt with at more length in later chapters. Here it need only be noted that, while thuggery is indeed essentially a policing problem, the person who contends that it has nothing to do with labor unions or labor relations is either misleading himself or trying to mislead someone else. Lola Freels, having been bookkeeper and secretary to Teamsters' Local 821 in Knoxville during 1955 and 1956, was in a position to contribute valuable information to the Committee on this issue—and she did. She testified to buying for the local, with union funds, various commodities which could be used for, among other things, immobilizing internal combustion engines. The goods were sugar and syrup (7171). She also informed the Committee of a curious relationship between telephone calls and violence. Striking locals would call different locals "and ask them to send somebody in to help out on the strikes," she said, and continued:

> Then after this would occur, after the people would come in, whoever they called, you could always pick up the paper the next morning or so and see where we had . . . violence. (7173)

The officials of Horn & Hardart would be surprised to learn that they were not having "labor trouble" in Philadelphia in 1955–56, when four unions, the Bakery & Confectionery Workers, the Meat Cutters & Butchers, the Restaurant Union, and the Teamsters undertook "organizational" picketing of their premises. Leonard W. Lowther, executive vice-president, told the Committee that "we had never been approached by any of the unions as to the signing of a contract or any communication whatsoever." But suddenly, on May 2, 1955, a picket line appeared—"a complete picket line was thrown around our plant which, of course, stopped all deliveries." Of 4,800 Horn & Hardart employees in Philadelphia, less than 100 left their jobs to join the picket line (10706–7).

When the police were around, their efforts to preserve the peace were conscientious; but unfortunately they could not be everywhere to afford protection, and when they were not around, a great deal of violence and property destruction occurred. "I would say," another Horn & Hardart official testified, "these acts of violence and so forth usually took place when the police escorts were not available." The full list of the unions' violence was fourteen pages long, too long for inclusion in the Record. Only a few of the many instances of arson, truck sabotage, and assault were given (10713–16).

One of Horn & Hardart's suppliers, McCray & Hunter, found itself in great trouble because it tried to continue to supply Horn & Hardart during the siege. The senior partner of McCray & Hunter, Solomon Freedman, felt that Horn & Hardart were "innocent victims," a fair concern which would have respected its employees' rights. "I felt," he said, "that I was going to continue on to help them as much as I possibly could." His scruples cost him a great deal:

> We suffered approximately fifteen or twenty thousand dollars' worth of damage. . . . they threw gasoline on some of our merchandise. They threw stink bombs in our stores. . . . Our main truck, the largest one, was dumped in the river, and we couldn't salvage anything out of it. (10729)

That big truck seemed to be the union's main target:

> Of course [said Mr. Freedman], there are different incidents at various times on this very same truck. As I say, what we did in this case here, since we found it almost impossible to operate under our own name, we took the name off the truck, and we assigned it to one of our employees, and he run the truck.
> We parked it at a different location every night. We finally resorted to parking it in back of the police squad, thinking that there they wouldn't molest it.
> But they towed it away from that location several times. The last time that they towed it away, that was the end of it. . . . They dumped it in the river. (10730)

There are heroes, too, as well as thugs, in these affairs. Solomon Freedman was a hero, and so was William S. Young, his only driver who, in spite of everything, went on, and on, making deliveries to Horn & Hardart. "He is the only one," said Freedman, "and he thought as I did, that right prevails over anything else. He knew it was a righteous cause, and that is the reason he went along, in spite of the fact that his life was in danger numerous times. He still continued on, and just wouldn't let down. Without him . . . we could have never effected our deliveries."

(10734) Young was threatened repeatedly, brutally assaulted, and "landed in the hospital on one occasion." (10735) Chief Counsel Kennedy seemed a little baffled by Young. He asked: "With the fact that you had rocks thrown through your windshield ten or twelve times and were beaten up, and these other threats, didn't you feel that you would want to stop driving?"

> Mr. Young. No, I didn't.
>
> Mr. Kennedy. For what reason?
>
> Mr. Young. Well, I had faith in that company. I stuck with them.
>
> Mr. Kennedy. You had faith in the company?
>
> Mr. Young. Yes, and I stuck with them, with the good Lord's will.
>
> Mr. Kennedy. The good Lord's will?
>
> Mr. Young. That is right. (10739)

Senator Goldwater undoubtedly expressed the feeling of many when he said to Mr. Young: "I want to congratulate a free American worker who has the guts to do what he thinks is right." (10739) While others may be more incredulous than admiring as they consider William Young's attitudes and actions, perhaps all but a few will agree that at least he ought not to be considered either an outlaw or a traitor.

Chapter 4

VIOLENCE IN
COLLECTIVE BARGAINING

I called the sheriff's office . . . and asked them when
they were going to open up the [picket] line and the an-
swer I got was, "What do you want us to do; go out there
and get our heads bashed in?"

* * *

Every man has a right to join a union and through it make
such demands upon his employer as he and the union see fit. If
the employer feels that the demands are dangerous or unreasonable, he has a right to refuse to concede them. The union
then has a firmly protected right to call a strike, and the employer has an equal right to try to keep his business going during
the strike. Employees, too, have their rights during the strike.
Under the law they may join in the strike, if they wish to do
so; or they may, if they feel with the employer that the demands
are unreasonable, exercise their right to work during the strike.

The public interest can be protected in no other way. To
make an employer shut down his plant and to force workers to
refrain from applying for jobs every time a strike is called—this
would be to assume that unions are entitled to have everything
they want and insist upon. As Chairman McClellan observed
at one point in the Record, "that means complete surrender [to
the unions]." (9679) On the other hand, it is impossible in a
free country to deny workers and their unions the right to call
strikes when they are dissatisfied with their conditions. The
employer can no more be trusted than the union with an absolute power to dictate on this issue.

47

If one party uses violence to deny the other's rights during strikes, the effect is to destroy the peaceful framework which civilization requires for the settlement of disputes. The party using violence to work his will upon the others assumes to himself the power of a dictator, the worst kind of tyrannical dictator at that. One or another basic right is destroyed: the right to strike, the right to work, or the right to carry on a lawful business.

The frequent occurrence of violence in labor disputes poses a fundamental problem for the nation. One might say, indeed, that there is no internal problem more critical than this one. It cuts deeply, poses a crucial challenge to our basic principles, and has an economic significance which cannot be exaggerated.

The Kohler Strike: What Happened

In some ways, therefore, the high point of the Hearings was reached when the McClellan Committee considered the long Kohler strike—a strike by the United Automobile Workers Union (UAW) which has lasted five years and has been characterized by mass-picketing, a nationwide secondary boycott, and perhaps by more instances of violence and vandalism than any other strike in American history. With these external features the Committee dealt exhaustively. But the deeper importance of the Kohler Hearings rests in the searching quality of the interrogation by the Committee and the philosophy of trade-unionism revealed by the union officials who appeared as witnesses. The Chairman, the Committee Members, and the Chief Counsel got down to basic issues, basic issues of law and society and the rights of the living human beings involved in labor disputes.

No racketeering unions were involved here. If there were thugs and ruffians, they were attached to a traditional union. And the union officials were not preoccupied with fattening their own bank accounts or embezzling union funds. The officials of the United Automobile Workers are, so far as an outsider can tell, as dedicated to trade-unionism as they say they

are. If their conduct raises a problem for society, therefore, it
cannot be dismissed as the old problem of how to keep racketeering down—it must be faced, instead, as a genuine trade-union
and labor-relations problem.

Two things should be made clear at the outset. First, this
chapter is not primarily intended to deal with the social philosophy of the UAW officials; that is the subject essentially of the
following chapter. Second, the Committee's job, in investigating the Kohler strike, was neither to settle the dispute nor
even to judge its merits. The Committee's fundamental job
was to determine *what* happened during the strike and who was
responsible for such unlawful and antisocial conduct as occurred.
Witnesses for the UAW repeatedly charged the Kohler Company with backwardness and unwillingness to yield concessions
sought by the union. However, Chief Counsel Kennedy was
not to be diverted. As he said to one such UAW official,

> You spent thirty minutes telling the Committee about
> what a terrible thing the company was doing in all of this.
> If the company did not want to sign with the union or felt
> that the demands of the union were too great, they had a
> right to take that position.
> Ultimately, when the strike came along, the first illegal
> act was done by the union, and that remained for fifty-
> seven days until the court intervened. . . . It was done by
> the international officers of which you were one, and of
> which there were at least a dozen others out there. (8549)

The total picture, in a general view, looked like this: Immediately after calling the strike, the UAW set up a mass picket
line which formed a human barricade, making entrance into the
Kohler plant impossible. In a gesture of ineffable arrogance, the
union gave passes to some persons, which permitted them entry
for narrowly limited purposes; all others were kept out, even
when the police tried to help them enter. Besides finding their
entrance to the plant barred, nonstrikers were harassed, assaulted, and humiliated, and hundreds of acts of violence and
vandalism against their homes and other property were recorded, to the point that a pall of fear and bitterness poisoned
the whole atmosphere. Large numbers of people were encouraged by the union to congregate at the Sheboygan docks

when a boat carrying clay for the Kohler Company put in there, and in the ensuing melee unloading the clay boat proved impossible.

The details of the Record fill out the foregoing summary. The strike was called by the union after a strike vote in early 1954. At the time, Kohler had a total of 3,344 employees. Of these, little more than a third (1,254) participated in the vote; but of the participants, an overwhelming majority voted to strike. That is, 1,105 voted to strike and 104 voted against striking (9567-68). It must be noted that the 1,105 who voted in favor of striking constituted just about a third of the Kohler payroll, and this fact must be borne in mind when considering the union leaders' theory of the duty of individual workers to follow the "will of the majority."

According to the testimony of numerous witnesses, including union officials, the picket line was composed of over 2,000 persons, and some thought there were as many as 2,500 at times. There was a difference of opinion among the various witnesses as to how many of the pickets were Kohler employees. Some thought there were as many as a hundred "outsiders," including international UAW officials, representatives, and others. Union officials uniformly took the position that there were no more than twelve to fifteen of such "outsiders."

Allan Grasskamp, president of UAW's Kohler local, was the Committee's first witness. He testified that the union had issued strict orders against violence and that the only unseemly conduct he had observed was committed by nonstrikers. As to violence, Grasskamp testified, the UAW "neither encourages it nor condones it." (8346) Let us remember these words, as we cover the Record—the union neither *condones* nor *encourages* violence.

The only violence of which he was aware involved depredations against the strikers, he averred. There were two instances, according to Grasskamp. One involved vandalism against his own home, the other damage to strikers' automobiles (8344-45).

Grasskamp admitted that the union had a practice of giving special passes to some who sought entrance to the plant (8344), but had difficulty following the Chief Counsel's inference that the union thus revealed an intention to keep all others out. Further probing made some progress, however. Chief Counsel Kennedy observed that the people who wished to continue working could not get in because "the pickets were walking so closely together or with their arms through one another's that it was impossible to get into the plant." (8351) Then the Chief Counsel asked:

> It is a fact that you kept the people out of the plant, did you not, when they wanted to come into the plant?

Grasskamp's answer to this was: "Yes."

But he had more to say:

> When I see people wanting to go into that plant to steal our jobs, and to take our jobs away from us, I suppose that maybe tempers are not always what they should be. (8352)

In considering this statement, the reader should be aware that the union treated nonstriking workers employed by Kohler before the strike precisely as it did the striker replacements who began their Kohler employment only after the strike had been called.

Fred J. Daley, the operator of certain vending machines under concession from the Kohler Company, told the Committee about the union's special passes. He testified that the massed pickets prevented him from entering the plant to service his machines. His only recourse, the pickets told him, was to get a pass from the appropriate union authorities—a strange situation, if it be true, as the union officials testified, that such obstruction as occurred was strictly spontaneous and not a part of union strategy. Daley was apparently willing to follow the procedures established by the "government" which the union had set up. When it was suggested by union agents, "why don't you come back to a board meeting [of the union] and *explain your case* to the committee?" that is what he did. His first pass, however, was a rigorously limited one, restricted to a right of entrance for the sole purpose of deactivating his equipment. He had to petition later for a broader permit (8429).

Those without passes could not get through the massed pickets, even with police escorts. Harold N. Jacobs, a long-time Kohler employee who parted from the UAW because he thought its demands upon the company unreasonable, gave the Committee a full account of his efforts to breach the blockade:

> I went down there the first morning at the regular scheduled work hour to go to work and approached my normal gate of entrance and I was blocked by some automobiles and by massed pickets. . . . So I did not try to enter that gate at all, because I realized it was impossible. I turned and went up on High Street to the main entrance of the plant, and there were anywhere from 1,500 to 1,800 people blocking that entrance there.
>
> So I parked my car, and I walked across the street, and stood there and I made no actual attempt to enter the plant that first morning, and I don't think that I did for 3 or 4 mornings. But I went down there every morning and tried to get into work.
>
> At that time there weren't enough of us, I would say, to really make a concerted effort to get in.
>
> But a few weeks later there were enough of us, and we tried to get in, and I tried to drive through in my car, and we were blocked and stopped, and we could not get in. (8394)

The local chief of police, while willing, was unable to do much for Jacobs:

> I asked the chief of police of the town of Kohler, Mr. Capelle, if he would try and he made an attempt. But they would not open the line. (8394)

Apparently from a belief that the massed pickets did not really mean to obstruct access, Senator Ives asked Jacobs whether the pickets had threatened him "personally." The reply presumably was instructive:

> They told me that if I drove my car in, they would tip it over, and I had phone calls, and I recognized the man's voice, and he told me I was going to get beat up if I drove across the line. He said, "We are not a bunch of kids. If you think you are going to get in, you are not going to get in today or any other day." (8395)

The sheriff of Sheboygan County, unlike the local police chief, did not seem very anxious to help Mr. Jacobs. Senator Goldwater wanted to know whether he had asked the sheriff for any help, and when Jacobs said that he had, the Senator then asked, "How did he react to that?" Jacobs' reply was:

> Well . . . he went across and talked to some of the people on the picket line. What their conversation was, I don't know. He came back and told me that if I attempted to get in, there would be bloodshed. (8398)

Senator Goldwater wanted to know whether Jacobs considered this a refusal of help. The reply:

> He refused, yes. We even offered one morning, when we became quite angry, and there were fifty or sixty of us, we offered our services as deputies to try to open the line to get through, and he refused to deputize us. (8398)

Jacobs apparently was never able to drive his car into the plant during the picketing; he would have had to run over "twenty or thirty people." When he tried to get through on foot, he said he was kicked in the leg by an "outsider," one Jesse Ferrazza, who, as Jacobs described him at another point, "was quite handy with his feet." Jacobs testified, too, that he saw Ferrazza "kick one man in the groin with his knee." (8399–8403)

A great number of other Kohler employees who had no sympathy with the UAW's strike objectives testified to the intimidating and obstructive effect of the mass picket line. One must bear in mind here that such picketing deprives nonstrikers of their basic rights even though no actual violence occurs. The moment that a man, through a reasonable fear of violent consequences, is compelled to refrain from going to work, he has become a victim. Marvin J. Harder, for example, testified that although he did not support the strike and went to the plant, wishing to work, the massed pickets kept him out. "I had been there on different occasions," he said, "and looked it over and seen I wouldn't get in, so I went home again." When Mr. Kennedy asked whether "it would be useless to even try to get through the picket line," Mr. Harder opined that "it would be healthier to stay away." When the mass picketing ended, Harder went back to work, a persuasive testimonial to the obstructive capacity of the picketing (8700).

Mrs. Alice M. Tracey, a widow with four children, apparently felt that she had enough at stake to warrant a go at the picket line. She learned what Mr. Harder apparently knew in advance: that she could not get through to her job. She rallied a group of women who like her wanted to get to work, and together they braved the massed pickets. "We got to the picket line, and we pushed them and they pushed us." No luck. And no luck even after the local chief of police did his best to help them through. "He tried to help us with his deputies," Mrs. Tracey said, "and they asked them to open up the lines and let us through, and they refused, and one morning I saw one of [the deputies] was pushed down." As for Mrs. Tracey herself, she "was tromped with something besides soft-soled shoes," and the tromper, she testified, was the ubiquitous Jesse Ferrazza, administrative assistant to UAW vice-president Emil Mazey, and a UAW member who had never been employed at Kohler, who had, indeed, never even been a Wisconsin resident. "He was standing right in front of me and he was stomping up and down like a racer would," said Mrs. Tracey (8388). Further attempts earned for Mrs. Tracey "a black and blue mark about the size of an egg, which I carried some six weeks." That blow came from a woman in the picket line, and Mrs. Tracey was angered enough to strike back "with the back of my hand." Whereupon the aggrieved pickets had the gall to charge her with having carried a weapon. Mrs. Tracey went directly to a deputy, however, and proved that all she was carrying was a plastic dinner sack with a drawstring on it, and a pair of slacks, a piece of fruit, and a sandwich in it. Furthermore, she testified, she did not even strike with the dinner sack, which was hanging on one arm by its string, but with the back of her other hand—the only one she could move in the crush (8389-90).

According to Mrs. Tracey, such "outsiders" as Jesse Ferrazza were mainly responsible for the violent obstruction of entrance to the plant. The strikers themselves, she thought, were in the background (8389). In fact, although she had worked at Kohler for almost thirty years, among the activists in the front ranks of the pickets she "didn't know a soul." She confessed that she was kind of poor at estimating numbers; but her best estimate was that the "outsiders," the pickets who had never been employed at Kohler, numbered more than 100 (8392).

Chairman McClellan asked Mrs. Tracey whether the purpose of "this massed group of people out there [was] solely to keep you away . . . , out of the plant?" Mrs. Tracey answered:

> Yes, sir; and they told us so. And they said, "You won't get through," and they just hollered that all of the time.

The Chairman, apparently intent upon finding out whether the officials of the international union were really responsible for what went on, then asked whether there could be any

> question but what the international representatives of the union who were there present knew at the time that mass picketing to prevent ingress and egress to the plant was going on?

Mrs. Tracey's reply was:

> They certainly must have, because they were standing there. Mr. [Robert] Burkhart [an international agent] was standing there right on the island, as they call it, and he certainly could see it. (8392)
>
> THE CHAIRMAN. From what you observed there in your efforts to get into the plant to go to work, could anyone have misunderstood the purpose of the tremendous crowd that was assembled there?
>
> MRS. TRACEY. If they did they must have been very, very ignorant. (8393)

It would be difficult to find clearer evidence of the violent and obstructive character of the UAW's picketing than the reason given by the sheriff's office for refusing to help Mrs. Tracey. She told the Committee:

> I called the sheriff's office. Who answered I don't know, but I called and asked them when they were going to open up the line and the answer I got was, "What do you want us to do; go out there and get our heads bashed in?" (8391)

Besides suffering assaults on the picket line, Mrs. Tracey, like a great number of other nonstrikers, was persecuted day and

night by threatening, menacing, and insulting telephone calls—
"I was called all of the filthy names you could lay your tongue
to." When she said that she had finally "put [her] telephone
down in an upholstered chair and put two pillows on top of it,"
Senator Ives' observation was: "In other words, they did not
bother you too much, did they?" (8390)

It soon became clear to most nonstrikers that they would
never be able to get to their jobs through the massed picket line.
The point was driven home when, according to the testimony of
Dale Oostdyk, the sheriff "said he would give us protection up
to the picket line, but he would not attempt to open it to get us
in the plant." (8417) For some, though, their interest in getting to their jobs was great enough to warrant further effort.
Mr. Oostdyk, who had been in the Navy for four years and
employed at Kohler for twelve, never joined the UAW because
he disapproved "the tactics they were using to try to influence
[membership]." (8410) Realizing that he could never get
through the picket line, he resolved, with four others, to try to
sneak into the plant one night through a back field. He did
not make it:

> . . . it was dark, and somebody spotted some of the pickets
> lying in the field and they started to chase us and so we ran
> and we came to a snow fence, and we separated and I
> jumped over this snow fence.
> It was quite muddy. This was in April of 1954, and it
> slowed me down, and I noticed some more pickets in front of
> me, and I turned and I almost ran right into them. One of
> them jumped on my back and about that time there were at
> least three or four more there and some of them kicked me
> in the back and on the side, and two of them picked me up
> by the arms. One picket was very small, and he hit me on
> the left temple while the other two were holding me, and
> . . . they swore at me and called me names and that I
> ought to be killed for trying to go to work. (8411)

Mr. Oostdyk told the Committee that he was then dragged to
the UAW's soup kitchen about a half-mile away, where he was
told that he had to join the union and participate in the picketing. He had a conference in a corner with Mr. Ferrazza in
which, he testified, Mr. Ferrazza

told me it was a good thing I was not in Detroit, because I
would have been killed for trying to go to work during a
strike. (8413)

Mr. Oostdyk was not having, and never did have, any part of
the UAW, despite the threats. That was his response to Mr.
Ferrazza's persuasion:

I told him that at that time I thought we had our rights to go
to work. The law stated that if you did not belong to the
union and if the doors were open for work, you could go
to work. That is what I had planned on doing. (8413)

One of Mr. Oostdyk's companions, Herman Miesfeld, proved
to have inferior resistance. Captured with Mr. Oostdyk, Miesfeld accepted union membership. As to whether or not his acceptance was coerced, there is some confusion between his
testimony before the Committee and the testimony he gave in a
Wisconsin proceeding. In the latter he had made no mention
of coercion, but before the Committee he declared repeatedly
that he signed up with the UAW, after its pickets had caught
him in the fields, only because he had been threatened with a
beating (8441-45). The actual enrollment of Miesfeld as a
UAW member occurred at the soup kitchen. The issue was
whether he went there willingly. Senator Goldwater set the
record straight. He said:

Here is a man who has been taken by force to a meeting
place. He did not go of his own free will, and he did not
receive an engraved invitation, and he did not call up somebody and say, "Boys, I am going to be down there in a little
while; I want to sign up." Somebody met him out in the
back yard and threatened him and escorted him down to the
kitchen. (8445)

Of the hundreds of Kohler employees who did not like the
UAW and who wished to continue working during the strike,
a goodly number testified before the Committee. All who testified, without exception, declared that the UAW's mass-picketing
constituted an impenetrable bar to entrance to the plant. Not all
actually tried to breach the line, it is true; but those who had
were enough to demonstrate that attempts by the others would
have been futile.

Numerous nonstrikers informed the Committee that besides being denied entrance to the plant, they were viciously assaulted away from the plant, and that their family lives were tormented by continuous, insulting telephone calls, demonstrations at their homes, and highly destructive vandalism. In all, more than 800 such instances were charged and recorded. A long list in the Record tells the tale of vicious beatings, kicks in the groin, paint bombings of homes, numerous instances of the "acid treatment," tire slashings, cars dynamited, and so on (8794–8816). Nonstrikers who also ran small farms said that some of their pigs and heifers had been poisoned.

Gilbert Moede had been working for Kohler for almost thirty years when the UAW called its strike in 1954. He wanted no part of the strike but found that he could not continue working because of the picket line. More than that, his little cottage in the country received severe treatment during the strike. Acid was sprayed on various objects, including his Bible, and his boat and its motor were damaged (8724–25). Finally, Moede gave up and quit his job with Kohler:

> It got so bad we would be laying there sleeping and if [my wife] would hear the sirens go past she would reach over and see if I was in bed, and she thought I was getting run over or something. Well, that is not living no more. When you have to have your window sheeted up and afraid that something will come in, that is not living. That is not America. (8730)

Willard Van Ouwerkerk is a little fellow, over fifty, who weighs 125 pounds and stands five feet six. He is also a Kohler employee who wanted to work during the mass picketing but could not. One night during the strike, he told the Committee, he and his wife went to a tavern in Sheboygan Falls, where he was accosted by a woman who identified herself as Mrs. Robert Burkhart. She asked why he did not want to join the union. When Willard indicated that he wished to continue working, she said, according to his testimony, "Well, I will call somebody." Things moved rapidly from that point. "As I got off the stool," he said, "somebody hit me from behind, in the back of the head." The next thing Willard knew, he was lying on the ground outside. The remainder of the story he learned from others. He was told that a man identified in the Record as William Vinson had hit him and then worked on him with his feet. The results were three or four broken ribs, and a punctured lung from which, Van Ouwerkerk said, he contracted pneumonia. He spent twenty days or more in the hospital (8868-71).

William Vinson was twenty-seven when he assaulted Van Ouwerkerk. When he testified before the Committee, in March, 1958, he said he was six feet three and a half and weighed "about 230." While admitting the assault, he insisted that he had used only his fists. He insisted also that he had got a raw deal in his trial for the assault on Van Ouwerkerk: "My position," he declared to the Committee, "is I think I got a very unfair and unjust trial on the sentence side of it." He did not deny that he had broken Van Ouwerkerk's ribs or punctured his lung. He only thought that the one-to-two-year sentence, of which he served thirteen months, was unfair to him (8876). One way or another, the professional unionist must make himself out the underdog.

John Elsesser was another of the nonstrikers who testified to the obstructive character of the picket line and to acts of violence and vandalism away from the picket line, threatening telephone calls, and all the rest. Among other things, he made it clear why it was advisable, as Gilbert Moede said, "to have your window sheeted up." On December 23, 1955, according to his testimony, Mr. Elsesser was sitting at home, watching television, with his daughter in his lap, when two jars came crashing through his windows, splashing paint over both his living-room and the adjoining bedroom. Nothing like that had ever happened to him before the strike, Elsesser said, and so far as he knew he had no personal enemies. He believed that all his misfortunes arose out of the strike. And they were many. He was kicked in the groin by some men he identified as strikers; an attempt was made to destroy his car with dynamite, and though the attempt was unsuccessful in destroying the car, it did result in a broken eardrum for his wife; and he was assaulted by a mob while taking his wife and family for a ride one day (8676-81).

The Record goes on and on with this kind of thing. Family life became a hell for the nonstrikers. Many of their wives became nervous wrecks, their children humiliated, their homes despoiled. Read the testimony of Warren Williams to get a sense of the bitterness (8771), or that of Peter Breu, who had worked for Kohler for thirty years (8779), or that of Mrs. Ole T. Pladson (8784). None of these had ever bothered the strikers. As a matter of fact, almost every nonstriker who testified was asked whether he had ever heard of any threats or harm done to the strikers, and each said that he had not. Of all the complaints registered with the police or the sheriff, thirty involved allegations of violence suffered by strikers (8834). Against these, nonstrikers swore in affidavits that they had been the victims of over 800 acts of violence and vandalism.

The kind of mass obstruction which went on around the Kohler plant was repeated at the Sheboygan docks when the Kohler Company tried to get clay, badly needed for its operations, unloaded from a boat. A vast number of people—some estimated the crowd at 3,000—had congregated there; there was also a compact picket line. In the absence of the crowd, and of the UAW's picket line, there would have been no problem in getting the boat unloaded. The Kohler Company had no difficulty in engaging the services of the Buteyns, a partnership which had all the necessary equipment and was ready and willing to unload the clay boat. Mr. Cornelius Buteyn testified before the Committee that as he approached the docks with his equipment, an international representative of the UAW—one Donald Rand—asked him not to unload the boat (9181). Peter Buteyn felt it his duty to do the job he had promised the Kohler people he would do. As he told the Committee,

> I primarily was interested and concerned about the obligation that I owed to the Kohler Co., who, for over a period of twenty years, had treated me as fair as any organization could. (9184)

But Mr. Rand said, according to Cornelius Buteyn, that "if you don't cooperate, we will pull out all the stops to prevent the loading and unloading of the clay." (9182) Meanwhile several Kohler officials had arrived at the scene, and, despite his brother's good intentions, Peter Buteyn felt bound to tell them that "it was impossible for me to unload the boat under these conditions." (9185) He agreed, however, to lease his truck and trailer to the Kohler people. As soon as the company tried to move the equipment into the dock area, though, the picket line closed in and all movement was impossible (9186-87). There in the street, outside the docks, the heavy equipment had to lie, in the midst of a yelling, milling, riotous mob—to the considerable embarrassment of all concerned, especially the political authorities, who exhorted both the Buteyns and the Kohler Company to move the equipment (9188). Finally, Peter Buteyn decided to make a stab at removing it—only to find that the big truck—an eighteen-wheeler—had ten flat tires. Getting that truck out of there proved quite a problem. Pickets were massed all around, and new flat tires appeared as quickly as the old were replaced. Peter Buteyn testified that

> The crowd kept on shouting, "Ask Mr. Buteyn to make the announcement over the loudspeaker system [which the Sheboygan mayor had used] that he not only is willing to pull this equipment back to the Kohler Co., but will promise never again to unload a clay boat." (9189)

It was a long time, and many things happened, before the Buteyns got their equipment away. Air lines were cut, rods hurled through radiators, foreign materials inserted in engines, and so on. When the Buteyns asked UAW representative Rand for cooperation in getting the equipment out, Rand is said to have replied in language which Cornelius Buteyn declared that he could not "repeat in the presence of this committee and ladies and gentlemen in this building." (9192) Furthermore, he testified, he was kicked so severely that he still carries scars (9193). Finally, after an epic struggle and the cooperation of a county agency which got permission "from the union hall," the equipment was removed (9190). The damage to his equipment Peter Buteyn estimated at between six and seven thousand dollars (9194).

*   *   *

The clay boat never was unloaded at Sheboygan. As we saw in Chapter 2, a boycott at Milwaukee prevented its unloading *there,* and indeed it had to leave the country before it could be unloaded. The mass picketing shut down the Kohler plant as tightly as a drum, notwithstanding the fact that at least 800 Kohler employees wanted to continue at their jobs. Even after the Wisconsin Employment Relations Board held the picketing unlawful, it was continued; it was continued, too, in spite of an agreement by the union to desist after a court hearing; until, finally, after several months, the Wisconsin court tired of the union's intransigent unlawfulness and issued an injunction. Indeed, the UAW appealed that injunction all the way to the U. S. Supreme Court, where it was ultimately upheld (9495–9503; 10005).

The damage done to principle, to persons, and to property in the Kohler strike was incalculable. One can say of it, positively, only that it was profound and devastating. In determining the full facts, the next inquiry must be addressed to the question of responsibility: Was the UAW responsible for what went on, or was it Kohler and the nonstrikers? The question may seem superfluous, but it should nevertheless be answered.

Was the UAW Responsible?

The uniform contention of all UAW officials before the McClellan Committee was that the International union had no responsibility whatsoever for the brutal assaults, the blockading of the plant, the vandalism, and the depredations summarized in the foregoing pages. On the contrary, all UAW officials were pious to an extreme, declaring that the UAW has a firm policy against violence, based on the alleged fact that the UAW president, Mr. Walter Reuther, had himself been the innocent victim in the dark past of management-inspired violence (9958 ff.; but see 9379-80).

Violence and vandalism suffered by the company and the nonstrikers, if there really was any, the UAW officials urged, must have been a spontaneous response of righteously indignant strikers to the reactionary attitude of the company and the "treasonable" character of the "scabs," that is, the nonstrikers. The worst that might be said of the International union, its officials observed, was that it did not take as much control over the conduct of the strikers and the picket line as perhaps it should have (10005 ff.). Had it not felt that control belonged exclusively to the local union, the officials felt, the UAW would have taken more responsibility. As it happens, the main burden of this is to assert in another way that the UAW did not bear any responsibility at all for what actually occurred.

It is well to attend to such contentions, but it is better to take a careful look at the facts. Perhaps the most important single fact is that, by the admission of all concerned, the International union—the UAW—spent at least $10 million of its funds in support of the Kohler strike (8342). It is possible that the UAW would spend that kind of money on a project over which it exercised no control; but it is scarcely credible.

Almost equally important is the fact that numerous witnesses testified to observing International officials, International representatives, and other agents of the International at the scene of each incident (except, of course, those incidents in which the guilty persons were undetected). Thus Emil Mazey, vice-president and second-in-command of the UAW, was identified on the mass picket line. Indeed, the Committee itself observed him there, in a movie exhibited at the Hearings, accompanied by eight other persons who were identified as agents of the International union. Lawrence O'Neil, a Kohler employee, testified under oath before the Committee that he saw some International officials on the picket line every single day (8454-56). This testimony was corroborated by a cloud of witnesses; it was controverted by not a single one.

Waldemar G. Capelle told the Committee that he recognized a number of International officials and representatives daily on the picket line and that he inferred from their conduct and other relevant circumstances that they were in control. Chairman McClellan, interested in getting this point clearly, undertook the following interrogation:

> THE CHAIRMAN. . . . You mentioned a number of labor leaders or representatives of the International UAW, I believe, whom you have identified as being present. Is that correct?
>
> MR. CAPELLE. Yes, sir.
>
> THE CHAIRMAN. I believe in answer to Senator Goldwater's last question you said that they appeared to be leading the strike or in charge of it, giving directions and so forth.
>
> MR. CAPELLE. Yes, sir.
>
> THE CHAIRMAN. Did they ever obey any orders that you gave in your official capacity as chief of police with respect to permitting the ingress and egress of those who wanted to work?
>
> MR. CAPELLE. No, sir.
>
> THE CHAIRMAN. In other words, all they gave you was opposition, obstruction, and mass picketing to prevent it?
>
> MR. CAPELLE. Yes, sir.
>
> THE CHAIRMAN. So they are bound to have known mass picketing was going on to the extent that it provided a resistance that denied those the right to go in who wanted to go in, and the only thing that could have been done, in your judgment, is to have used greater force in order to open the way up?
>
> MR. CAPELLE. Yes, sir. (8540)

Even Sheriff Mosch—he who, according to the testimony of many nonstrikers, had a very faint heart when it came to opening up the picket line—testified (a) that the picket line physically obstructed entrance to the plant and (b) that it seemed to be directed by "outsiders" from Detroit (8490-97).

A cursory reading of the Record is all it would take anyone to form a firm conclusion that the "outsiders" were the active leaders and—more than that—active participants in the UAW's violent obstruction of entrance to the plant. Consider the position and the role of only three such "outsiders": Jesse Ferrazza, William Vinson, and John Gunaca. None of these men had ever been employed at Kohler, or anywhere else in Wisconsin for that matter. All came to the Kohler strike from their respective locations in other states upon order or request of the International (8986, 10370). Each played a leading role on the picket line or in personal assaults upon nonstrikers. Jesse Ferrazza seemed to be everywhere on the picket line, as we have seen; he is the "stomper" who, according to Harold Jacobs, was "quite handy with his feet." (8400) William Vinson, the 230-pounder, admittedly assailed diminutive Willard Van Ouwerkerk, breaking several of his ribs and puncturing his lung (8868–70). In a dramatic confrontation at the Hearings, William Bersch, Jr., accused John Gunaca of a brutal assault (9079, 9119). During the same assault, Mr. Bersch testified, his father, then sixty-five years old, was beaten so badly that not only did he have to stay in the hospital for eighteen days, but he had to return seven times after that, and never thereafter fully recovered his health to the day of his death (9078–80). Joseph Rauh, the UAW's Washington attorney, made much of the fact that the senior Mr. Bersch's death certificate did not state as the cause of death the beating he had received (8694–95). Mr. Rauh's certificate gave "congestive failure or heart failure" as the cause of death. But no great acumen is required in order to see that such a certificate is not evidence that the senior Mr. Bersch did not die ultimately as a result of the beating. The certificate could not possibly eliminate the beating and its resulting injuries as causes leading to heart failure, a point attested to by the physician who treated the senior Mr. Bersch's injuries after the assault (8928–29).

Be all that as it may, the Record, even so much of it as has thus far been covered here, inexorably establishes the responsibility of the International UAW in the unlawful mass picketing. It financed the whole affair; some of its principal officers and many of its agents were continuously on the scene, participating in the mass picketing; and a number of witnesses, some of them clearly disinterested, were convinced that the Inter-

national officers and agents were in control. How could anyone reasonably infer anything else?

The point is established beyond any reasonable doubt by the
admissions of the high-ranking UAW official, Emil Mazey, in
his answers to a series of questions put by Chief Counsel Kennedy. Mr. Mazey's presence at the picketing has already been
established. In this colloquy he admits to knowing that the
picketing intentionally obstructed entrance, concedes that he
did nothing to discourage the illegal conduct, and even defiantly
asserts at the end that he felt the pickets had a right to keep the
nonstrikers out by violent and unlawful obstruction. Because of
the critical character of these admissions, the interchange between Chief Counsel Kennedy and Mr. Mazey is reproduced
here at length:

> MR. KENNEDY. Just answer my question, Mr. Mazey.
> Did you know, during the period of the strike, that they
> [the massed pickets] were keeping the nonstrikers out of the
> plant?
> MR. MAZEY. Yes; I knew they weren't going in, and
> so they must have kept them out.
> MR. KENNEDY. Didn't you know, as a matter of fact,
> that they were keeping the nonstrikers out of the plant?
> MR. MAZEY. Well, I think if you would come right
> down to it, they probably were.
> MR. KENNEDY. You knew it at the time?
> MR. MAZEY. Yes, sir.
> MR. KENNEDY. Did you, as a representative of the Inter-
> national, the person second in charge of the International
> UAW, take any steps to prevent this illegal, or at least
> improper, action of keeping the employees who wanted to go
> to work from their jobs? Did you take any steps to in-
> sure that the picket lines were open for those who wanted
> to go to work?
> MR. MAZEY. I did not. . . .
> MR. KENNEDY. Now, is it the policy of the International
> to condone this kind of at least improper action of keeping
> people from their jobs when they want to go to work?
> MR. MAZEY. It was my opinion that every worker out
> there had a right to protect his job.

Mr. Kennedy. And do you feel that they have a right to protect their job by physically stopping those who want to go to their jobs?

Mr. Mazey. Well, there was court action.

Mr. Kennedy. Just answer the question. Do you feel that that is proper?

Mr. Mazey. I do. (9058)

The International UAW did not rest content with mere approval of violent and unlawful conduct; it actively encouraged such conduct. Robert Burkhart was one of the principal International representatives during the Kohler strike. While his authority was somewhat vaguely defined, there can be no doubt that he exercised real and substantial authority. As he himself put it to the Committee: "I was in general charge of the situation." (8625) Among his other duties, it seems that he was chief propagandist for the UAW during the Kohler strike (8629). He insisted that he had "no authority to tell this local union [of the striking Kohler workers] what it had to do." (8627) But Mr. Burkhart seemed to be a past master in the art of speaking out of both sides of his mouth at once. His skill may be observed by reading some excerpts from one of his speeches to the Kohler strikers which was later broadcast in Sheboygan. He refers to the nonstrikers as "germs which would pollute [our union] solidarity," but insists that "the type of germs that I saw go into the plant the other day, in my estimation, are not going to pollute the solidarity of our strike." (8640)

These "germs," he went on,

> are the ones who are prolonging this strike, and anything that happens to these people will—and I am not saying this as any plea to violence against them in any sense of the word —but anything that happens to them as being accursed from now on out, if I can use such a term as that, certainly they have got to live with it. They have made their bed and they have got to lie in it. (8644)

Upon occasion, in spite of himself, Burkhart's double-talk became single-talk, and could almost be called straightforward. This is one such occasion:

> Now we know who they are. We have taken pictures of them. We have taken down the license plate numbers, we have made notes of what their names are, and just like anything else in life, every action has a reaction. You cannot do anything in this life but that something happens in consequence for your actions *and those people should not go without those consequences.* (8644, italics added.)

As this speech wore on, Burkhart apparently decided to leave as little as possible to the imagination of his listeners. He pointed out that in his home town, Toledo,

> it isn't necessary to have a picket line around the plant, not 35 pickets, not six pickets. We usually station one or two guys out there and sometimes, as I said before on other occasions, we merely put a sign on the gate. I predict to you that the time is coming in Sheboygan County, after these people learn the lesson they have coming to them, that it will not longer be necessary for us to have large picket lines either. They will have learned their lesson and will have learned it well. (8645)

When interrogated by Senator Mundt about these ominous words, Burkhart protested that he was referring only to the "lesson" which *social ostracism* would teach the nonstrikers. He did not say, he needlessly pointed out, that violence should be used against the nonstrikers. But he failed to explain why it was necessary to have "large picket lines" in order to establish "social ostracism," or how "social ostracism" would work when, if his goal was reached, there need not be any pickets at all at the scene of a strike, only signs.

One more example of Burkhart's rhetoric will be of assistance. After the usual double-talk of advising against threatening or coercing anybody "or anything like that," he exhorts his audience to keep after the nonstrikers, especially by calling them on the phone; "expressive language" is what he recommended, and then he went on:

> . . . let's do everything we can to keep them away from the plant before they get to the picket line. As for the smaller number of them who would have even courage enough—and I hate to use a decent word like courage in this respect—to come to the picket line in spite of the fact that they know

the picket lines will be fully manned, as for them, they are
going to have to take their chances when they get there.
(8646)

Burkhart's speech, despite the careful qualifications, was not
only a clear incitation to violence, insofar as it was addressed to
an audience of strikers; it was also *in itself a clear threat of violence to the nonstrikers.* Since it was broadcast by radio, there
can scarcely be any doubt that it was heard by many nonstrikers, and that the word got around to even more. A nonstriker
hearing, or hearing of, this speech, and knowing the way the
picketing had been conducted in the past, would have reasonable grounds to fear an assault from the pickets. The speech
constitutes proof, therefore, not only of the International's responsibility for unlawful obstruction, but of participation by an
agent of the International in such obstruction.

Burkhart's speech also tends to establish International UAW
responsibility for the demonstrations at the homes of the strikers,
for the vicious vexation of the "telephone campaign," and for all
the other persecution of the nonstrikers, including the acts of
vandalism. It was, in short, a general direction to the strikers to
make life as miserable as possible for the men who felt that they
had no quarrel with Kohler—and for their wives and children.
No qualification of this conclusion is called for by the fact that,
upon interrogation, Burkhart attributed responsibility to the
Kohler Company. His view, expressed to Senator Mundt, was
that

> when the perpetrators of these outrages were found, they
> would be found to be people unfriendly to the labor move-
> ment, people attempting to harm us in our collective bar-
> gaining. (8636)

After a while, the company had begun indemnifying nonstrikers whose homes were being despoiled by the acid treatment, the
paint bombs, rocks, and gunshot. Against the $10 million spent
by the International UAW in support of the strike, Kohler had
expended $21,297.88 in compensating nonstrikers for uninsured
damage to their homes, furnishings, and other property (8838).
Such company contributions, Burkhart suggested, raised the

possibility that "some of these things were self-inflicted," for "They came to a peak immediately after the company offered indemnification of these people." (8636)

Burkhart's reference to the company's indemnification proves only his special capacity to speak out of both sides of his mouth at once, his skill at double-talk, and his tendency toward double-think: qualities shared by all the UAW officials and agents who testified at the Hearings. The strong-arm men who traveled to Wisconsin for the Kohler strike admittedly engaged in brutal assaults upon nonstrikers. In some instances they were apprehended, tried, and convicted. The UAW paid for their legal defense; it even continued their salary while they served time (8877–78; 9600–3; 10062).

When UAW vice-president Emil Mazey made the same argument about Kohler's responsibility that Burkhart had made, Senator Curtis raised a question concerning his consistency:

> Now, Mr. Mazey . . . you said that the Kohler Co. encouraged vandalism by subsidizing the injured parties.
> If we assume this to be true, don't you agree that the expenditure of union dues for court costs, fines, attorney fees, and sustenance for convicted felons is, to say the least, the passive condonation of violence? (8958)

Mr. Mazey's response was a first-rate example of evasiveness, indirection, and irrelevance—referring to matters having nothing to do with the Kohler activities at all. He said:

> No, I don't think so, sir. We have been the victim of violence. . . . The president of our union, Walter Reuther has been a victim of violence. His brother has been a victim of violence. I have been threatened. (8958)

UAW president Walter Reuther's handling of this hot potato demonstrates why he has progressed so far in life so fast. Confronted with Vinson's brutality and with the ambiguous role in which the UAW was cast when it compensated him during his imprisonment, Reuther's condemnation of Vinson was vigorous; yet he still managed to make the UAW's compensation seem but a humane act:

I think Mr. Vincent [Vinson] hurt our union no end. I for
not one second will defend what he did, because I think he
was wrong. He was punished. He should have been punished. Things that we did [were] to help his family. His
family didn't make the mistake. I did not think they should
be punished. (10007)

Vinson was punished all right; but not by the UAW. There is
a more important point: if continuing the compensation of a
convicted assailant was only the human thing for the UAW to
do, by what twisted course of reasoning could Kohler's indemnification of the innocent victims of bullies and thugs be characterized as a bad thing, or, still more, as an incitation to vandalism?
We do not know precisely what Mr. Reuther would say on this
specific question. But the Record demonstrates that he, like
Mazey, Burkhart, and other UAW officials and agents, took the
position that Kohler and the nonstrikers—not the UAW—were
responsible for all the bad things that went on during the strike.
He waved aside the possibility that the inflammatory speeches
by Burkhart and other UAW agents were responsible for the
violence and the vandalism (10049). The company was responsible. It was responsible, he thought, by a process of reasoning which would do credit to his aides, Burkhart and Mazey.
According to Reuther, the company's duty was to shut down the
plant when the strike was called. When it insisted on operating, it was guilty of attempting to break the union. That being
the case, it followed, in Reuther-logic, that the company was
responsible for every single thing that happened thereafter, not
the UAW.

Now one must bear in mind here that a company's decision
to continue operating during a strike is well within its legal,
social, and moral rights—as those rights are understood in this
country; that, indeed, it is the duty of a company to resist what
it considers unreasonable union demands: a duty to itself, its
owners, its employees, and the general public. It must also be
borne in mind that neither reason nor legal authority holds that
a decision to operate during a strike means that the company is
attempting to break the striking union.

Reduced to its essentials, then, Reuther's course of reasoning goes something like this: when a union calls a strike, it is the duty of the company to shut down its plant and of employees to subordinate *their* wills, too, to the union's decision. If they do not, they must bear, not only such harm as the union sees fit to wreak upon them, but the responsibility for that harm.

Lest it be thought that no one could seriously take such a position, that somehow Reuther's attitude has been misrepresented here, it is best to present his view verbatim. This is how he put the matter, in indirect response to Senator Goldwater's request for his opinion as to whether or not Burkhart's speeches were inflammatory. Evading that question, Reuther delivered himself of the following observations:

> I believe that when a company deliberately and willfully embarks upon a labor policy designed to break a strike and destroy a union, that it must assume the prime, moral responsibility for anything that happens. There is not one enlightened modern management group in America who, where a responsible union takes a strike vote democratically, even though management may question their judgment, when they go on strike—management may feel that they are wrong in what they are doing, but if they democratically choose to go on strike, there is not one responsible management in any industry that attempts to break that strike.
>
> We had a strike in General Motors for 113 days. The company never made any effort. They told us they would not attempt to operate until the strike was over. We had a strike in Chrysler in 1950 where we didn't have a single picket at a single plant in the whole of Detroit.
>
> Why?
>
> Because everybody knew the company wasn't going to try to break the strike. It was an economic contest. We wanted so much for our labor power, and the company was only willing to pay us so much. So we had a reasonable, sensible argument about this. But they didn't try to destroy us and we didn't try to destroy them. But the Kohler Co. gets in trouble because they want to destroy the union. (10049)

Let no one be misled. These are Mr. Reuther's honest and heartfelt convictions. The thoughts expressed in the foregoing are repeated throughout his testimony, which fills a large portion of Part 25 of the McClellan Record. His is the view—well hidden, it is true—of all those men who insist upon unlimited power—always, to be sure, to be exercised in accordance with what he believes to be the "public interest"; yet always blind to the possibility that there is another side to the story, that maybe the person he vilifies and condemns as an eccentric enemy is the only true servant of the public interest. Reuther's ideal, responsible businessman is one who submits, to the union —not to the wishes of stockholders, not to employees out of sympathy with the union, not to cost consciousness, not to his own judgment, and not, least of all, to the public interest in uninterrupted production and prices as low as possible.

Moreover, his references to the situation in Detroit are misleading in a high degree. No one can know the facts completely, aside perhaps from the top managements of the automobile manufacturers. But there is room for doubt that the complete shutdowns characteristic there during UAW strikes are voluntary on the part of either the manufacturers or the workers. As several vivid demonstrations in the Record reveal, the UAW's long history and pattern of strike violence are centered in Detroit (9267 ff., 9379 ff.). Dale Oostdyk testified, it will be remembered, that Jesse Ferrazza told him how lucky he was not to be in Detroit because if he were there he "would have been killed for trying to go to work during a strike." (8413) The situation in Detroit may be like the one which Burkhart ascribed to Toledo: no one will work there during a strike because Toledo workers have already "learned the lesson" which the Kohler nonstrikers were in the process of learning (8645).

The importance of these considerations in the formulation of labor policy cannot be exaggerated. They reveal the UAW convinced of the righteousness of imposing everywhere the kind of sovereignty and power which it has fastened upon Detroit and upon Toledo. No expense is too great, no methods will be spared, when it comes to an employer, such as Kohler, who insists upon lawful resistance to union demands. He must be shut down. If he will not do so himself, we will shut him down. If our conduct hurts someone, it's their fault, not ours. All right is on our side. We are the sole and exclusive guardians of truth, justice, and humanity. We are the protectors. Big Brother is speaking.

The UAW's tactic of attributing to Kohler responsibility for conduct instigated and directed by UAW agents is nowhere more evident than in the "clay boat" incident." The bare facts are these: at least partly through incitation by UAW agents, a large mob congregated at the docks; there was also a UAW picket line; one way or another, the Kohler people found it impossible to get the clayboat unloaded; and, as we have seen, it took extreme effort even to get the disabled unloading equipment away after it became evident that the boat could not be unloaded.

Robert Treuer, an agent of the International UAW, admitted to Senator Curtis that it was his intention in a radio broadcast "to invite Kohler strikers and others down to the dock when this clay boat came in." (9159) A great crowd, some estimated it at 3,000, turned out, presumably in response to the broadcast and to "a telephone campaign . . . by the strikers, calling one another down to the clay boat." (9406) All disinterested witnesses testified to the effect that Donald Rand, another International UAW representative, seemed to be in charge for the union (9407, 9358, 9194). For example, Walter H. Wagner, Sheboygan chief of police at the time of the incident, said—when asked by the Chief Counsel whether the "picket line was being directed by Mr. Rand"—"Absolutely." (9423) The Buteyns, as we have seen, were approached by Mr. Rand and excoriated by him when they refused to "cooperate." (9192) Mr. Rand of course denied that he was any more than an interested spectator; such effort as he expended was directed, he said, toward keeping the peace (9274). Chief Counsel Kennedy found this incredible. He reminded Rand that:

> You were there at 7 o'clock in the morning at the arrival of the equipment, at 11 o'clock in the morning at the arrival of the crane and where all the damage was done, and 6 o'clock at night when they came to try to pick up their equipment. . . .

> You were there three times, and three incidents oc-
> curred. . . . (9276–77)

Mr. Rand replied: "Yes; I was disturbed about it." The Chairman had difficulty with Rand, too, as indeed did all the other
members of the Committee. Senator McClellan put it this way:

> You were in charge, giving the directions and refusing to
> let them get their equipment out, and you were threatening
> them if they did; were you not?

Rand's answer: "No." (9277)

Against the evidence, and against incontrovertible facts,
Rand, Treuer, and all the other UAW agents who testified on
the issue declared that the responsibility for the obstruction and
the riot at the docks belonged to the Kohler people. What
touched it all off, they said, was the appearance of Edmund J.
Biever, the Kohler plant manager. Treuer declared that Biever's
appearance was as though someone had "dropped a bomb in
that crowd." (9168) According to Mr. Treuer, Biever was an
object of hatred because he was thought to have been responsible for firing the first shot in a dispute between Kohler
and another union some twenty years earlier (9166). The position taken by Treuer and other UAW agents at the Hearings
was that Biever's appearance at the docks was an unusual thing,
out of the line of duty, and designed for no purpose other than
to incite a riot and thus to discredit the UAW (9174–75).

Mr. Biever testified that inspecting the clay at the docks was
a normal and regular part of his duties. He had been doing it
continuously since 1949. Moreover, he had been doing it continuously during the strike which began in 1954 (9471). Even
during the height of the mass picketing of the plant itself, he
had never had any trouble getting into the plant (9472). According to Mr. Biever, the excitement had already started at the
docks when he arrived (9475). This is borne out by the weight
of all the evidence, for it was the appearance of the Buteyns
with their equipment which set things in motion. And the
Record establishes that the equipment was already there when
Mr. Biever arrived (9472).

* * *

The general responsibility of the UAW for the unlawful conduct during the strike seems clearly established by the Record. The single gap in the structure of direct proof relates to the individual instances of vandalism against nonstrikers' homes and other property. As to them, expert inferences from the nature of the acts are the best the Record can supply. Steen W. Heimke, captain of police for a part of the period of the vandalism and chief of police of Sheboygan for the remainder, was unable to pin down the guilty parties, but he was convinced that there was a uniform modus operandi which "established a pattern" and that "it was a small, closely knit organization." (9343) This closely knit organization could have been an instrument of either the Kohler Company or the UAW. There is no direct evidence in either case. The reader must make up his own mind.

As to the rest, the Chairman seems greatly to be understating the true situation when he says:

> I am not convinced that this big union and all of its international representatives are so innocent in this thing. . . .
> (9241)

Senator Mundt seems to be much closer, in saying:

> I have shared a feeling with Senator Curtis—the feeling that a strike, any strike, has to be master-minded and directed by someone, and that we have been listening to a lot of guff by some of these [UAW] representatives who would have us believe that they simply wound up in Sheboygan on a happy Sunday evening with no idea of where the union headquarters were, what they were supposed to be doing, and they meandered their way around for three or four months at the rate of $90 a week.
> I have listened to it, but I haven't believed a single word of it. (9191)

The trial examiner of the NLRB, who heard all the evidence— in a different proceeding—apparently felt the same way. He found responsibility in the UAW for all the unlawful conduct except the individual acts of vandalism (10227 ff.). No disinterested person of common sense could come to any other conclusion.

Kohler's Position

Perhaps in a commendable effort to appear perfectly objective and evenhanded, some members of the Committee and its Chief Counsel dealt severely at times with those of the Kohler management who testified at the Hearings (9467, 9528, 9678, 8856). But no evaluation of the Record would be worth much which did not bring attention to the uprightness and unvarnished straightforwardness of the conduct of the Kohler management throughout the affair. It is true that Kohler had strongly armed itself in preparation for the strike. Yet, as more than one witness testified, it is entirely possible that but for its having been equipped to defend itself, Kohler might have suffered the same kind of assault upon its plant that occurred in 1934, when another union had called a strike and engaged in mob action resulting in two deaths. Whatever else may be said of the 1954 strike, no one, with the possible exception of Mr. Bersch's father, was killed.

Furthermore, the arms acquired by Kohler were lawfully acquired, for a lawful purpose: self-defense. They were never used (9491). When the sheriff canceled the deputyships of Kohler personnel, the company voluntarily turned over to the chief of police of Kohler Village the tear gas which it had in its possession. Contrary to the UAW's false accusation, the sheriff did not have to seize the tear gas (8499, 9492).

Much has been made of Kohler's alleged wrongdoing during the 1934 strike. A thorough analysis of that affair would take us too far afield. It is enough to say here that no one who reads the Record objectively can help concluding that Kohler was much maligned. Several witnesses in the McClellan Hearings told factual, documented stories concerning Kohler's conduct in the 1934 strike. It was unexceptionable and purely in self-defense (9195 ff., 9457 ff.). Two men were killed, but there is no evidence that they were killed by Kohler management personnel or nonstriking employees. Gilbert Moede, an eyewitness, declared that he could see firing coming from what another witness described as "a howling mob of thousands." (9457) People were shot in the back, all right, but who did the shooting was another matter. Mr. Moede thus described the affair:

> Across the street . . . you could see the fire coming from the spectators. One of them I know for sure that was shot, was shot in the back and he was coming toward the plant.
> They say "shot in the back." They should find out which way they were running when they say "shot in the back," and who was liable for it. (8729)

Against the clear and convincing evidence of several eyewitnesses that Kohler had only defended itself against mob action in the 1934 strike, the UAW was able to produce at the McClellan Hearings but one eyewitness—and his testimony, besides being challenged by Lyman Conger, Kohler counsel, as pure perjury (9620, 9749), is so confused, garbled, inconsistent, and nonsensical that it cannot really be understood, let alone credited or discredited (9871 ff.).

Kohler's only dereliction in the 1954 strike was that it refused to respond properly to the UAW's cues. It would not shut down its plant when the UAW called its strike. And it would not accept the compulsory unionism contract which, in the opinion of Mr. Conger, was what the UAW wanted most. Conger expressed the opinion that

> the issue that caused the strike, and the union will contest this, but this is my opinion and the opinion of my associates —the biggest issue was union security, the union shop.
> The union was very insistent on having the union shop, because they had gotten in by about a 2.6 percent majority, and in our estimation hadn't made the gains in membership that they thought they were going to make, and they were very anxious to have some way of forcing people into that union.
> In my opinion, we could have settled all of the difficulties quite readily had we been willing to concede a union shop. (9532)

The Committee investigated one other recent UAW strike involving the same kind of violence that occurred at Kohler— the Perfect Circle strike of 1955. William Prosser, president of

Perfect Circle, testified that the basic demand of the UAW there again was the union shop. He said:

> we did not believe that any of our employees should be forced to join the union as a condition of work in our plants. We recognized that we would minimize trouble and violence by closing our plants for the duration of the strike. But we believed that the strike would not be widely supported by our employees, and thought those who wished to work had a right to work during the strike. (10260)

If the judgment of Messrs. Conger and Prosser concerning the underlying motivation of the UAW in the Kohler and Perfect Circle strikes is sound, the UAW must be viewed in a new light. It must be viewed, not only as an organization which feels that no employer has a right to resist it, but as one which, like so many investigated by the Committee, will use whatever methods are necessary in order to impose unionization upon unwilling employees. A good many union leaders view nonunion workers as outlaws and union members as serfs. The UAW may not be in as strong a position to make a complete and candid disavowal of that view as its preachments would suggest.

On the other hand, those who take the long view may consider the Kohler position—far from being the reactionary, vicious, antisocial thing which the UAW officials would have us believe—was courageous, honest, and honorable in the highest degree. The Kohler management, by common reputation and the consensus of the press, are not skilled in the wiles and arts of "public relations." Mr. Reuther, when confronted with overwhelming evidence of violent and obstructive conduct by his subordinates, charmed and disarmed some viewers and the press by his "boyishly" frank acceptance of a fact that no one could have any doubt about: that his union had been guilty of viciously unlawful conduct. The Kohler people made no such disarming admissions—because they had done nothing wrong. They were blunt and direct even when persistently unfair attempts were made to put their entirely justifiable attempts at self-defense in a bad light (8854 ff., 9524 ff.). They never lied, cheated, or led the Committee on a merry-go-round.

That may or may not be good "public relations." But if it is not, the fault lies with the public, not with the honest men who refused to go along with the deceptive and destructive view that "everybody shared guilt in this affair." If the McClellan Record means anything at all, it means that the guilt was all on one side.

Chapter 5

EVERY NONUNION MAN
AN OUTLAW

*The people who have returned to work are traitors
to our cause. They have joined the ranks of the enemy,
and they ought to be treated as such.*

* * *

*I have nothing to offer but my labor. I sell that to them
and they pay me for it, and I think the agreement is
fair.*

* * *

*I think he is not the kind of person who helped build
America. I think he is not the kind of a person who
helped make social progress in America, to make America
strong.*

* * *

It is the purpose of this chapter to examine the thinking
which animates the conduct of one of the four or five most
powerful unions in the United States—the United Automobile
Workers—and to observe and evaluate the methods by which
that philosophy is expressed in action. The reader will find exposed here a series of distortions seldom equaled and perhaps
never surpassed—of fact, of language, of truth, of political and
social theory. He will see honest, hard-working, self-reliant
persons transformed into enemies of society, while cheap thugs
and demagogues are spirited into the ranks of those who have
made America great. Under his eyes an organization which has
proclaimed itself a defender of civil liberties will emerge as a
destroyer of civil liberties. If the reader concludes that the
UAW's pompous philosophizing merely rationalizes a thor-

81

oughly unscrupulous lust for power, he will have a great many facts with him.

Lynch Law and Mob Violence at Perfect Circle

Kenneth Griffin, a supervisor at the Perfect Circle plant in New Castle, Indiana, was driving two co-employees home from work one night, much as usual, when a strange thing happened to him. It didn't seem so odd, at first—just a Studebaker truck up ahead of him in the middle of a lonely road, blocking it. "At first," Griffin said, "I never thought too much about it. I thought maybe a farmer had got stuck on the hill, having engine trouble, because he started to back down." He took his eye off the truck for a moment, to look in his rear-view mirror—"to see if I had anybody behind me so I could get out of his road." When he looked back up, there were about "fifteen people with hooded masks" charging out of the truck toward him—"hooded masks over their head, clear down to their shoulders, black." They were loaded with rocks "to their chins." Griffin had a shotgun in the car. Though it was unloaded, he had shells in the glove compartment, so he swiftly loaded the gun, stuck it out the window, aimed it at the masked assailants, and fired. They ran. They "vamoosed as fast as they could." (10328-29)

Upon reflection, Griffin realized that the assault squadron could not have been a part of the Ku Klux Klan, because the Klan members, although they wear the same kind of hood, favor white material, not black. Members of the Committee bore him out on that, although Chief Counsel Kennedy thought it proper to ask whether the hooded assailants might not be of the Klan (10328).

It is hardly likely that they would be. The event occurred in September, 1955, during a UAW strike against the Perfect Circle Company in Indiana which exceeded the contemporaneous UAW strike against Kohler in the intensity of its violence, though not in duration or scope. How did it happen, Chairman McClellan asked Griffin, that he was carrying a gun? Griffin replied:

The reason I was carrying a gun then, there were several, I will say two or three incidents in the country of things happening like that, and Mr. Hoover, who is a supervisor there almost got blocked on a bridge, and he happened to see it in time and turned around and got away. As to Charley Alexander, another supervisor, they had logs across the road that he was traveling on, and he saw it in time, and he got away. (10336)

Between July and October, 1955, more than two hundred incidents of violence occurred in the area of the struck Perfect Circle plants, against the person and property of nonstriking employees. It built up, this reign of terror, to a savage peak on October 5, 1955, when a mob, composed only in part of strikers, hurled itself at the New Castle plant. Clyde Hoffman, an attorney who represented Perfect Circle, described the build-up to the Committee:

The people at the New Castle plant bore the brunt of the pressures of violence. As a result of this, tensions were built up and they feared for their safety and the safety of their families. By October 5, 1955, the people working in the plant were in a frame of mind to expect further and more drastic violence. . . .

On Tuesday, October 4, 1955, there were strong rumors that on the following day there would be a big demonstration by the union; that demonstrators would be brought in from all over the State of Indiana and adjoining states.

The reports were that they would come into the plant, drag the people out, and destroy machinery and equipment. Employees were warned not to go into the plant on the following day by workers from other plants in the city, and police authorities had information that such a demonstration would occur. . . .

On the morning of October 5, 1955, between 8 and 8:30 A.M., unusual activity was observed in the south of the plant on A Avenue and two blocks to the west of the plant on 25th Street.

As time went on traffic in the area increased out of all proportion to normal conditions and by 9:30 A.M. the streets were congested for blocks by parked and slowly moving vehicles. . . .

Women employees were sent to the cafeteria in the basement of the building. The men gathered in groups and

silently watched the activity on the outside. I believe that
every person in the plant was extremely apprehensive and in
fear of what was to come. (10350-51)

What came was a literal invasion of the plant. Signaled by
the firing of guns, two contingents of the mob, each numbering
hundreds, converged on the plant, charged forward, crashing
through the gate. One assault group headed for a car parked
inside the plant area and turned it over; another, numbering
forty or fifty men, according to Hoffman, having breached the
gates, "started toward the plant entrances." Outside, meanwhile,
a mob of at least two thousand was gathered. Hoffman's description continues:

> As the men turned over the car, an employee stepped out
> on a platform, a fire-escape platform, in the northeast cor-
> ner of the office building, and fired a 20-gauge shotgun low
> and in front of the men who were turning over the car, and
> continued to fire in front of the people who were approach-
> ing the plant entrances.
> With this, the demonstrators hesitated, turned, and ran
> out of the gate.
> In all, the man who fired these shots fired three shots.
> All of this I observed personally. I observed the break-in, I
> observed the shooting, and the turning over of the car. . . .
> Immediately upon the firing from the inside, firing from
> the outside commenced. A woman standing in the window of
> the shipping room . . . was shot in the upper left leg, the
> bullet lodging in the bone just below the hip joint.
> At about the same time, one of the supervisors from the
> Hagerstown plant, standing in the payroll office, . . . was
> hit in the abdomen by a bullet from the outside that came
> through the window.
> . . . After the demonstrators were driven from the plant
> yard, the shooting from within the plant ceased. Later, how-
> ever, the police did fire in the direction of snipers who were
> shooting high-powered rifles at the plant from vantage
> points within or behind buildings in the area.
> I saw the man that was shooting from across the rail-
> road track at one time, and I saw a man standing out to the
> east of the east gate, on the outside of the fence, firing into
> the plant.
> At one time he got behind a woman and reached behind
> her and fired his gun. It has been mentioned here, I believe,

that woman was shot in the legs. As I understand it, he was shot through both legs.

We have information, and strong reason to believe, that that shooting was done by a police officer of the New Castle City police force. I believe that he would testify to the fact that he shot this man through the legs. (10352–53)

The union's contention was that only a peaceful and spontaneous demonstration had occurred, and that the shooting from the plant was unprovoked. Here is more of Hoffman's testimony:

> This shooting from within the plant was not the firing into an innocent group of demonstrators as the union might like for you to believe. It was provoked by the particular group that had demonstrated by its actions that it did not have peaceful intentions.
>
> We do not know of any shooting from within the plant toward or into the large mass of demonstrators that congregated in the front and near the main entrance to the plant.
>
> This group of demonstrators was estimated to be in excess of 2,000 persons. I would, myself, estimate that there were at least that many people present on that morning.
>
> Following the break-in, the demonstrators barraged the plant with stones and other objects, shotgun blasts and rifle fire for more than an hour and a half.
>
> Nearly all of the windows in the office building were broken and many cars inside the fence were damaged.
>
> Stones were hurled into the windows, shotgun blasts into the windows. The shotgun blasts were from some distance and didn't have much effect. But I happened to be in one room when pellets came into the room.
>
> Also, they virtually demolished a house across the street from the plant, which had been occupied by the police prior to this riot. Later they set fire to the house and burned it down. (10354)

The mob included a great many people who were not strikers, and who were not even New Castle residents. Many were UAW members employed in other Indiana firms, some from more than twenty miles away. The UAW disavowed all responsibility in connection with such "outsiders," precisely as it had in the Kohler mass picketing. Yet, according to Hoffman's testimony, E. J. Kucela, an official of the International UAW (assistant regional director, 3d region, UAW) "said that the union would be willing to go back to peaceful picketing if the management and city and state police would cooperate and stop protecting nonunion workers." This was said, according to Hoffman, at a meeting held later on the day of the riot, with several high officials of the various governments involved, including Lieutenant-Governor Handley of Indiana. Moreover, Hoffman testified, another International UAW representative, William Caldwell, said that "if management only was allowed to enter the plant, the union would agree to peaceful picketing with but five men on the line." When the Lieutenant-Governor made it clear that declaring martial law could not involve closing down the plant, as the UAW officials insisted, "Mr. Caldwell then warned," according to Hoffman, "that if the plant operated there could be more violence of the same kind that occurred earlier in the day." (10355)

In a meeting held on the following day, said Hoffman, Caldwell refused to give any assurance that there would be no more rioting. "He warned," Hoffman continued, "that plants at Hagerstown and Richmond could become the targets of the same sort of violent demonstrations that erupted at New Castle on Wednesday, October 5." While Caldwell disavowed any UAW desire for such violence, Hoffman said he found this hard to believe:

> The many demonstrations of violence over the preceding two-month period, the size of the demonstration planned for that day, the turning over of the car and breaking through the police line, the unhesitating advance on and breaking into the plant enclosure, and, finally, the apparent determination of the union to stop production in the New Castle plant did not give credence to any peaceful intent. (10355)

One of the "outsiders" who participated in the New Castle riot was Paul Carper, an official of a UAW local in Anderson, Indiana, some twenty-four miles from New Castle. When asked how it came about that he participated in the New Castle riot, Carper said that a group in his local

> decided that maybe it would help out the morale of the Perfect Circle boys, the union boys, if we would go over

there, in a mass parade, and show the solidarity of the union
members, and kind of boost the morale a little bit, to show
that we were behind them in their sincere effort to get their
strike settled and them [sic] just demands straightened out.
(10364)

So he and "maybe fifteen or twenty-five" of his fellows "declared
a one-day holiday" in their plant to go to New Castle, to build
up morale there, and help out in the securing of the UAW's just
demands. When they got there, they merely had a good time,
nothing menacing, all peaceful, until the company opened fire
upon the happy and jolly crowd which had congregated. After
having listened to Hoffman's story, Chairman McClellan seemed
to be in no mood for Carper's. When Carper said that there
had not even been any shooting from the mob, the Chairman
said: "I just don't believe your story, if that is plain enough."
(10372)

Traitors to Their Class

There were no economic issues of any significance in the
Perfect Circle strike, any more than there were in the Kohler
strike, according to William Prosser, Perfect Circle's president.
The crucial issue was the union shop—the union's insistence that
the company compel the employees to join the union as a condition of employment. Mr. Prosser testified before the Committee that "Mr. Carl Batchfield, president of the New Castle
[UAW] local, said they would strike unless they got the union
shop and added that they had to have a union shop because
they couldn't persuade enough employees to join the union
voluntarily, so they had to have a means of forcing them."

The tremendous violence, the enormous crowds gathered at
the various plants, Prosser felt, could only have been designed to
force union membership upon unwilling employees, to make
those reluctant to join the union change their ways, "to intimidate them and their families." (10258–81) Perfect Circle employees were not the moving parties in any sense, Prosser felt—
not even those who were active in the UAW. "There is no
question in my mind," he declared, "but that our strike was

instigated by the International union [UAW] to force us into a
union-shop agreement. They expected us to be a pushover and
became desperate when the majority of our employees refused to
support them and the company could not be intimidated."
(10264)

In fact, Prosser said, one Perfect Circle employee who was
on the UAW bargaining committee resigned from that committee upon hearing that the UAW was intending "to bring in thugs
to do their dirty work." According to Prosser, this employee
"went on our guard force . . . and worked during the entire
strike." (10281)

Against the clearest possible evidence of flagrant violation of
law and of the rights of nonstriking workers, even of defiance of a
court injunction against mass picketing, UAW officials disclaimed all responsibility for the violence which went on during
the Perfect Circle strike, just as they had in connection with the
Kohler strike (10282-308). Chief Counsel Kennedy reminded
one UAW official that "on occasion, members of the UAW were
brought in from other plants in the neighborhood and massed
in front of these various Perfect Circle Co. plants." "It seems to
me," he went on, "that those actions speak louder than your
words saying 'We are against violence.'" (10306)

The usual evasion was the only response to this observation.
Now to expect from UAW officials a candid acknowledgment
of their responsibility for the violence which occurred in connection with their strikes would be wholly unrealistic. Yet one
must be, to use Mrs. Tracey's expression, very ignorant indeed
to accept at face value the UAW's disavowals and protestations.
The pattern of violence is too clear. Of course the UAW does
not use violence when plants are shut down during its strikes;
there is no need of violence then. But if a plant stays open,
and if employees show an inclination to work during a strike, the
violence occurs. Numerous instances are to be found in the
Record (9365-9400), and a great many more may be found
outside the Record.

This continuous presence of violence is no accident. It is of
a piece with the philosophy expressed by the UAW officials and

agents. It is, in short, their philosophy in action: the philosophy that every nonunion man is a traitor to his class, an enemy, a person who has no rights, and should have no protection. Emil Mazey, second-in-command of the UAW, puts it rather plainly. Walter Reuther says the same thing, only less straightforwardly. And the UAW propagandist, Robert Burkhart, gives the philosophy its active form.

One thing that can be said for Emil Mazey is that, unlike a good many UAW officials, he speaks his mind plainly, at times. Upon one occasion, during the Kohler strike, he said: "No one has a right to scab despite the law." (8980)

As we have seen in the preceding chapter, Mazey also thinks that pickets have a right to prevent nonstrikers from going to work. That thought is but a logical extension of what he expressed in one of the Kohler strike bulletins:

> The people who have returned to work are traitors to our cause. They have joined the ranks of the enemy, and they ought to be treated as such. (9000)

Senator Mundt wanted to be sure that Mazey meant what he said:

> Now let us take one of these men. He has a job, and a family, and a career of experience working in the plant. If he goes to work or if he went to work during that strike, do you consider him a traitor?

Mazey's answer:

"Yes."

When asked the basis of his feeling, Mazey replied:

> The purpose of the strike is to improve the wages and working conditions for all of the workers in the plant, whether they are members of the union or not. Anyone who aids the company, who makes it more difficult to achieve economic and social justice at the bargaining table, are betraying the cause of all of those workers, and therefore they are traitors. (9001)

Two things must be kept clearly in mind here. First, it will be noted that Mazey is speaking as though the issues in the

Kohler strike were exclusively economic, whereas the Kohler management took the position that the union was mainly interested in forcing unionization upon unwilling employees. Second, the inquiry into Mazey's views was not merely abstract and philosophical; the question was not whether the nonstrikers *ought* to have gone along with the strikers. It was whether the UAW had a right to prevent the nonstrikers from going to work by *physical force*. It is true that Mazey would not accept responsibility for the violence and vandalism at Kohler. But it is also true that he, and other UAW officials, made it perfectly clear that, in their opinion, the nonstrikers were outlaws against whom any kind of reprisal would be no more than they had earned. According to Mazey, if a majority of employees vote to strike, it is exactly the same as when Congress votes to go to war. On one occasion when he made such a comparison, Chairman McClellan caught him up:

> We are not talking about war. We are talking about the right of an individual to make a decision to follow a livelihood for himself or his family. (9064)

When Mazey said, "there is a great deal of similarity, Senator," the Chairman responded with:

> I do not think so. I think a man who has a job, who wants to go to work, should have the right. I think you should have the right to strike and you should have a right to put those pickets out there . . . but you do not have any right to mass them in front of that gate where a man who wants to work cannot get in. (9064)

Mazey's supremely arrogant response to this clean statement of law and morality was: "You have a right to your opinion and I have a right to my opinion." (9064) He went on to say that the law ought to be different—that it should prohibit the operation of a plant during a strike. When pushed, however, he receded a bit, saying that "perhaps" he would be willing to *go along with* a law which prohibited only the hiring of new employees during a strike (9065).

Mazey and his fellow UAW officials feel that they have or should have the power of government: when a union decision is reached on a majority-rule basis, it should, like an act of Congress, bind everyone. They may think that way if it suits them, but their own arrogant assumptions are not sufficient to constitute them a duly authorized government. Much less can they serve to establish for the UAW the power—greater than that possessed by any legitimate government—which Mazey tried to assert. The power over nonstrikers which he claimed for the UAW goes beyond the power of any legitimate government. Government decisions and laws bind only people within the boundaries of the government. The laws of the United States do not control the conduct of Germans; the laws of the State of Wisconsin do not control the conduct of New Yorkers. Even if unions were entitled to governmental powers, therefore—as of course they are not—they could not have the power to control nonmembers, people who refused to go along with union decisions. Clearly understood, therefore, Mazey's position is that the UAW is entitled to more power than the United States government. Ours is a government by consent of the governed. Mazey does not think that the UAW should be a government by consent of the governed. He believes that it is entitled to pure powers of compulsion; that it is and should be a government by compulsion of the governed. There is a government which believes that all should yield to it. It used to be called tyranny in other days. The current version—with which we have become all too familiar—is known as a totalitarian dictatorship.

Mr. Reuther's position, though stated much more guardedly, reduces to fundamentally the same thing. Senator Goldwater read to him the previously quoted Mazey theory:

> The people who have returned to work are traitors to our cause. They have joined the ranks of the enemy. . . . During the war, when they joined the enemy, they [were] shot, when convicted.

"Do you agree with Mr. Mazey's statements in that instance?" Senator Goldwater asked. Mr. Reuther would not say "no." He would not say "yes," either; but the more important thing is that he would not say "no." Instead, he became "cute":

> Well, I would choose my words much more carefully than Mr. Mazey did. I think that his words are very descriptive, but I would think that they were not chosen too carefully. (10047)

He and Senator Goldwater went back and forth on this for a while, with Reuther adopting the stock debater's evasion when the Senator pressed for an unequivocal answer:

> If you don't know my position after telling you these things, I will have to draw you pictures. (10047)

Reuther's final position seemed to be that, while he wouldn't have used the words "enemy" and "traitor," he would have found another way "to describe this fellow." And how would he describe the nonstriker? The best we get from Reuther is:

> I think he is not the kind of person who helped build America. I think he is not the kind of person who helped make social progress in America, to make America strong. (10048)

We shall presently look into the character and accomplishments of some who, presumably, in Reuther's opinion, "helped build America." Here we need only recapitulate that Mazey's "traitor" and Reuther's "enemy of progress" became in Robert Burkhart's inflammatory speech a "germ." He warned, it will be recalled, that those "who come to the picket line in spite of the fact that they know the picket lines will be fully manned . . . they are going to have to take their chances when they get there." (8646)

It is not easy, after studying and pondering the opinions of nonstrikers held by UAW officials, to state clearly and briefly what their attitude is. If all were as indiscreet as Emil Mazey, it would be easier. But the facts being what they are, one can offer only somewhat hesitantly a one-word description that would fit the conception of nonstrikers held by the UAW officials. The word offered here is: *outlaw*.

This word is chosen because it denotes a person who has refused to go along with the rules of society, and because the society he has spurned usually denies the outlaw the rights of other persons, and feels virtuous while doing so. Such, to this writer at any rate, is what the opinion of the UAW officials as regards nonstrikers and nonmembers of the UAW seems to come to. They treated, and seemed to want others to treat, the nonstrikers as though they were outlaws not entitled to the full rights and privileges of citizenship.

The UAW as an institution, its president, Walter Reuther, and indeed its Washington lawyer, Joseph Rauh, have all made names for themselves as vigorous advocates of civil liberties. They have repeatedly gone on record in vigorous castigation of the deprivation of the rights of Negroes which, according to their accounts, is a common occurrence in the South. They have been especially vehement in condemnation of the Ku Klux Klan. They have stoutly maintained that there should be "no second-class citizens in these United States."

The best clue to the character of some persons is often to be found by looking carefully at the ideas and the actions about which they make the most noise. This rule may apply to the UAW and its officials and agents. It will be remembered that Kenneth Griffin was attacked on a lonely Indiana road by fifteen hooded men. There was one difference between those men and the Klan; they wore black hoods, while the Klan wear white. It is difficult to find any other essential difference. Griffin had violated no law; he had merely exercised a right normally associated with first-class citizenship: the right to work, a right which Senator McClellan stoutly defended more than once during the Hearings as among the most important of civil rights. For that he was persecuted.

The Record does not establish that Griffin's hooded assailants were acting upon UAW orders. But there can be no doubt that the attack grew out of the UAW's strike and that it fitted into the pattern of other attacks during both the Kohler and the Perfect Circle strikes. One more thing seems reasonably clear—the attack was not inconsistent with what might be expected from an organization whose leaders expressed the views which we have been examining.

An outlaw status—perhaps second-class citizenship would be better—seems to have been what some Kohler nonstrikers had, too, insofar as the Sheboygan authorities were concerned during the Kohler strike. On the one hand, they were denied the protection to which they would have been entitled as first-class citizens; on the other hand, they were persecuted frequently on trumped-up charges, a common mode of treatment of second-class citizens.

Whom the Authorities Protect

The mayor of Sheboygan during the clay-boat riot was Rudolph J. Ploetz. The sheriff of Sheboygan County at that time was Theodore J. Mosch. Both were indebted to the UAW for financial and other support during their political campaigns. Both seemed to be much more preoccupied with insuring the success of the UAW's efforts to obstruct the Kohler Company and its nonstriking employees in the exercise of their lawful rights than with enforcing the law.

Sheriff Mosch testified that in his 1954 political campaign he and his "club" spent about $1,000. Of this amount $300 was contributed by the UAW's Kohler local. In addition, the CIO's Political Action Committee (PAC) spent $200 on mailing out campaign literature for him. There was at least one political advertisement in his behalf paid for by a "farm-labor political group." Sheriff Mosch told the Committee that "I have always been a friend of labor." (8487–89)

Sheriff Mosch also told the Committee that he could never get anyone through the mass picket line and that upon several occasions his deputies "went down" as they tried to get through (8481). He agreed when Chairman McClellan said that "there was sufficient force used in the picket line by massive assembly, by pushing and shoving, that you were unable to get any workers into the plant during the period of that mass picketing." (8490) When asked what he did about all that, he said a few arrests were made, but no convictions were secured (8491).

Those arrests were not identified at that point in the Record, and the Committee therefore did not get a clear impression of the character of Mosch's law enforcement. It was only much later, when Kohler attorney Lyman Conger filled out the details, that a true conception could be formed. Conger described some of the arrests made by the sheriff's men. There was Reno Federwisch, a nonstriker. Evidence in the Record is that he was arrested when, after being kicked in the groin by UAW agent Jesse Ferrazza, he struck back. The verdict: not guilty (9575). Then there was Adam Gulan, who was arrested for chasing some strikers off his property with a shotgun, when they menaced him (9576). One of Mosch's deputies arrested another nonstriker, Gilbert Loersch, for responding in kind when pickets called him vile names. The deputy said he had heard only Loersch (9576). Kohler's plant manager, Edmund Biever, was arrested for assault and battery when a picket bumped him (9576). Another nonstriker was arrested when, after being followed by three strikers for a mile and a half and then being forced to the curb, he drew a knife on his assailants. He was charged with carrying a concealed weapon. This case, too, was dismissed (9577). Perhaps the sharpest of these travesties of law enforcement occurred when one of Mosch's men arrested a nonstriker who, tormented by pickets and the tobacco juice they were spitting at him, drove his car over the barricade that they had—unlawfully—placed before the plant. He was picked up for violating a traffic ordinance (9576).

Hundreds of acts of vandalism were committed against the homes and other property of nonstrikers. In not a single instance was the guilty party convicted. The Record contains one proved instance of vandalism against the property of a striker: Conrad Holling's car was sprayed with paint (9337-38). Unlike the expert vandalism against the nonstrikers, this job was so amateurishly done that the culprit, William Bonanse, was apprehended, tried, and found guilty. But that is not the whole story by any means. Bonanse said he lost his head when Conrad called him a "scab" and made an insulting reference to his brother who had just died (8775-78). Holling admitted to the name-calling but denied the insulting reference to Bonanse's dead brother. Chairman McClellan pursued the point with Holling in an interesting way.

THE CHAIRMAN. If a fellow called you a scab, would you resent it?

MR. HOLLING. I believe I would.

THE CHAIRMAN. Do you think Bonanse had the right to resent your calling him one?

MR. HOLLING. I imagine so. . . .

THE CHAIRMAN. I asked you if you would resent being called one and you said you thought you would. I just thought it might also cause resentment in others to be called names like that.

MR. HOLLING. It may.

THE CHAIRMAN. That is the purpose of calling them that, to make them mad, to make them resent it, wasn't it, that is why you called them names, to insult them.

What other purpose is there to calling them names, except to insult them, to offend them? Can you think of any other purpose?

MR. HOLLING. None that I can think of. (8776–77)

The point is clear. Through some queer twist of reasoning, pickets acquire a special privilege to insult and to provoke the nonstrikers. If the nonstrikers resent the insults, as men will; and if they retaliate, also as men will, then they are prosecuted and found guilty—while their tormentors receive the protection of the authorities. The "human rights" all apparently belong to the bullies and the mob. Senator Mundt tried to make Robert Burkhart see the other side when he said:

Just as one good ordinary American to another, Mr. Burkhart, can't you imagine that the other fellow had a little difficulty feeling kindly, too. . . . He had been going along working at a place, and there was a vote to strike . . . and he was locked out of his job. His income was reduced. . . . You say that some of these fellows on the picket line got to feeling pretty bitter. I can understand that. But I am wondering about the fellow who is locked out, who goes to work some morning, who had a good job, who had a place to live, a good income, the door is closed, and the picket lines are moving back and forth.

He tries to get in, but gets pushed back. He might get to feeling kind of bitter, too, especially after he turns on his radio after the Holy Rosary Hour and hears himself called a germ. . . . (8641–42)

Mayor Ploetz is another great defender of "human rights" as against "property rights." In his thinking, "human rights" are associated with the mob, or with strikers and pickets at any rate; while "property rights," which he believes to be inferior, are what belong to beleaguered businessmen and nonunion workers (9435–36). Mayor Ploetz has always been, like Sheriff Mosch, a good friend to the "labor" movement—by which he means, of course, not all workingmen, but the big affiliated unions such as the UAW. He demonstrated his friendship by his conduct during the riotous clay-boat incident.

Like Mosch, Ploetz was indebted to the UAW for a large proportion of his total campaign funds, and for other support not calculable in money terms (9438–42). Walter H. Wagner, chief of police of Sheboygan while Ploetz was mayor, during the clay-boat incident, testified that Ploetz had assumed all responsibility for policing the dock area the day of the riot (9407). He also testified that the mayor had told him two police officers would be sufficient to handle the affair (9404). Steen W. Heimke, a captain of the Sheboygan police at the time of the clay-boat affair, testified before the Committee that, during the incident, he overheard a conversation between Mayor Ploetz and Sheriff Mosch:

> I heard the mayor say to the sheriff, "How much are you obligated to the union for?" And the sheriff turned around, and he was going to say something when he saw me, and he stuttered and stammered, and he said, "Let us go someplace where we can talk." (9313)

Mayor Ploetz later appeared before the Committee and in reference to Heimke's testimony said:

> I charge Steen Heimke with being a perjurer. I never made such a statement that day or any other day, or anything similar to it. (9424)

No one will ever know with entire certainty whether Steen Heimke or Rudolph Ploetz was the liar and perjurer in this affair. But impressions may be gained by further analysis of the Record. Heimke was a good witness who testified straightforwardly and gave direct replies to all questions by the Chief

Counsel and the Committee. The Senators seemed to be satisfied with both his demeanor as a witness and his skill and devotion to duty as a law-enforcement officer (9311-52).

No such favorable comment may be made concerning Ploetz's performance at the Hearings. Some facts are clearly established. *First*, the Kohler people had informed Ploetz that they were expecting the clay boat, that certain conduct of the UAW indicated the possibility of a riot, and that the Sheboygan authorities had a duty to prevent any "mob or riot interference with the unloading of the boat." (9477-79) *Second*, Ploetz by his own admission expended no effort toward getting the crowd dispersed so that the boat could be unloaded (9434 ff.). *Third*, on the contrary, Ploetz directed all his efforts toward preventing the unloading, going so far as to exhort federal authorities to forbid the unloading of the clay boat (9443-46). *Fourth*, the Committee obviously considered him an unsatisfactory witness. Consider these excerpts from the Record:

> Mr. KENNEDY. Didn't the union tell you then or earlier that they were not going to permit the unloading of the boat?
>
> Mr. PLOETZ. The union?
>
> Mr. KENNEDY. Yes.
>
> Mr. PLOETZ. No, sir.
>
> Mr. KENNEDY. No representative of the union told you that?
>
> Mr. PLOETZ. No, sir.
>
> Mr. KENNEDY. Certainly, early in the morning you found out that they were not going to permit the unloading of the boat.
>
> Mr. PLOETZ. When I got down there—
>
> Mr. KENNEDY. Could you answer that question? Didn't you find out early in the morning that they were not going to permit the unloading of the boat?
>
> Mr. PLOETZ. No, sir, I did not.
>
> Mr. KENNEDY. Didn't you find that out from the chief of police?
>
> Mr. PLOETZ. I had no such discussion with the chief that the boat was not going to be unloaded.

THE CHAIRMAN. Let me ask you something. Do you mean to sit here before this group and before this whole audience and the whole American people and tell them after going down there that morning you, as mayor, didn't know what the situation was? Is that what you are swearing?

MR. PLOETZ. Mr. Chairman, the question was asked whether or not I knew whether the boat was not going to be unloaded.

THE CHAIRMAN. You knew that they didn't intend to let it be unloaded after you went down there and saw the situation, didn't you?

MR. PLOETZ. When I went down there in the morning, the situation was not such that it might not be unloaded.

MR. CHAIRMAN. Well, you knew it was the intention of the union at that time not to let that boat be unloaded, didn't you?
They had pickets out there for that purpose.

MR. PLOETZ. No, I did not know what the intent of the union was.

THE CHAIRMAN. Do you mean to say you were that dumb? Are you swearing that?

MR. PLOETZ. I did not have a conversation with the union, that they didn't have the intention of unloading. (9430–31)

Later in the interrogation, Ploetz, perhaps unintentionally, conceded that his efforts were expended largely in helping the union prevent the unloading of the clay boat (9443). According to his own testimony, however, his conduct was motivated by a desire to prevent any harm to the mob! He did not care very deeply about the harm done to the person and property of the Buteyns; it did not concern him that he was under a sworn duty as mayor of the town of Sheboygan to protect the Kohler Company's right to secure its clay. Senator Curtis asked him:

> Did you feel that the constituted authorities had any obligation to the Buteyn Co. to see to it that they could carry on their business? (9435)

Ploetz's reply:

> Well, Senator, my primary concern was the safety and
> welfare of the people in that area. It simply was against
> my religion and against my principles and religion at this
> time to have placed property rights above human rights,
> when I remembered, and I was an eyewitness also, to the
> 1934 episode, when I saw what happened at that time.
> [For another eyewitness's version of what happened in 1934
> —describing it as a duplicate of what happened in New
> Castle and Sheboygan in 1955—see pages 9456–71 of the
> Record.]
> I definitely did not want to see anyone injured, blood
> shed, or anybody shot, in that dock area. (9435–36)

Senator Curtis insisted upon a reply to his question concerning
the existence of a duty to the Kohler Company and the Buteyns.
All he could get was more about "human rights" as against
"property rights." "I definitely would not allow the clay to
be unloaded," Ploetz said, "as long as the safety and welfare
of the people was in jeopardy." And again, "I think the obliga-
tion was more to protect the human rights than the property
rights at that particular time." (9436)

The Committee would not accept this mendacious and
fraudulent misuse of the term "rights." Its Members clearly
understood that Ploetz was doing what all those do who prate
so much about "human rights." He was declaring that those
he favored had a special privilege to deny and destroy the
human rights of those he opposed. Senator Mundt pointed out
that the Buteyns and their drivers were assaulted, that a nonstriker had his head bashed in (9443–44), and he asked the
crucial question: "Who was threatening the safety and welfare
of the people?" (9443) Senator Mundt went on:

> Let's stop at that point a minute. You mentioned a
> great many times, that you were against bloodshed and
> against killing, and that certainly is a commendable position.
> But just who did you think was going to create the
> bloodshed down there? . . . to have a riot, to have killing
> and to have bloodshed, it takes somebody going in there de-
> liberately trying to engage in some kind of personal attack.
> Who did you think was going to make that attack? (9446)

Getting Ploetz to see anything—or state anything—clearly was extremely difficult, but persistence sometimes is rewarded, and in this instance Senator Mundt did get a fragmentary and guarded admission from Ploetz that the UAW's determination to prevent the unloading of the clay boat created the danger of bloodshed. Ploetz said, with characteristic evasiveness:

> Let me put it this way, Senator, that after all it takes two to have, shall we say, a fight, and if the attempt would have been made to unload the clay, it would have excited the people that were in sympathy not to have the clay unloaded, and one thing perhaps would have led to another. (9446)

There are many things to be learned from Ploetz's position and his testimony. Careful consideration of the facts and of his attitudes should demonstrate to all that the determination of unions to force themselves and their demands upon employers and employees is what lies at the bottom of violence in labor disputes. One must apparently be on guard when one hears it said that employers or nonstrikers have harmed innocent bystanders. At least this question should be asked: which party was simply going about its lawful business, and which was trying to prevent the other from doing so?

Equal alertness is required when one hears someone preaching about "human rights" being more important than "property rights." One must remember that there are only human rights —that a "property right" is itself a "human right," and that the person who makes a great point of the difference is, like ex-mayor Ploetz, usually intent upon establishing a special privilege in one person or group to destroy the human, property rights of someone else. Kohler's attorney, Lyman Conger, reminded the Committee that nonstrikers are human beings of flesh and blood, too. He said, referring to himself and other nonstriking Kohler employees during the mob assault upon the Kohler plant in 1934:

> I thought the brick that was directed to my head was directed to a human being. I want to tell you that there were human beings endangered that night. This is not just a question of property rights. We are human beings too. (9201)

The UAW philosophy that only union leaders and strikers are full citizens, that only their human rights are entitled to consideration, would deny to nonstrikers a right to the protection of the laws. It would make them second-class citizens, outlaws, from whom good citizens should turn their faces, and against whom the hands of the righteous should be raised. This philosophy can only result, as it always has, in violence and bloodshed, so long as unions have a special privilege, secured through corruption of public officials, to form great mobs of demonstrators and to incite them to hatred and disgust.

There can be no doubt that the philosophy is an evil one, and that equally evil implementation through rabble-rousing speeches and other union conduct is inevitable. Both the philosophy and the implementing conduct must be eradicated. Perhaps attainment of that goal will be aided if some attention is directed to the character of the people whom the UAW philosophy would make outlaws, the human beings whom Emil Mazey called "traitors" and "enemies," whom Walter Reuther thought of as enemies of progress, whom Robert Burkhart addressed as "germs."

The Outlaws

Alice Tracey did not approve of the UAW, or of the strike it called at Kohler. She had worked there for thirty-one years, ever since her husband had died, and had raised four children by herself, without any assistance. She could not get through the UAW's mass picket line and was injured when she tried. In a seemingly endless series of telephone calls thereafter she was called "all the filthy names you could lay your tongue to." (8386–93) She is one of the persons, as Reuther would put it, who did *not* help "build America."

Harold N. Jacobs is another. He had worked at Kohler for 26½ years. He did not like the UAW, either, and felt he did not want to be associated with it. "My treatment at the hands of the Kohler Company has been very good," he testified. "I had every reason to go back to work, and none at all to stay out."

(8396) When asked whether he had received especially good treatment from the company, he replied that his treatment was no better than that of other Kohler employees, and then he added, simply: "I have nothing to offer but my labor. I sell that to them and they pay me for it, and I think the agreement is fair." (8398) He too found it impossible to get through the massed pickets on repeated attempts. He too was on the receiving end of the brutal, vicious, and dirty telephone campaign. Undoubtedly he had no right to expect anything else, this enemy of the working class.

Dale Oostdyk had worked at Kohler for only twelve years. He wanted no part of the UAW, mainly, he said, because he didn't like the "tactics the UAW was using to try to influence people to sign up." (8410) We have already seen that he received unusual attention. Caught while trying one night to get into the plant, commando-style, through a back field, he was savagely beaten and dragged into the union headquarters, there to be given another opportunity to mend his traitorous ways. But he still refused to join. He was a particularly hardened enemy, having been on active duty with the Navy for four years during World War II. The callousness to his country's needs which he developed in those four years was undoubtedly increased by his subsequent training. He is now a captain in the Army Reserve.

Robert Hensel, a twenty-year man at Kohler, was a special case. He was actually a UAW member, but he declined to participate in the strike vote and went to work as soon as the picketing was somewhat alleviated as a result of a court injunction. For these derelictions he received the full treatment: not only the eternal, insulting telephone calls, but mob demonstrations at his home, paint bombs, and the acid treatment as well (8751-53).

Carl Yerkman, father of five, did not have much seniority at Kohler, only seven years, but he liked his job and as soon as it seemed that he could get by the pickets he went back to work. He had never joined the UAW, but he too got the full treatment reserved for the enemies of progress: paint bombs, telephone calls, and rocks thrown at his home. Not much property damage was done, he observed, but there was some human damage. It scared the life out of his kids. "By golly," he told the Committee, "the children, I couldn't get them to sleep for about five or six nights after that rock attack." (8760) His youngest, an infant, was in a crib in the living-room as a rock crashed through the window. "The glass from the window, yes, it laid into the crib. I call that a dirty, lowdown, sneaky trick." (8760)

Peter Breu, with thirty years at Kohler, had no interest in the UAW, never joined, and he too went back to work as soon as it seemed safe to do so. He was treated to a home demonstration by a howling mob of 400, continuous, nasty telephone calls, and the paint bombs (8779).

Mrs. Ole T. Pladson was stunned by it all. She just could not believe that all this was happening to her. She never did work at Kohler, but she was the wife of a twenty-year man at Kohler and the mother of his four children, and he went back to work as soon as the mass picketing ended. So she too learned about the telephone calls and the paint bombs, at first hand (8784). As Robert Burkhart said, "every action has a reaction." "You cannot do anything in this life but that something happens in consequence for your actions and those people should not go without those consequences." (8644)

Mrs. Arleigh Gosse committed an especially grievous offense against her fellow-men. The wife of a farmer, she took a job at Kohler after the strike began. For this, she and her husband naturally had to pay. For them, paint bombs and telephone calls were not enough. Retribution had to be tailored to their situation. "They put a good-sized bolt in a cornstalk," she told the Committee, "and when my husband went to chop, it ruined our whole chopper." (8763) Among her other mistakes, she took the job at Kohler during harvest time.

Warren Williams was another UAW member, a father of three, and employed at Kohler since 1951. He took no part in the strike vote and went to work as soon as the mass picketing was enjoined. The effect on his family life, he said, was terrifying, especially the telephone calls, although the paint remover poured on his car was not easy to take, either (8769).

Gilbert Moede would never in a million years understand how he could be considered a traitor for trying to continue what he had been doing for thirty-three years, namely reporting for work at the Kohler plant. Moede appeared to be something of an old-fashioned type, someone with whom the Chairman felt a particular sympathy. Senator McClellan asked him: "Do you feel you are fighting for your rights just as much as the union men claim they are fighting for theirs?" Mr. Moede could only say—"well, here is the Constitution. . . . It gives me the right to earn my living. If I can't work, how am I going to exist?" The Chairman understood. "I agree with you," he said. "I think it is one of the highest civil rights we have, the right to work." Two men, these were, getting on in years, who have not kept up with the latest developments in thought, who do not realize that what to them seems the greatest virtue is really, in an up-to-date and more realistic view, the greatest vice. For his complicity in such vice and such obstruction to progress in America, Mr. Moede had to be brought to account. He was threatened repeatedly, and when he persisted he was given the full-scale acid treatment, family Bible and all. Finally he had to quit, for his wife, whose father had been a flag-bearer in the war between the states, could not take it any more. So much for one of the "highest civil rights." (8723)

The list is long, of these outlaws, traitors, enemies of progress, and germs. There were more than a thousand at Kohler, an unassorted group, united by only one characteristic—they tried to work at Kohler during the UAW strike, and for that they paid. Wilmer Mentink: a shotgun blast while his sixteen-year-old daughter was home alone (8696). Marvin Harder: another shotgun blast, plus windows broken (8701). Fred Yurk, thirty-year man at Kohler: one car completely wrecked by dynamite (8716). James J. Holsen, special account, striker-replacement, four small children: telephone calls; two cars, successively owned, sprayed with acid; a third car, dynamited; house stoned, windows broken (8721). Herman Miesfeld, beaten up, dragged to union headquarters, there allowed to sign up "voluntarily." (8421) Guenther Voss, one of those who succeeded in sneaking into the plant through a back field: car stoned (8432). Bernard M. Daane, striker-replacement, farmer: vulgar telephone calls, kids called "everything" when they answered; shotgun blast through living-room window when drapes were drawn, pure luck that no one was killed (8688).

There were well over 800 such instances of retribution. If Robert Burkhart was right, the day should not be too far off when the people of Kohler Village and the City of Sheboygan, like the people of Detroit and Toledo, will have learned their lesson. If they have not already, it is only because of the unusual profundity of their treachery. It could not be because of any deficiency in their teachers, for their teachers have had much experience in their work and gave of their best in the effort to bring to Sheboygan the enlightenment they have already brought to Detroit.

Men Who "Helped Build America"

The McClellan investigation was not directed toward filling out the details of the careers of the UAW's officers, representatives, and agents. But there are in the Record bits and pieces which provide a little information.

Jesse Ferrazza, the "stomper" of the Kohler picket line, the man who said, according to Dale Oostdyk's testimony, that Oostdyk would have been killed had he tried to sneak into a struck plant in Detroit, ought to know. A photograph introduced in the Record shows five pickets beating up a timekeeper who was trying to go to work during the UAW strike against the Ford Motor Company. Ferrazza was identified as one of the five assailants. That strike occurred in April, 1941. Representative Clare Hoffman introduced the picture and in his accompanying testimony declared: "that boy has been a member of the UAW, acting under orders—and Reuther is in this outfit—and for sixteen years he has been beating people." (9388)

William Vinson, the 230-pounder who assaulted little Willard Van Ouwerkerk, had been a member of the UAW for ten years in 1958. Besides being a chief steward of the UAW Briggs local in Detroit, Vinson said he was a "voluntary" member of the UAW's "flying squadron," an organization which, according to Senator Goldwater, has been identified as a "goon squad." (8885) Although he had never been in a strike involving his own employer, Vinson testified that he had participated in a number of other strikes, "four or five, maybe," but always on his own motion, never because he had been ordered to do so. Referring to himself as a "morale builder" (8884), Vinson said he couldn't remember the details of how he came to travel to Wisconsin for the Kohler strike, and that he simply returned to Detroit when he thought he had been gone long enough (8896).

John Gunaca admitted to being one of the progressive builders of America, with a career and an occupational background much like Vinson's. He too operated out of the Briggs Detroit local, where he was a chief steward. He too was a member of the UAW's "flying squadron" (9110). Again, he participated in a number of UAW strikes not involving his own local. He had gone to Sheboygan when one of his local officials asked him if he'd like to go. While no formal arrangements were made concerning his pay, it turned out that his salary and expenses were continued during his services at Sheboygan. Among those services, according to a direct accusation at the Hearings, was a vicious mauling of a nonstriker and, allegedly, also of the nonstriker's aging father. When asked why his services were needed during the Kohler strike, his answer was a genuine classic, an overwhelming demonstration of one of the possible meanings of Reuther's reference to people who "helped build America." Gunaca said:

> Well, . . . the conditions under which the people were on strike, and the conditions that they lived under prior to the strike, [indicated] that they were not advanced in the labor movement as far as someone like myself would have been. (9111)

We move to an even higher level of advancement when we consider Robert Burkhart, the man who was so dismayed by the ignorance and backwardness of the Kohler workers, and who was so anxious that they be taught the lessons they needed in order to join the ranks of those who have helped build America. If Ferrazza, Gunaca, and Vinson may be regarded as rank-and-file instructors, Burkhart should be regarded as at least a dean. Between 1944 and 1947, he testified, he had been a member of the Socialist Workers Party, an organization identified elsewhere in the Record as a revolutionary Trotskyite group. "I left the organization because I no longer believed in its principles," he told the Committee. "I felt," he continued, "that the solutions to our problems lay within the framework of our free-enterprise system and our constitutional form of government." (8617) Lyman Conger did not believe him, and he left the Committee in no doubt of his view of Burkhart's present political faith. He said:

> I say to you that I do not believe a word of his testimony —let me put [it] this way: That he may have left the Socialist Workers Party, but my dealings with him showed very clearly that the Socialist Workers Party had never left him, that his attitude and approach to all these situations was the attitude and approach of a confirmed Communist, which I believe, whether he is an active party member or not today, he still is. (9548)

* * *

Mr. Reuther undoubtedly intended to include himself, Mazey, Burkhart, Gunaca, Ferrazza, Vinson, and all the other UAW officers, agents, and representatives among the people who "helped build America" and "who helped make social progress in America, to make America strong." That is his right and privilege. But when, while including himself and his associates, he excludes the Kohler nonstrikers, and the Kohler management, he must not be allowed to go unchallenged. He has not the slightest rational basis for doing so. America is made strong by its free institutions, its workers, its capital investments, and its enterprisers. All workers, Kohler workers included, all businessmen, Kohler included, have had a share. But Reuther and his associates have done, mainly, a great deal of talking. They have never tired of patting themselves on the back and of issuing self-serving statements. They have in twenty years of violent strikes managed to impose a sovereignty of terror in a number of areas in the United States. They have prevented and discouraged people from working and investing. They are making a mockery of our free institutions. Surely that is not the kind of conduct which has "helped build America."

Reuther's arrogant and insulting references to the Kohler employees and management must therefore be bluntly rejected. But while recognizing his statements for the distortions that they are, we must also recognize them as something more—an expression of the philosophy which promotes and condones violence in labor disputes.

Chapter 6

EVERY UNION MAN A SERF

*I told him that 30,000 taxidrivers, whoever controlled
them in New York City would be a powerful figure.*

* * *

*You are saying under oath that the men who came to
visit you at night are afraid not only that they would
lose their jobs and their means of livelihood, but that
they might also be subjected to physical violence?*
    Yes, sir.

* * *

*. . . there was a fellow there and he would get up on
the floor and he would try to put his two cents in on
something, and the business agents didn't like it, and
Robert Malloy gave Robbie Hubshman orders to beat
the fellow up. So when the fellow was walking out the
door Hubshman walked up and clipped the guy a couple
of times . . . and the fellow never opened his mouth
[again].*

* * *

The McClellan Committee was frequently dismayed by the
conditions of virtual serfdom which it found in the unions under
investigation. The tens of thousands of letters it had received
from union members, describing abuses suffered at the hands
of union officials, were some preparation but by no means
enough for the appalling succession of disclosures at the Hearings.
Time after time the Committee ran into power plays by trade
union officials which suggested that union members were important to them only as tools, victims, or perhaps as chessmen,
not as principals to whom they owed the highest kind of fiduciary duty. Embezzlement of dues money, trading of members

back and forth, rigging of elections, rank theft, and, most ominous of all, an accelerating tendency on the part of crooks and
racketeers to infiltrate the unions—all these—"the rascality, the
thievery, the very scum of union behavior," as Chairman Mc-
Clellan put it once in insuppressible indignation (10790)—
parade time and again across the thousands of pages of the
Record.

Finding an intelligible pattern in this welter of chicanery,
violence, and racketeering is as difficult as it is vital. The conditions are intolerable; still it would make little sense to swing
into action with a program of indiscriminate "reform." Evil
results have causes, and unless those causes are perceived and
remedies appropriate to their eradication effected, the results
will remain the same. The Record is rampant with evidence of
dictatorial and tyrannical conduct on the part of union officials.
In many instances, however, the dictatorial conduct has been
consistent with by-laws and constitutions passed strictly in accordance with democratic, majority-rule principles. Such dictatorship will not be remedied by insisting that all unions operate
"democratically." Dictatorship by majority vote is as old as mankind. A deeper question must be asked, and a deeper cause
sought.

The conclusion to be drawn from the evidence surveyed in
this chapter is that the causes of the evils which the Committee
has found are two—violence and economic compulsion in the
from of closed-shop and union-shop agreements. The cause and
effect relationships between these and the conditions which so
exercised the Committee are the subject of this chapter.

Rich Pickings—on the Road to Serfdom

Sam Zakman wistfully described the power and security
which would fall to the man who "organized" New York City's
30,000 taxi drivers. He and John Dioguardi, ostensibly only an
associate but actually his master, were considering the prospect
together. "I told him," Zakman recalled, that "30,000 taxidrivers, whoever controlled them in New York City would be

a powerful figure." Thirty thousand drivers, at dues of, say, $3.00 per month per head, become $90,000 per month, and Zakman wasn't far off, therefore, when he told the Committee that "it would have brought in a legitimate [sic] million dollars a year in income." And more than that, Zakman thought, as he allowed his imagination to roam, "the taxidrivers would have helped us organize anything that was unorganized. You know how the taxidrivers are." Senator Kennedy apparently felt that the Record would not be complete on this episode unless Zakman were given the opportunity to indicate that there was also some regard, in his plans, for the welfare and well-being of the cab drivers. Perhaps Zakman's response was not entirely satisfactory, however, emphasizing as it did that power and money were the primary motivations:

> Well, it was a combination of both, sir. I didn't kid myself. Whoever had the 30,000 members would make a nice living and would have a powerful organization and would be secure. Basically, when we started, it was primarily for some security. (3657)

Sam Zakman was born in Russia, raised among the Bronx underprivileged, became a Communist, and achieved one of the heights of his career when he became a commissar during the Spanish Civil War (3610, 3638). Such training richly equipped him for his future career as an organizer in the "labor" movement. He was welcome in both AFL and CIO unions. United Automobile Workers (UAW-CIO) Local 259 seemed an especially appropriate spot for him; referring to the officers of that local, Zakman said "they were all Communists." (3668) He served as an organizer also with the Hotel and Restaurant Employees union and the International Brotherhood of Electrical Workers (IBEW-AFL) (3639). Yet he had not done well, financially; and finally he decided to go into business for himself. As Chief Counsel Kennedy put it, he went "looking around for a charter." (3610)

A charter, the Chief Counsel explained, is really a license, a commission to organize the unorganized (3623). Whenever Zakman ran into a person of influence in the "labor" movement, he let it be known that he would like a charter. He put it this

way: "the only way to get a charter is if you know someone
from within a union, and you might know the second vice
president or somebody like that and he would use his influence
to get it for you and if you made a private arrangement with
him that would be it." (3659) Zakman himself had never
bought a charter, of course, but he had heard of the practice
(3655). Normally, he said, one would have to pay if one were
looking for a charter before one had any members, but "once
you have membership, they are only too glad to give you a
charter." (3655)

Zakman finally got lucky. Through one person and another
a charter came to him from the AFL's United Automobile
Workers (not to be confused with Reuther's UAW-CIO).
Partly through coincidence and in part sentimentally (3701–2),
his local was designated UAW-AFL Local 102. The original
connection in getting the charter, he testified, had been Sam
Berger, business manager of Local 102 of the International
Ladies Garment Workers Union (ILGWU). The play went,
according to Zakman's story, from Berger to Paul Dorfman, a
Capone alumnus, through a person identified variously in the
Record as Dave Previant (3675) and Dave Privian (3610),[1]
till finally Anthony Doria, secretary-treasurer of the UAW-AFL,
was reached. Zakman had no funds with which to finance his
organizing campaign. But he was in business, anyway (3640–
62).

Money was what Zakman needed and Dioguardi could supply. The Committee's files revealed loans in all of $20,000 to
Zakman's local, and, according to Zakman, Dioguardi was its
only creditor (3613). Originally, Dioguardi had had no formal
connection with or authority in Local 102. But he was an avid
student, Zakman said, who asked a great many questions and
never said much, at first (3648). Later, Dioguardi developed
ideas of his own, whereupon the relationship grew strained.
Zakman's organizing methods had managed to get 700 members
signed up (3648). Perhaps Dioguardi thought things were not
moving along as rapidly as they should. An application was

[1]Mr. Previant filed an affidavit later, disavowing any acquaintance with
Dioguardi. Record, 13378.

made for a new charter, this one carrying Dioguardi's name. The new charter was issued in April, 1951, and shortly there-after Dioguardi was named—by International headquarters—business manager of the new Local 102. As such, oddly enough, he had more real power than Sam Zakman, the president of the local. Zakman put it this way: "he could not fire you from your position if you were elected, but he would take you off the pay-roll." (3658)

Dioguardi then began questioning Zakman's organizing methods and his choice of organizers. Zakman described the controversy:

> Well, he wanted to organize, but I told him that the only proper organizer to put on the staff is someone who would come from the industry. He felt that anybody could be an organizer who wanted to be one. I told him that when you organize an automobile worker, you should send an auto-mobile worker after him, and the same for dress workers, that you take them right out of the shops. He felt that he could hire them from the street if he felt like it and train them to be organizers. (3652)

Dioguardi's taste in organizers seemed to run to ex-convicts, if the Record is accurate (3634); their methods were extortion-ate (3719-34); and Zakman was not pleased with them—except, possibly, Benny the Bug Ross. "There is a fellow," said Zakman, "that did everything wrong and organized better than the rest of them." (3652) At first Zakman didn't think too much of Benny, but he changed his mind "after I saw what he did." How did he work? "Well, Benny, as we call him, used the methods that were used about forty or fifty years ago. He would just walk into a shop and pull the switch and say, 'Everybody out on strike.' That is all there was to it." Benny must have been the wonder of the New York organizing professionals and a pure phenomenon to the workers he "organized":

> Everybody thought he was crazy and they would walk out and the boss would sign a contract. It was as simple as that. I know it sounds unbelievable, but he organized many shops by the same methods. . . . He didn't believe in elections. . . . He was a hard worker. He just ran from shop to shop. . . . He did a lot of yelling and made in-

nuendoes, but I have actually never seen him get into any physical disputes, not while I was with him, anyway. (3653)

One thing leads to another. Before long Zakman was out; the UAW-AFL had issued fourteen additional charters to Dioguardi and his associates, of which seven or eight proved viable (3615); and, Zakman felt, something like 5,000 workers had been "organized." (3661) They were all paying dues, even though either no contract at all had ever been negotiated with their employers or, if there had, it was of the sweetheart variety. But what happened to the dues is something of a mystery. The Committee investigators could discover no records. Chief Counsel Kennedy explained to the Senators:

> We have had a rather difficult time with the books and records of these unions. We find that we will come to one of these locals, for instance, and find there was a fire the day before and the records have been destroyed. Or, again, that the janitor threw the records out, or . . . it happened that the district attorney was subpenaing the records at the time and to make sure they were turned over to the district attorney . . . bright and early, they took the books and records out and put them in their automobile and then some burglar broke into their automobile and stole the books and records. (3620)

George Meany, then head of the AFL in New York, did not like anything about Dioguardi or his associates. He therefore ruled that the taxi drivers were within the Teamsters' jurisdiction, and that Dioguardi would have to give them up (3617–18). Mr. James R. Hoffa enters the story at this point, with a suggestion that Dioguardi, with his locals and their members, come into the Teamsters. The New York Teamster leaders then in power, Tom Hickey and Martin Lacey, however, had a different idea. They felt that Dioguardi had, in Chief Counsel Kennedy's words, "a bad background and the wrong kind of friends." So, the Chief Counsel continued, "they had a meeting about it, and subsequently, Dave Beck [then president of the Teamsters] ruled that Johnny Dio should not be brought into the teamsters organization at that time. Jimmy Hoffa was overruled." (3618, 3711–12)

For such a man as Hoffa, reverses and overrulings are only challenges. He had his way, ultimately, in New York, just as he has had in most other places. Tom Hickey and Martin Lacey were men of tremendous power. They were in control of Teamster Joint Council 16, an aggregation of fifty-eight locals (numbering some 125,000 members) which is in a position at any time to throttle New York City and to guarantee the success or failure of any strike or organizing drive on Manhattan by the attitude it takes toward crossing picket lines (3597). Senator Kennedy put this matter clearly when he said: "that gives . . . that joint council . . . free power not only over the economic life of New York but over all of the other unions who might be completely unconnected with the teamster leadership." (3598)

In spite of all that, the man now at the top in New York is John O'Rourke, the man Hoffa backed against Tom Hickey's desire to keep Martin Lacey at the head of the Council. Furthermore, the charters and the locals which were at first the product of Sam Zakman's aspirations to power and security and then became the barony of Dioguardi, only to suffer a setback at the hands of George Meany, Tom Hickey, Martin Lacey, and Dave Beck—those same charters, according to the Record, were instrumental in bringing Hoffa's candidate to power in Joint Council 16.

Members, if Any, Irrelevant:
Of "Paper" Locals and Mergers

Hoffa and Dioguardi seem to have been close associates, with a certain fondness for each other. "In 1954," Chief Counsel Kennedy told the Committee, "Johnny Dio, . . . supposedly, resigned from the [UAW-AFL]. It was shortly after, in October, 1954, that he met with Jimmy Hoffa in New York City, and in front of the press at that time Mr. Hoffa put his arms around him, and Johnny Dio said, 'I am looking for a job, Jimmy.' And Jimmy said, 'Any time you want a job, Johnny, you can come to me.' During 1955, Johnny Dio remained, in fact, in control —or his lieutenants remained in control—of the [UAW-AFL locals]." (3622)

The Record indicates that Hoffa was to find use for Dioguardi and for the UAW-AFL locals over which he retained control. A crucial election was coming up early in 1956 which would determine the control of Teamsters Joint Council 16, in New York. In that election each Teamsters local in the Council could cast seven votes, whether it had one or 10,000 members, or none. By tradition, no new charters within the Joint Council's jurisdiction could issue without notice to and approval of the Joint Council. Hence the Council must have been astonished when, in Chief Counsel Kennedy's words, "on the eve of the election, the joint council received notification that seven different locals that they never knew existed suddenly requested permission to affiliate with the joint council, and, therefore, to vote in the coming election. . . . These locals evidently had been chartered . . . without the notification to the joint council and without notification to the general organizer, the international organization in that area. . . . They [had] been chartered at first at the request of Mr. James Hoffa and that request had been made to Mr. Einar Mohn in the international headquarters here in Washington, D.C., and those charters had been granted and given to the seven different locals." (3623)

The issuance of these charters was all in proper form, signed by Dave Beck and other officers of the International. Everything was fine—except that five of the new locals had no members. But even so they could each cast seven votes in the overwhelmingly important Joint Council election; that they were phantoms, ghost unions, made only of paper, made no difference. The names of the officers of Dioguardi's empty UAW-AFL locals were simply transferred to the new Teamsters locals. In two instances, members were transferred as well; but in the rest, a name, an address, and a list of officers were all the locals amounted to. There was a mad scramble to distribute members around to all the paper locals, when somehow news of the operation's duplicity leaked out. There were other anomalous features, too—for one, some of the persons named officers of the paper locals did not even know of their existence, much less that they themselves were officers (3627-29).

As it happens, Hoffa's candidate, John O'Rourke did not need the votes of the paper locals; he would have won without them, if certain challenged ballots other than those of the paper locals could have been counted. A court ruled against him on that, and Martin Lacey was declared the winner. But he occupied the post for only a short while; he soon resigned in favor of John O'Rourke on the ground of ill health.

After digesting the facts and pondering them, Chairman McClellan observed that:

> This was a power fight, in other words, internal union power fight, and the interests for O'Rourke undertook this procedure in order to get control of the joint council. (3630)

Counsel Kennedy immediately interjected "which controls all of these things that we have discussed earlier," meaning the economic life of New York City.

Among the persons transferred from Dioguardi's UAW-AFL locals to the Teamsters were employees of a restaurant equipment manufacturer, a toy manufacturer, a rubber products company, a maker of Christmas tree lights, and some sixty other companies having not the remotest relationship to the Teamsters. There were even employees of a manufacturer of vitamin pills (3632-33). Senator Curtis observed that these union members "were moved about like they were chessmen." Chief Counsel Kennedy put it another way: "These individuals decided these members should be transferred and they were transferred." (3631)

It happened often, this moving of union members around as if they were pieces in a game of chess, with about the same volition as a chessman. Employees had almost nothing to do with the sometimes petty, sometimes funny, sometimes large and dramatic facts we have been surveying. Actually, all they did was pay dues, although they had a bit of excitement now and then when Benny the Bug would burst into a shop, "pull the switch," and yell—"Everybody out on strike." But as a reading of the whole of Part 10 of the Record would reveal, their normal role was that of the exploited victim or the leverage for either an extortion gambit or a big-power play. They come into the picture as a materialization of Sam Zakman's dream of power and security, and they go out of the picture as incongruous digits among the 1,500,000 human beings who, largely unwittingly, constitute the entire basis of the tremendous power wielded by the president and other officers of the Teamsters.

They were a part—even if pretty silent—of the "labor" movement. They are a part of the big-labor movement in precisely the same way that A & P's grocery clerks became a part of Max Block's Meat Cutters. It will be remembered from Chapter 2 that there were indications of a deal between the Butchers and the Retail Clerks, pursuant to which A & P's clerks were eventually to go to the latter. Of that affair, Senator McClellan said: "I am sure we don't know all of the story, but they got together and made some kind of a deal where at the end of this contract all of these employees, again, were pawns, and would be delivered over to the Clerks Union." (11298)

How much of this sort of thing goes on, nobody will ever know. But that a great deal goes on is subject to no doubt at all. While all the Senators deplored manipulation of membership whenever it turned up in the Record, none has ventured any opinion at all of the AFL-CIO's greatly publicized "no-raiding" pact. That pact is an agreement, among unions belonging to the AFL-CIO, largely of the kind which, when made by Max Block and the Retail Clerks, caused the Senators to become indignant. It provides that, quite without regard to the preferences of employees, they "belong" to certain unions, and no others may seek to represent them. The "no-raiding" pact becomes no less cynical a manipulation of the human rights of workingmen merely because it has been praised and publicized so widely, because it is the creation of the AFL-CIO, or because it has not been a part of the Committee's investigation.

The essential feature of serfdom lies in the control of one human being by another. It is not yet possible for union leaders completely to enslave their members; but they come closer and closer.

Harold J. Gibbons is, by common repute, the heavy thinker of the Teamsters Union, the Teamsters' challenge to the ideological pre-eminence of Walter Reuther and his UAW associates. According to a biography of Gibbons distributed by the Teamsters, he is "a student of economics, history, and the labor movement; a writer of textbooks; a pioneer in free medical care, the guaranteed annual wage, and non-discrimination clauses in the labor movement." (14555 ff.)

According to testimony before the McClellan Committee, and the accusation of Chief Counsel Kennedy, Gibbons brought violence into St. Louis on an unprecedented scale (14254 ff.); he tolerated no opposition within his union, or without (14259); and he bought his Teamsters Local 688 from its previous officers. That local was originally formed by Lawrence J. Camie, in 1941 (14238). Camie apparently met Gibbons in Chicago, while the latter was seeking an entry into the Teamsters from the CIO, whence, perhaps, his ideological propensities trace. When he and Camie met in 1949, Gibbons was chief of the United Distribution Workers, at that time an independent union which he had but recently cut loose from the CIO's Retail, Wholesale, and Department Store Employees. Dragging his 5,000 members along with him, Gibbons had told Dave Beck, according to Camie's testimony, that he wanted in with the Teamsters (14239).

Camie's story continues: He himself had suggested the merger of his 2,500-member Teamsters Local 688 and Gibbons' 5,000. The deal worked out to the satisfaction of everyone concerned—that is, of all the union leaders concerned, for the Record indicates that the members were not consulted. Gibbons became president of the merged local, and Camie received $36,360 in "severance pay" which was disbursed in three annual installments. All other members of the executive board of old Local 688 were also given "severance pay" if they chose to resign (14240).

To Chief Counsel Kennedy the operation seemed nothing more than a purchase by Gibbons and a sale by Camie of the

2,500 Teamster members. When Camie protested that he would not have "the right to sell the property that belonged to someone else," Kennedy remarked: "That's why you are here today." The transfer of members—or the "merger"—involved in all a payment of $78,410 to Camie and other leaders of old Local 688 (14247–48).

Chairman McClellan liked nothing about the deal. When he asked Camie why the Local 688 members were not consulted, not even notified in advance of what was happening to them, Camie testified that it was "past the regular meeting." And anyway, he added, "the cold weather wouldn't have brought out a handful of members." Now there are a good many reasons for the failure of union members to turn up at even the most important union meetings, and we shall consider some of the possible explanations later in this chapter. For the present, however, it is sufficient to notice the Chairman's reaction to the affair. He thought the membership ought to know "when it's being traded off or merged." The Camie-Gibbons deal, he declared, was "quite typical," with "the membership . . . handled like they were chattels, and not human beings, and not given a chance" to decide their own fate. It seemed deplorable to him that "a few labor leaders [could] get together and make a deal out of which they expect to profit." (14252) When Camie remarked that corporations are always merging, the Chairman observed that stockholders have a right to vote on mergers, that no merger could ever be accomplished simply on the basis of a decision by the corporate management. Senator McClellan's conclusion should be considered carefully:

> That is exactly what is permitting all of this corruption . . . in some unions. . . . You officers take the position that you own [the union] and can run it and do what you please with it. (14253)

Confronted with the foregoing charges, Gibbons later insisted to the Committee that the $78,410 was severance pay, not the price paid to purchase Local 688. Severance pay was proper, he contended, because "We don't run a business. We run a movement." (14565)

Rigged Conventions:
Manipulations of the Mighty

Besides his learning, Gibbons brought with him to St. Louis in 1941, as has been mentioned, more organizing violence than any other trade-union leader had ever introduced in that strongly organized city—such was the testimony of Captain Thomas L. Moran, of the bombing and arson squad of the St. Louis Police Department. According to Moran, "practically every union [Gibbons] has been connected with has had one incident after another of violence and disturbances on picket lines." (14254) As we shall see, the testimony indicates that Gibbons no more tolerated differences of opinion within the union than he did resistance to his organizing efforts. Brutality, the Record shows, was the prescription in either case (14645).

But it has not been all brutality in Gibbons' rise to eminence from a mere student to great power in the "movement." He is now widely regarded as "No. 2 man" in the Teamsters. His offices in that segment of the "movement" are many: executive assistant to Hoffa, International vice-president, secretary-treasurer of the twelve-state Central Conference of Teamsters, director of the National Warehouse Division of the Teamsters, president of the Missouri-Kansas Conference of Teamsters and of Joint Council 13 of the Teamsters (St. Louis Joint Council), and, last but by no means least important, president of Warehouse Local 688 (14556).

All the eminence and intellectual stature in the world, however, are of no great value to a man in the "movement" who cannot get elected. Elections naturally mean votes. Fortunately, one need not be too scrupulous about who does the voting, or whether the votes are voluntarily cast. What matters is that votes be counted for the right man. It was charged before the Committee that Gibbons owes his position as president of the St. Louis Joint Council—the organization holding power in St. Louis comparable to that held over New York City by Joint Council 16—to the votes of six men who had no intrinsic relationship at all to Teamster members in the St. Louis area or even to any Teamster locals in that area (14492 ff., 14669 ff., esp. 14679). Committee investigators dug up evidence which induced the Committee to level the following accusations at Gibbons: that six carnival foremen were hauled from Tampa, Florida, on Monday, January 13, 1958; named trustees of a St. Louis Teamster local which has been under International Union trusteeship (see below) from the day it was chartered; voted for Gibbons in the Joint Council election held on Wednesday, January 15; and returned to Florida the next day, each with $150 in his pocket which the Teamsters had provided. It was further charged that not one of these men had paid dues steadily for two years, as the Teamsters' constitution requires before a man is entitled to cast such a vote (14675).

Gibbons refused to waive these votes (14678). All the Floridians were appointed to their trusteeships; as appointed trustees, they were entitled to participate in the St. Louis Joint Council election. At most, he conceded, there was only a technical violation of the constitution in the fact that these men had not paid dues for the required two years. As Gibbons put it several times, the Teamsters could not operate in accordance with their constitution (14674, 14677). Yet a far less serious technical violation of the Teamsters' constitution has been the means of disqualifying voters and candidates to whom the mighty in the Teamsters have been opposed; for example, a failure to pay dues a month in advance, owing to no fault of the disqualified members, whose dues were checked off by their employers in time but not deposited in time to the Teamsters' account; yet Gibbons felt that this particular technical violation should certainly not, among large-minded men, provide the occasion for undoing an election.

Careful consideration of the whole McClellan Record bears out Gibbons' point that there is no great future in spending time and energy on the technical details of the inner operations of trade unions (14674 ff.). The facts in the Record bear out an old truth—that nothing is much easier than to establish the legitimacy of a dictatorship through democratic processes, if only the bullies and the aspiring dictators are allowed to use violence and compulsion on the way up. Tyranny through majority rule is an old process. Hitler came to power through a majority vote. The rulers of Russia hold sway in accordance with the Soviet constitution. It stretches back through history. Karl A. Wittfogel tells us, in *Oriental Despotism:*

> Nor does the regime become less despotic because the ruler attains his position through election. . . . The Byzantine custom of determining the emperor through election goes back to republican Rome. . . . When, from Diocletian on, the Senate took a more prominent part in the election of the emperor, the political center of gravity shifted from the military to the civil branch of the officialdom. Election was not the best method by which to establish a new emperor, but wrapped in the cloak of tradition and legitimacy it proved definitely compatible with the requirements of bureaucratic absolutism. And the frequent changes in the person of the supreme leader deprived neither his position nor the bureaucratic hierarchy, which he headed, of its despotic character.[2]

The problem which statesmen and the public face is, not whether tyrants and demagogues and racketeers are governing in accordance with written rules and constitutions voted by a majority, but how, if the results are shocking, such rules came into existence, and why rules which are not in themselves bad can so often be used to reach atrocious results.

The power of the internationals to impose trusteeships upon locals, a power which is genuinely needed and which can lead to good results as well as bad, illustrates the point. The Hotel and Restaurant Workers Union, for example, has recently placed all eleven of the locals constituting its Chicago Joint Board into a trusteeship, following the McClellan Committee's disclosures of the conditions there. That trusteeship is designed to clean up a very bad situation.

On the other hand, the Bakery & Confectionery Workers Union has used its trusteeship power to suck the blood of a good many local unions, if convincing evidence presented to the Committee is credited. George M. Kopecky, a Committee investigator, testified that George Stuart, a vice-president of the Bakery Workers, did very well for himself during his trusteeship

[2] (New Haven: Yale University Press, 1957), p. 104.

of Bakery Workers Locals 100 and 300. Among other things, the Record indicates, he came into possession of three Cadillacs and a Buick. Chief Counsel Kennedy summed up with a statement that the Committee has proof of an illegitimate gain by Stuart of something like $40,000 (2646-57). Anthony J. Conforti, business manager of Local 300, told the Committee that he had no real alternative to following Stuart's instructions and to making opulent gifts. He had to play ball with Stuart even after the trusteeship was lifted, he said, for fear that it would be reimposed. Senator McClellan summarized Conforti's position in a comprehensive question:

> [The international officers] were still your masters. . . . You were afraid not to do what they told you to do. . . . Because you had seen them remove others and you were afraid they would put you back in trusteeship. . . . So instead of serving the members of the union, even after the trusteeship was lifted, what you were serving was a national dictatorship?
> MR. CONFORTI. Yes, sir. (2614)

The national dictatorship to which the Chairman referred was reached through democratic processes and majority rule—a fact which must be kept carefully in mind. In its Interim Report, the McClellan Committee had some harsh words to say of the career of the Bakery Workers:

> . . . retrogression has been the bakers' lot, a grim fact directly traceable to the ruinous stewardship of International President James G. Cross.
> Stewardship is, in fact, a misnomer for the Cross brand of administration, for it implies accountability, of which the bakers have had less and less, to the vanishing point, since Cross took over in 1953. In its place they have had double-talk and dishonesty; their constitution has been abused and perverted; their hard-earned funds have been plundered; tyrannical and swindling trusteeships have crushed their local freedoms.
> As an exemplar of a labor autocrat, Cross, in the opinion of the committee, conjures up few rivals. Such has been his cynical and rapacious grasp on the bakers union that in all the misdeeds uncovered by the Committee's hearings he seldom plays other than a starring role; in the instances when

> he does not, his handpicked henchmen do. The Committee
> is of the emphatic belief that the culpability of James G.
> Cross is central to the corrosion of the bakers union. (Re-
> port, 128)

The Interim Report went on to enumerate the various items
of chicanery, extortion, collusion, and misuse of union funds
of which the administration of the Bakery Workers was guilty
(Report, 128–31). It made special note of Cross's "authoritarian
philosophy" and how "under his callous direction use of the
secret ballot to elect international officers was abandoned." (Report, 130) It might have emphasized, too, that Cross secured
power for the international president to set the salaries of his
executive board and for the executive board to fix the salaries of
the president (Record, 2802–3).

All these facts are significant, but even more significant is
the process whereby Cross secured the changes in the constitution which permitted him to put his "authoritarian philosophy"
to work. The delegates, voting strictly in accordance with the
constitution, gave him the power he sought. Senator McNamara
focused attention on this absolutely vital point when, at the
Hearings, he observed that "nevertheless, [the Bakery
Workers' constitution] was changed through democratic processes in the 1956 convention." Joseph G. Kane, president of one of the Bakery Workers locals, had to agree
that the changes were secured in accordance with the procedures
set forth in the constitution (2802).

The important topics for inquiry, to repeat, are still before
us: How does it happen that dictatorial and autocratic powers
are vested in trade-union leaders? How does it happen that even
good union constitutions come to be perverted and abused in
practice? Why do union officials do, and union members tolerate,
these things? Senator Goldwater emphasized the real problem
when he said:

> About four years ago I made a study of union constitu-
> tions and bylaws to find out how democratic the processes
> were. By and large most unions in this country have pro-
> visions in their constitutions and bylaws calling for the demo-
> cratic processes and elections.

> I would say probably 95 percent of them do. The prob-
> lem, . . . is one of making any organization use its demo-
> cratic practices. (328–29)

The Committee's Interim Report did not use up all its superla-
tives in describing James Cross's administration of the Bakery
Workers. It saved some to describe what it had discovered about
the serfdom of the members of the International Union of Operating Engineers (IUOE). These are some of the Committee's
findings:

> Of all the unions subject to committee inquiry over the past
> year, none has proved more backward, more indifferent to
> the changing times, more incredibly feudal, than the Inter-
> national Union of Operating Engineers.
> Under a constitution unworthy of the name and, even
> so, seldom observed except in the breach, IUOE members
> have dwelt in a state of servitude scarcely imaginable in the
> midst of a democratic society. (Report, 371)

The Report notes that "neither in locals under trusteeship nor
in those free of it does any accountability exist for union funds.
Literally millions of dollars have vanished from the IUOE treasury often reappearing in the form of improved living standards
for union bigwigs." (Report, 372) All of the Committee's conclusions concerning the IUOE should be studied:

> 1. Democracy within this vital union is virtually non-
> existent. Through an international constitution designed
> to give the membership as little voice as possible, only 46
> percent of the union's 280,000 members are even allowed to
> vote for their own officers. Where elections are held, union
> leaders have shamefully deprived their members of their
> democratic rights through the indiscriminate stuffing of ballot
> boxes and rigging of elections.
> 2. Trusteeships have been imposed—for no apparent
> reason—as a means of continuing domination over the affairs
> of a number of locals. . . . The locals under trusteeship
> have been looted and their members deprived of their rights.
> Two locals in Chicago, Ill., have been under trusteeship for
> 29 years.
> 3. There has been extensive collusion between union of-
> ficials and management which has resulted in the emergence
> of a class of "favorite contractors" who, testimony showed,

were permitted to pay lower wages and ignore other established contractual arrangements.

4. Union officials have entered into business arrangements with the very employers with whom they negotiate in what the committee feels are clear conflicts of interest.

5. Vast amounts of union funds have been misused and diverted to the personal profit of union leaders for their extravagant entertainment and luxury. (Report, 437–38)

The manipulations of the mighty in the "movement" are so endless, so labyrinthine, and sometimes so incredibly cheap, that one tends at times—lost in the foul mess—to forget that working men are involved at all, and that the fancy living and coarse harlotry come out of the pockets mainly of men whose wives have to skimp and strive in order to make ends meet. Great, showy buildings rise in Washington, D.C., in which are found offices of imposing dimension, and large staffs, a multitudinous personnel, sitting at expensive, shining desks, looking important as they twiddle their thumbs. Back home, the business agents drive around in new cars every year. Expense money of as high as $1,000 a week is not unknown. Truck drivers and bakers and factory workers do their best to keep little houses from falling apart, while the union bosses live in palatial homes in the best part of town—not because they have earned honest profits in competitive business—but through extortion from businessmen and plain stealing from union treasuries. And then there are the conventions, the final mockery, held in the most opulent hotels of the most garishly expensive resorts of the nation. There, swimming in luxury, hard-faced delegates roar with approval, and they roar the louder the more cynical the manipulations become, the more firmly the masters weld their iron power structures together.

At the moment when the Committee was revealing to the nation some of the most grotesque contortions of the union bosses, and not too long after it had uncovered to public view the legendary defalcations of Teamster president Dave Beck, the Teamsters were in the convention, in Florida, from which James Hoffa, a man who in some ways makes Beck seem like a rank amateur and buffoon, emerged as president of the Teamsters—

and thus as the holder of the greatest unrestrained economic power in the United States.

This election of Hoffa, Senator McClellan charged, was a fraud. In fact, on the opening day of the Teamsters convention, September 30, 1957, before the election took place, Senator McClellan announced that his Committee had evidence indicating that over 50 per cent of the voting delegates were not selected in conformity with the Teamsters' constitution. He offered this evidence to the Teamsters, and the then president, Dave Beck, accepted it. Nevertheless, the credentials of the challenged delegates were approved and Hoffa was elected by a large majority.[3]

The letter covering the Senator's evidence declared that the Committee had definitely established wrongdoing in the selection of delegates in twenty-four locals, and that similar evidence existed with respect to forty-four other locals, though not as yet fully confirmed. After a remarkable runaround, the Committee managed to secure from the Teamsters' convention, by subpena, the credentials data. Of this data, Senator McClellan said:

> Even a preliminary examination of the records furnished by the Teamsters in connection with their Credentials Committee revealed a shocking situation. Not only are their records missing, but the records that are available are, to say the least, inadequate. Furthermore, we have found several instances where Mr. Dave Beck, the International President, instructed the Credentials Committee to disregard the Teamsters constitution. Without this dictatorial action on the part of Mr. Beck, Mr. Hoffa, the candidate of his choosing, could not have been elected president of the Teamsters.[4]

Among the locals in which Senator McClellan found the selection of delegates particularly defective was Philadelphia Local 107. Of this pillar of support of Hoffa he said:

> . . . on September 30, 1957, I notified the Credentials Committee through the Teamsters attorney here in Washington, that we had information that the delegates of Local 107 in Philadelphia were not properly chosen under the

[3] For this and further information on Senator McClellan's efforts to prevent Hoffa's taking office, see The McClellan Hearings, 1957 (Washington, D.C.: Bureau of National Affairs, 1958), pp. 315–18.
[4] Ibid.

Teamsters constitution. The minutes of the Credentials Committee show that they considered this matter and accepted the explanation of the officials of the [local] that they had been properly chosen as delegates at a general membership meeting held September 15, 1957. This, on its face, violates the [Teamsters] constitution in that the delegates had to be selected prior to September 1st.

Furthermore, we have found that the credentials were issued to the delegates of Local 107 some three months prior to the date they claim they were chosen, namely on July 11, 1957.[5]

It would be astonishing if the Local 107 delegates had been properly chosen, for, as we shall soon see, the Record discloses that very little else was done properly in that local.

The Principles of Serfdom

We approach at this point the operating mechanisms of the system of servitude, the machinery of power, by means of which the Teamsters—or the Operating Engineers, or the Bakery Workers, or, for that matter, any other union and indeed any other private association—can bind their members to serfdom, clamping upon them a dictatorship within the forms and procedures of majority rule. It is a three-stage affair.

1. The immediate instrument of power lies in control of a majority of the delegates to the national conventions, where the power of the leaders is formalized and their acts given a specious legality.

2. Convention delegates come from the locals. Control of the convention therefore requires control at the local level.

3. Control at the local level is established in one or both of two ways: physical violence and economic compulsion.

*　*　*

Trade-union serfdom's principle of operation may then be generalized as follows:

[5] *Ibid.*

A condition of servitude is formally imposed upon trade-union members by control from the top of a majority of delegates to the national convention. Intermediately this control of the selection of delegates is established by the co-operation of henchmen at the local-officer level interested in sharing the spoils, or by specific instruction in the case of trusteed locals, or by reluctant acquiescence in the case of the relatively decent local leaders who feel that the odds are stacked so greatly that they must go along with the men bent upon establishing the dictatorship. Fundamentally, however, a continued condition of servitude requires, indispensably, the availability of two special privileges: the privileges of violence and economic compulsion. Men will rebel against servitude if they can. This is true of "bad" men as well as good. The bad will fight in order to share in the spoils, the good in order to be free. Such rebellion can be quelled only by force and violence or by control over the rebel's means of livelihood.

Rx for Rebels

Hoffa could see only one thing wrong in his having dipped into the Michigan Teamsters' treasury to contribute $5,000 to one of the two rivals for the top job in Teamsters Philadelphia Local 107. He could not agree with Senator Kennedy's suggestion that this might be an improper use of the Michigan members' dues no matter who the candidates were. His only mistake, Hoffa felt, was that he had backed the wrong man:

> I might say that in this instance, Senator, the man who won the election turned out to be a better man for the members than the man that we supported. And I don't mind admitting that. (5054)

The "for the members" in this statement might have been a slip of the tongue. Hoffa might have meant to say "for Hoffa." The man who won was Raymond Cohen. His delegates to the 1957 convention, challenged, as we have seen by Senator McClellan, helped Hoffa to the Teamster presidency. But what he did "for the members" is something else again.

Committee investigator John B. Flanagan testified that, after a careful scrutiny of all books and records kept by Local 107 in the period 1954–1957, it appeared to him that something on the order of $250,000, *in cash,* of the members' money had been disbursed questionably. Raymond Cohen was top man in 107 during that period. There were no explanatory vouchers, only "lists of names with amounts set beside them, which purportedly supported the disbursement of this cash." In tracking down the men whose names appeared on these lists, Flanagan said, they "told us that they received either less than the amount indicated opposite their names, or they did not receive any of the money." The local's records did not indicate either who had disbursed the cash or the purpose for which it had been used (10597–602).

Disbursements by check were also pretty plainly felonious. James C. Cadigan, an expert on questioned documents in the Federal Bureau of Investigation's Washington Laboratory, testified before the Committee that in numerous instances checks were issued by Local 107 to one person in a certain amount but were altered to much higher amounts and then cashed by other persons, who forged the signatures of the payees (10474–77). This testimony was backed up by the direct evidence of witnesses whose names had appeared as payees on some of the checks but who swore that they had never seen the checks. One such witness declared that the endorsement on the back of a check ostensibly issued to him was a forgery. This check—for $1,000— was a complete mystery to him (10482).

When Raymond Cohen appeared before the Committee, he was confronted with such facts as the foregoing, and was asked how he had secured the funds for the purchase of a yacht, clothes, cameras, etc. He took the Fifth Amendment on every question (10393). His hirelings and associates in the local did likewise (10484, 19493).

Cohen may have been a good man "for the members" in Hoffa's opinion, but many members themselves thought differently. The Record discloses that the members did not get an uncoerced chance to vote against him in the first place and that his continuance in office did not rest upon their volition. It discloses that he secured his office at first by a power play and later through liberal use of brutality, maintaining it in the same way, with an assist from the control over employment which Local 107's area-wide union-shop contract gave him.

Cohen's rise to power in Local 107 was vivid and dramatic. He had been only one of several somewhat lowly business agents as of November, 1953, when nominations were opened for candidacy to higher office in the local. Raymond J. Kelly, a charter member of the local, described to the Committee how Cohen got started, during the nominating meeting. The attendance at that meeting, he said, was extraordinary. "The auditorium was crowded and members were standing out in the street and couldn't get in, which was really unusual." When nominations were opened for the secretary-treasurer's post, the top job in the local, Kelly continued, "someone jumped up and nominated Raymond Cohen; there was a quick second, . . . and all hell broke loose. They jumped on the seats and started stomping and shouting 'Cohen,' and nobody could be heard." Nominations were immediately closed, without giving the backers of the incumbent, Ed Crumboch, a chance. Kelly went on to say that:

> Of course, a man who wanted to nominate Crumboch just wasn't seen, and he had his hand up and standing there through this "young riot," I would call it, and they jumped all over the place. . . . Eddy wasn't nominated. (10406)

The election hall had been stacked, Kelly was sure, "because we never had that kind of a meeting before in the whole existence of the union." The International apparently agreed, for the local was put into trusteeship and a new election ordered, with Crumboch and Cohen the two contenders. Strangely enough, Kelly observed, Crumboch did not campaign actively, while Cohen seemed to have unlimited funds to spend and "a hundred or better" people working for him (10408).

These people campaigned for Cohen mainly with their fists. Samuel Gravenor, a Crumboch supporter, told the Committee that John Myhasuk, a Cohen campaigner, came up to him and asked whose side he was on. "Before I could give him any explanation . . . Myhasuk starts swinging and the other two fellows grabbed me. I received a black eye and a bloody nose."

(10468) William G. Roberts, another Crumboch supporter, told the same kind of story: "I walked out the door and this John Myhasuk, he said, 'You rat,' and . . . I turned around to face him, and I got hit with something, or with his fist, but that was the last I remember, and I woke up inside the union hall. . . . When I got home my face started to blacken up and that night my wife was in the hospital . . . and I had to get myself together enough to go visit her. . . . When I walked into the hospital I had a hat on, and I never wear a hat, and she hollered, 'Oh, my God, what happened to you?' So I told her, and I went home after the visit and I went to bed, and the following day I felt lousy and my face was all black and all and so they admitted me to the University of Pennsylvania Hospital, and I was in there . . . four days." (10460) John Myhasuk did not deny that he slugged these people; he took the Fifth Amendment instead (10463).

Cohen won the election easily, by a 9 to 1 margin. Chief Counsel Kennedy wanted to know how it was that Cohen won so easily after Crumboch's long and popular tenure in office. Kelly's answer was succinct: "Well, there was only one word for it. It was fear." (10410)

If fear won the election for Cohen, it solidified his power thereafter, and operated also to keep members in line who did not like the way the Local 107 treasury was being raided. Cohen got rid of all the local officers and agents who had not been supporters, using threats and violence in some cases, and relying on those to induce others to leave "voluntarily." Vincent Minisci was a Crumboch man, an elected steward. After the election, Minisci told the Committee, another of Cohen's supporters, Armand Palermi, beckoned to him one day from the curb. When he reached the curb, he said, "Someone hit me from behind, and I fell on my hands and knees, and I rolled over to see who it was, and somebody kicked me, and just kept beating me around, and I managed to get away on my own power after a severe beating." (10423)

Among his assailants, Minisci identified a Joseph Cendrowski. When Cendrowski was asked to testify, he took the Fifth Amendment (10429). The Record indicates that he had been arrested seventeen times, and that his convictions included larceny, disorderly conduct, inciting to riot, unlawful assembly, and burglary (10428).

A good many Crumboch men, including Kelly, left Local 107 "voluntarily" after that. "They would have gotten me the same as they had gotten others," one said (10417). Cohen had literally driven them out of their jobs, indeed in some instances completely out of the state (10470). Some remained, to make futile efforts at getting rid of Cohen when his maladministration became evident. Theirs is perhaps the most pitiful and tragic story. Robert Rifkin had a meeting at his home with some rebels who hoped to unseat Cohen. After the meeting, Rifkin told the Committee, "the doorbell rang, and I went to the door to see who was there, and there were two fellows standing in the hallway." Rifkin refused to open the door. Chief Counsel Kennedy asked him whether he recognized the men as members of "the goon squad of Local 107." Rifkin's further testimony strongly suggested that he had been put in mortal fear of his life. He did admit that he was in fear of a beating (10447), but he declined to make any identification, and he confessed that on the advice of an older and wiser man, he had gone cringing to Cohen, to "make his peace":

> Mr. Rifkin. . . . I went down and told Mr. Cohen what had happened, and made restitution, or whatever you would call it, I guess, and got things straightened out.
>
> Mr. Kennedy. You made restitution to the union? You made apologies, is that it?
>
> Mr. Rifkin. Yes, sir.
>
> Mr. Kennedy. Do you mean for having allowed this meeting to take place in your apartment, or what? What did you apologize to him for?
>
> Mr. Rifkin. For causing trouble that I shouldn't have, I guess. (10448) . . .
>
> Senator Ervin. In other words, you, who are presumably a free American citizen, go to Mr. Cohen and apologize to him for using your home for purposes which he disapproved of, although under our law your home is supposed to be your castle; is that right? . . .

> Mr. Rifkin. Sir, I don't know if he was misusing funds. It was what Mr. LaVelle had told me.
>
> Senator Ervin. You believed it at the time you allowed these people to hold a meeting in your home, didn't you?
>
> Mr. Rifkin. Yes, sir.
>
> Senator Ervin. And you go and apologize to Mr. Cohen for making the use of your home that you were entitled to make as a free American citizen? Is that what you are telling us? . . .
>
> Mr. Rifkin. I apologized to Mr. Cohen for the trouble that I caused, not for using my home, sir.
>
> Senator Ervin. What was the trouble you caused? That is what I am trying to get at.
>
> Mr. Rifkin. I don't know what the trouble was. (10449–50)

There is more to this pitiable colloquy, but enough has been presented to show what happens to those who rebel against union leaders intent upon establishing a condition of serfdom. Some are brutally assaulted, some are hounded out of town, some give up and leave, others come begging forgiveness for having tried to hold up their heads like men. Committee investigator John Flanagan, who interviewed a good many members of Local 107 while the Cohen phase of the Hearings was going on, testified that many of them were wallowing in fear, and that Cohen had threatened at a meeting to "fix" anyone who testified before the Committee (10528). Senator McClellan summed up the situation in a series of questions, to all of which the witness answered "yes":

> . . . the rights, the democratic rights and privileges of the members [of Local 107] have been completely denied them? They have no control, no authority, no contact, no entry to the union's affairs? They are virtually captives. They have to do what they are told to do, if they are to work? (10415)

No one could possibly be surprised to hear that Local 107 delivered its delegates illegitimately to Hoffa at the 1957 Teamsters' convention. The surprising thing to hear would be that anything it did was clean.

At another point in the Hearings, Senator Kennedy confronted Hoffa with the fact that at any given time some 12 per cent of the Teamsters locals are in trusteeship (5055). These trustees must do what they are ordered to do, in the way of appointing local officers and agents. If they do not obey orders, they will be replaced, as was true of the man named trustee of Minneapolis Teamsters Local 548. The story there is a long and sordid one, involving a manipulation of union affiliation much like that of Gibbons' local in St. Louis, all unknown to the membership, who learned that they "belonged" to the Teamsters only after Teamster dues books had been given them (5368). It involves also a story of tyranny much like Cohen's in Local 107, with Gerald Connelly allegedly playing the role in Minneapolis that Cohen played in Philadelphia. How is it, Arthur Morgan was asked, that the Minneapolis members went along with Connelly? The former vice-president of Local 548 gave a one-word answer: "Fear." (5366) The first trustee appointed to Local 548 immediately ousted Connelly. According to the Record, Hoffa directed that trustee to reinstate Connelly. When he refused, he was replaced with another trustee who forthwith put Connelly back into office (5373-79).

When James M. Ford seemed to be getting too much power among the members of Harold Gibbons' St. Louis Local 688, he ran into real trouble. He was ejected from a Local 688 meeting, but that was by no means all that happened to him. The next thing he knew, after the ejection, he was in a hospital with his front teeth knocked out, a fractured cheek bone, a punctured lung, and several ribs and his nose broken (14259).

Paul Bradshaw gave the Committee the tried and tested prescription for rebels who think they have any rights in an enserfed local:

> Yes, there was a fellow there and he would get up on the floor and he would try to put his two cents in on something, and the business agents didn't like it, and Robert Malloy gave Robbie Hubshman orders to beat the fellow up.
> So when the fellow was walking out the door Hubshman walked up and clipped the guy a couple of times . . . and the fellow never opened his mouth [again].
> (1743)

Serfdom—or Outlawry

It is a remarkable fact that the McClellan Committee was told—on the first day of its hearings—all it needed to know about the basic causes of serfdom in trade unions. This is not to say that the enormous documentation of the succeeding two years of hearings has been of no value. On the contrary, the subsequent piling up of massive detail has established the dimensions and emphasized the gravity of the problem. Yet, it would be disastrous if the detail should be allowed to cloud the vision of the basic causes which Wallace Turner, a reporter for the Portland *Oregonian,* set forth for the Committee back there on February 26, 1957. He testified, that first day, as follows:

> MR. TURNER. I mean the members of the union are scared to death to get out of line.
>
> THE CHAIRMAN. They are afraid to tell the truth and to reveal what they know?
>
> MR. TURNER. Yes, sir.
>
> THE CHAIRMAN. Their fear is what?
>
> MR. TURNER. That their union cards at least will be taken up and they will be out of employment.
>
> THE CHAIRMAN. You are testifying under oath that that is what they have revealed to you in the course of your investigation . . . ?
>
> MR. TURNER. I have been so told by members of that union.
>
> SENATOR MUNDT. . . . by retaliation you mean that they fear that they would lose their means of livelihood?
>
> MR. TURNER. That is one thing that they fear; yes.
>
> SENATOR MUNDT. To be deprived of their jobs, and they could not support their families?
>
> MR. TURNER. Yes, sir.
>
> SENATOR MUNDT. There are other types of retaliation which they fear?
>
> MR. TURNER. Yes, sir; that union has a history in our state of physical violence to people who disagreed with them. . . .
>
> SENATOR MUNDT. You are saying under oath that the men who come to visit you at night are afraid not only of the

fact they would lose their jobs and their means of livelihood, but that they might also be subjected to physical violence?

MR. TURNER. Yes, sir. (6–7)

The forty-odd volumes of the McClellan Record may accurately be summed up as an overwhelming documentation of Mr. Turner's point: the servitude of union members rests upon two kinds of fear, the fear of violence and the fear of loss of their jobs. It is fear of one or the other alone that keeps them bound in a union when they know their officers are cheating and abusing them. Some would of course remain in the union regardless of their condition of servitude. That all—or even most—would stay is unbelievable. But there is an even more important point: union officers would not be so highly tempted to abuse members who were free at any time simply to quit paying dues; and, still more important, thugs and racketeers would not find unions so attractive.

Most of Part 29 and all of Part 30 of the Record deal with the ramified and esoteric activities of Max Block, head of two locals of the Amalgamated Meat Cutters and Butcher Workmen's Union, Locals 342 and 640, in the New York City metropolitan area. Block's career is of the same kind as Beck's and Hoffa's, though perhaps on a smaller scale. According to the Record, he lived very well; he also accepted an extremely generous dues-financed pension for himself, had a great number of employers eating out of his hand, and strictly controlled the employment of his members. It would not do any member much good to complain, if he felt like complaining, about Block's conduct. Daniel Beatson, a former business agent in Block's two locals, described the unions' control of employment in the wholesale meat industry:

> [Locals 342 and 640] control practically 100 percent the wholesale meat industry in New York City. Practically all the meat from all over, for that area, comes into the 14th Street Market, the Westchester Market, or the Ford Green Market, and then disbursed to the supermarkets and retail markets in a 100-mile area.
>
> MR. KENNEDY. You say that is the control that it has over the business, [but] what about the individual employees?

Is that an important organization as far as an individual getting a job?

MR. BEATSON. Yes, because the hiring, with the exception of Swifts and Armours, the hiring is done exclusively at the union hall.

MR. KENNEDY. It is a union-hall operation?

MR. BEATSON. That is right.

MR. KENNEDY. You have to go to the union in order to get a job?

MR. BEATSON. That is right.

MR. KENNEDY. Can you transfer from one job to another?

MR. BEATSON. Not without the approval of the union.
(11604)

Mr. Beatson went on to say that if meat cutters transferred from one employer to another or went out on their own to find jobs, "they would be thrown out of the union and would never secure another job in the industry again." (11604)

Chairman McClellan summed up his conclusions on the Block operation. They were not favorable. Among other things, he said:

> The conclusion seems inescapable that Max Block and and his family treated these two unions as their own private property, and thousands of dues-paying members were made to suffer accordingly.
>
> They engaged in empire building in the most evil connotation of that term. In this case are the same overtones of denial of democratic process, the seizure and consolidation of power and the concentrated drive for perpetuation in office which the committee has encountered in other cases.
> (11760)

The Chairman might have added that this case shared one other essential feature of the others in which abuse of the membership was rampant: namely, power in the union leader over the employment of the members through one form or another of union-shop contract. Perhaps the Chairman failed to mention this because Senator Curtis, earlier in the hearings on Block's activities, had focused attention on the key role played by Block's control over his members' employment. Senator Curtis said:

It is morally wrong to have a situation, to have contracts, that make it impossible for members to withdraw from the union and stop paying dues, when the union is following a course that they do not like. Sometimes they may be in collusion with management and sometimes not.

I believe that workers of the country are entitled to absolute freedom to run their own union, and if the union top leaders do not take workers into [their] confidence, let them know what is in the contract, or otherwise push them around, they should have a remedy of withdrawing and stop paying their dues without losing their jobs.

I think to do otherwise is most unfair. . . . these union bosses voting themselves pensions without knowledge of active members, . . . is an indication that they are disregarding the wishes of the people and they are doing it because of the power they have over individuals to destroy their jobs and hold a captive membership. (11371–72)

Raymond Cohen had area-wide control of employment of the same kind that governs butchers in New York (10642–44). Without such control it is doubtful that he could have imposed so tight a serfdom on his members. Brutality alone would probably not have sufficed, for brutality, in the nature of things, has a narrow impact, is costly, and carries risks with it. But if an insurgent's card is taken away from him, and if without that card he can get no work in the area, he soon becomes no problem at all. Vincent Minisci, the rebel who was severely beaten, tends to prove the point. The brutality alone did not get rid of him. After the beating, he found employment with the Fox Transport System. However, Mr. Fox told him that he would "have to get clearance with the [Local 107] steward." The steward, a man Minisci had known for years, took his time when Minisci sought "clearance," and told him finally that he would "have to be hired out of the hiring hall." That was like the crack of doom for Minisci. The hiring hall was operated by his assailant, Cendrowski, and he knew he would never get a referral. He never did:

. . . being out of work for quite a number of months, I lost everything I had, mortgaged my home, and I was, well, I would say I was practically run out of the State . . . there was no use hanging around, and I couldn't find anything, and I knew if I went to the hiring hall I would get nothing. (10440–41)

Minisci finally moved to California. He moved only because the union had made Pennsylvania uninhabitable for him. There was no other reason for him to move, he said: "My home was paid for and everything in Philadelphia, and I had no need to move." Summing up, Minisci said:

> There wasn't too many that would be at liberty to speak and voice their opinion, which is their God given right, and they are not allowed to. I just tried to exercise my rights, and I finally ended where I am at. (10441)

On one of the few occasions when he did not take the Fifth Amendment before the Committee, Raymond Cohen ventured the opinion that the members were in Local 107 because he had done so much for them, not because he controlled their jobs. Senator Curtis disagreed. He said:

> I am not so sure about that. . . . I do not think for a minute that, if the Commonwealth of Pennsylvania would protect the workers of Pennsylvania in their constitutional right to work, they would stay in any organization that spent their money like it has been alleged here that they spent it.
> While I concur in . . . [Senator Kennedy's] recommendation that you ought to resign, I think the poor fellows who are paying the bill ought to be permitted to resign from your union without becoming unemployed and losing their livelihood. (10644)

Senator Curtis might have added that of the nearly 100,000 letters which the Committee has received, most have come from union members, and they tell a bitter tale of frustrated resentment toward their condition of serfdom.

* * *

The unions in which the Committee found the worst abuses, the most dictatorial policies, the most profligate misuse of membership dues were all what are known as "closed-shop" unions. The butchers, the bakers, the engineers, the carpenters, the teamsters—all work under union control of employment, and in all the Committee found much to concern it. This is not to say that every closed-shop union is guilty of such abuses. For one thing, the Committee did not investigate all the closed-shop unions. For another, it is believed that some such unions, for example, the International Typographical Union, operate internally in a business-like way.

Yet to recognize that serfdom does not prevail in every closed-shop union does not mean that control over employment has no operative significance in the imposition of such a state. The great probability is that very special circumstances prevail in closed-shop unions which do not abuse their members: they are small, their members are highly skilled, there is stability and continuity of employment, or something else of that kind. But the fact remains that there is a perfectly clear, logical, and rational relationship between control over a man's employment and exploitation of that man. He is in a weaker position to react against exploitation than he would be in the absence of such control. To deny that would be, not only to reject compelling logic; it would also be to blind oneself to the plain facts of life. It would amount to saying that all the sorry disclosures in the McClellan Record either did not happen at all, or that they add up to nothing more than an incoherent jumble of unrelated events. But there is still another phase of the matter: the tendency of the closed-shop union to increase the temptation to wrongdoing, to corrupt the union official who might otherwise operate decently and honestly, and to draw to it men who have already been corrupted by crime.

Chapter 7

CORRUPTION UNLIMITED

*Well there is some times . . . we hire people to do
certain jobs for us, but we don't let them get on the
inside of the organization.*

* * *

*. . . if anyone is in business, and you know that
a person stands well in labor circles, you don't try to
incur any ill will . . . not to get any benefits that you
are not entitled to . . . but merely to be sure that you
don't create ill will.*

* * *

*I make mayors and I break mayors, and I make chiefs
of police and I break chiefs of police. I have been in
jail and I have been out of jail. There is nothing scares
me.*

* * *

This society is too large and too complicated—its unions,
industries, and governments are too ramified—for anyone to be
able to tell precisely how far the corruption has gone. But there
can be no doubt that it has gone far and that it is pervasive, in
unions, in business, and in government.

The circle is almost complete. Special privileges accorded
by citizens to unions through government have drawn to unions
men of insatiable appetite for power, for money, or for both.
These men have raided union treasuries and abused union members in a thousand ways; at times directly and at times through
"middle men" they have extorted from some businessmen, cowed
others, and conspired with still others to cheat both workingmen
and the public; they have given "breaks" to the acquiescent and
terrifying experiences to the resistant; they have bribed, sub-

sidized, and otherwise influenced government officials in order to secure special privileges over and above those already provided by law; they have pilloried and excoriated public officials who maintain that the law should be neutral in labor disputes, that it should apply equally to ordinary citizens and to union officers and agents.

Closing the circle, the men who have come to power in trade unions are increasing their control of industry and government and subverting the basic institutions and principles of society. When the circle is finally closed, the general public will reap as it has sown. It will find confronting it a vicious and extortionate colossus, before whom all must cower. Even today, after two years of disclosures by the McClellan Committee, the question is, not how shall the government restrict the overwhelming power of the trade unions, but how favorable to unions can legislation be made without arousing the resentment of a public whose ignorance seems to be exceeded only by its apathy. Perhaps it is already too late.

"Power tends to corrupt and absolute power corrupts absolutely." This dictum of Lord Acton's, now almost a hundred years old, has had its inner truth demonstrated in a hundred ways these past years. The McClellan Record demonstrates that truth yet once again. From the unlimited power of trade unions is growing an unlimited corruption—in unions, in industry, in government, and in society.

Unions

The hearings revealed among unions a spread of corruption extravagant enough to shock even those who had, or who ought to have had, a good idea of what was going on. George Meany, president of the AFL-CIO was stunned. "We thought we knew a few things about trade-union corruption," Meany acknowledged, "but we didn't know the half of it, one-tenth of it, or the one-hundredth part of it." That confession was made after the McClellan hearings had been going on for less than a year. Presumably the diminishing fraction has become infinitesimal, now that more than another year of disclosures have been forth-coming. However, Meany's summary of the various categories of corruption upon which the Committee enlightened him is still accurate:

> We didn't know that there were top trade union leaders who used the [union] funds for phony real estate deals in which the victims of the fraud were their own members.
>
> And we didn't know that there were trade union leaders who charged to the union treasury such items as speed boats, perfume, silk stockings, brassieres, color TV, re-frigerators, and everything else under the sun.
>
> We didn't know that we had top trade union leaders who made it a practice to secretly borrow the funds of their unions.
>
> We didn't know . . . that we had unions where a criminal record was almost a prerequisite to holding office under the national union.[1]

It was not till later that Chairman McClellan, pretty nearly fed up, lashed out at "the rascality, the thievery, the very scum of union behavior" which was coming to light during the hearings (10790). And it was still later, during hearings upon a few phases of the administration of the United Brotherhood of Carpenters and Joiners, that the Chairman said:

> These hearings have shown without any question of doubt that the trust reposed in these persons has been violated; that the union members' dues money, funds in the treasury of the union, derived from dues and assessments, had been exploited. (11929)

It is not a pretty story, and there is no joy in the telling. In numerous instances trade-union officers cheated and defrauded their members. Some union leaders at both the national and local level made free use of the union treasuries for personal expenditures. They did this notwithstanding the fact that they were drawing substantial salaries and generous expense allowances, to boot. Dave Beck's use of the Teamsters' treasury need not clutter these pages; it has been publicized enough and is the subject of court actions. But it is less well known that the officers of many local unions engaged in similar conduct. A few

[1] *The New York Times,* November 2, 1957, p. 1, col. 2.

examples will be sufficient to indicate the kind of thing which has been going on.

The funds of Meat Cutter locals 342 and 640 were used to send twenty-eight officers and agents to a convention. The cost for one week was $20,000, more than $3,500 of that total going to the local president alone (11727). In the period 1955-1957, a total of $86,507.02 in checks was drawn on the bank accounts of the same two locals—without any explanation of the nature of the expenditures (11749). Beyond that, checks were issued to the president of those locals, during the same period, in a total amount of $26,705—again without explanation (11749-50). The same man, with his wife, took four trips to Florida, on the union. The cost of one, according to the Record, was $2,800; of a second, $4,400; of all four, $9,372.65 (11752).

The business manager of another local affiliated with the Meat Cutters, Local 627 of the Provision Salesmen & Distributors Union, while drawing a salary of $275 and expenses of $100 a week, plus the free use of a Cadillac supplied by the local, took the Fifth Amendment when asked to turn over his personal books and records (11811). So did Raymond Cohen, the man Hoffa declared had done so much "for the members," the same man who insisted that the members stayed in the union, not because they were compelled by closed-shop agreements, but because their benefits were so great. So did countless other union officials when faced with unexplained draws on union treasuries, amounting to millions and millions of dollars.

A man will, in spending his own money, feel it unduly burdensome to record and explain every expenditure. On the other hand, honest men will account scrupulously and exhaustively for the expenditure of other people's money with which they have been entrusted. Most of the union officials investigated by the Committee disposed of union funds as if they were personal funds: no records, loss of memory, and ultimately the Fifth Amendment. The Chairman said:

> . . . we come in here and we try to check these things, and officers know nothing about it, and they have no records, and the records are destroyed, and you get these big checks for cash, and no one can explain it. . . .

> The men who pay these dues are entitled to know
> how that money is spent. We have just found it throughout
> our investigation, transactions of this character, just marked
> on the book "organizing expense" or "strike expense,"
> and a big check, a lump sum taken out in cash. (11723)

The awesomely corrupt betrayal of fiduciary duties by Teamster officers and agents is certainly the most widely known of the Committee's disclosures. But that corruption is by no means in a class by itself. The same *kind* of corruption is evident in other unions investigated by the Committee. The scale may be smaller, but then all other unions are smaller, too. Moreover, on no other union has the Committee spent the time which it has given to the Teamsters.

In its fragmentary investigation of one phase of the activities of the officers of the Carpenters, the Committee found much the same kind of thing. Over a twenty-one month period, a high official of the Carpenters drew expense money of $25,600—to a considerable extent in unexplained withdrawals from *petty cash* —in addition to a salary of $20,000 per year (12082). On a trip to Europe, the same official drew upon the union treasury for $14,070, in spite of the fact that all his expenses while he was in Italy were paid by the Italian government (12083-84). The Carpenters' treasury, in a deal which would require a chapter to describe fully, was tapped to the tune of $310,000 for a biography of a deceased president, *Portrait of an American Labor Leader: William L. Hutcheson* (11861-79).

Most estimates agreed that during the first year of the hearings the Committee had uncovered evidence of corrupt misuse of membership dues in an amount not less than $10 million. That this estimate is conservative admits of no doubt. The Committee investigated only a few international unions and a still smaller proportion of the 70,000 or more local unions. As to the ones it investigated the best it could do was to track down leads; undoubtedly, not even the remarkable perseverance of its investigators could either get a lead on, or track down, everything. The estimate will vary, too, depending upon one's definition of "corruption": what *is* a corrupt misuse of membership dues?

When Hoffa spent $5,000 of the *Michigan* Teamsters' dues to support Ed Crumboch's election campaign in *Philadelphia* against Ray Cohen, was that a corrupt misuse of the Michigan members' dues? Hoffa could see nothing wrong in it (5054), it is true, but does that really settle the question? If the Michigan truck drivers had known of this expenditure, and if, knowing of it, they had approved, it could scarcely have been called a corrupt misuse. But if they had not known of it, and had no reason to expect their dues to be spent for a purpose so absolutely unrelated to their own lives, then it was a misuse. And if they could not even resign from a union which used their funds in such a manner, without losing their jobs—as was actually the case—then the corruption seems unlimited.

Again, all the officials of Walter Reuther's UAW boasted freely of the expenditure of $10 million in order to break the Kohler Company. The Kohler Company manufactures mainly plumbing equipment. The members whose $10 million were spent to "break Kohler" were preponderantly employed in automobile factories. Could they have had a reasonable expectation, when they paid their dues, that the money would be used in an attempt to force unionism upon unwilling workers, to limit the supply of bathroom fixtures, to cartelize an industry, and to raise prices—the fundamental objectives of the "break Kohler" campaign? The answer, plainly, must be "No." Again, the auto workers were no more free to resign from the UAW and to quit paying dues to it than their fellows in the trucking industry were free to quit financing Hoffa's plans of personal greatness.

Walter Reuther's $10 million expenditure of union funds was no more related to the interests of the auto workers than Beck's brassiere purchases or Hoffa's campaign contributions were related to the interests of the truck drivers. The auto workers are compelled to continue to pay dues to the UAW, if they wish to keep working in the auto plants, just as the truck drivers are compelled to continue to pay dues to the Teamsters if they wish to keep driving a truck. The only substantial difference between Reuther's $10 million expenditure and the equal amount attributed to corrupt misuse on the part of all the other unions investigated by the Committee is that the money did not go into the personal bank accounts or expenditures of UAW officials; it was spent in large part to support the Kohler strikers.

That is a substantial difference, all right, but only from one point of view. From the point of view of the UAW dues-payers, it is not substantial at all. The best that can be said of the situation, viewed from their standpoint, is that they were compelled to make a charitable contribution, the effect of which was to prolong beyond all reason a strike which should never have been called in the first place, or which could have been terminated at an early date if the UAW leaders, intent on getting a compulsory-unionism agreement from Kohler, had had the wisdom and moderation which the dictatorial type never seems to have.

If there is little difference between the $10 million spent to break Kohler and the $10 million attributed to all other corrupt misuse of union funds uncovered by the Committee in its first year, there is even less between Reuther's expenditure and the $800,000 which the Teamsters are said to have spent in the 1958 elections in order to defeat the "right-to-work" propositions which were offered in six states. In fact, there is really no difference at all. The UAW expenditure involved the use of dues money which members were compelled to pay in order to fasten the same compulsion on others—the Kohler workers. The Teamsters' expenditure of $800,000 likewise came out of the pockets of members working under compulsory-unionism agreements and was directed to the defeat of proposals which would prohibit such compulsion. The evil spirits must surely chortle at such a play: serfs compelled to contribute to the spreading of serfdom.

No honest attempt to establish the true dimensions and character of corruption in trade unions can gloss over these matters. There was nothing corrupt in the bare fact that Dave Beck bought shirts for himself; there was not necessarily any corruption even in his buying shirts with money contributed by truck drivers. Dave Beck's corruption, if any, resided in the fact that the money was not contributed to him voluntarily, and that when contributed, there was no expectation that it would be used to buy shirts. Of the $10-million "break Kohler" campaign, exactly

the same may accurately be said. It came from a forced contribution, and it went to a purpose never conceived by the dues-
payers. In some ways, the Reuther expenditure on the Kohler
strike is much worse than the Beck expenditures, though no
worse than the Teamster expenditures to defeat the right-to-work
laws; for at least Beck got shirts for the money, and it is good
to have shirts, especially such good shirts. But nobody got anything out of the Kohler strike. Its purpose—to fasten compulsory
unionism upon unwilling employees—was morally and socially
evil. Its method—violence, vandalism, and terrorism—was morally and socially evil. And its results, too—loss of employment,
bitter resentment on all sides, and the searing of a community's
relations—were morally and socially evil. In any reasonable cal-
culation, the sum adds up to corruption of the worst kind.
Rationalizing it with a pompous and thoroughly sophistical
"philosophy" of trade unionism does not help a bit. And it
becomes no more acceptable, when properly understood, by
being associated with men dedicated to the "movement." That
only makes it worse, for then to corrupt abuse of power are added
fraud and hypocrisy.

No matter how much "real trade-union leaders" may decry
the findings and revelations of the McClellan Committee, the
fact remains that they have practically all been guilty of either
the Hoffa, Beck, or Reuther varieties of corruption. One of the
most ominous trends perceived by the Committee was that of
infiltration of the unions by professional crooks and racketeers.
This trend, the Record suggests, began when the so-called real
union leaders found it useful to employ thugs in connection with
"legitimate" union activities. At one point in the Record, the
Chairman said:

> . . . the evidence will disclose that hoodlums and racketeers
> came into the labor picture with the aid and assistance of
> certain high-level union officials. (3592)

David Dubinsky, president of the International Ladies Garment
Workers, must undoubtedly be included among the genuine
trade-union leaders. Yet, according to the sworn testimony of
Lester Washburn, onetime president of the UAW-AFL, Dubin-

sky was instrumental in introducing John Dioguardi, a convicted extortionist, to the "movement." Washburn narrated that, casting about for a way to get rid of Dioguardi, he went to Dubinsky for information which might help to demonstrate Dioguardi's undesirability. Dubinsky replied at first, according to Washburn's testimony: "I don't even know the man." Thereupon, Washburn testified, "I named the plant and the city in which he worked, and [Dubinsky] got very excited." The only reply he got, however, Washburn said, was this:

> Well there is some times . . . we hire people to do certain jobs for us, but we don't let them get on the inside of the organization. (3702)

It remains to be seen whether, after inviting them in, keeping the thugs and racketeers out has proved possible. To list the number of union officers and agents who have long criminal records, and, what is more important, who have persisted in criminal conduct while acting as union officers and agents, would require a book in itself. It would take volumes, at least, to describe their criminal careers in any detail. But the point of present concern is that the thugs and racketeers are brought in by the "legitimate" union leaders.

Joseph G. Kane, an honest man and president of Bakery Workers Local 525, contributed a great deal to the Committee's understanding of the process. During his description of a beating he took from Bakery Workers president Cross, Kane explained the basis of selection of organizers in at least one union:

> Gardone, the boy that was [charged with] beating the young 14-year-old [son of a resisting employer] was one of the ones . . . in the room standing by as a goon to protect President Cross. . . . [Vice-President Stuart put him on the payroll] because he . . . can really slug. He put him on because of the fact that he came to his aid in goon-squad activities with the CIO . . . and protected Stuart. That is the qualifications of Gardone for an organizer in this international union. (2806)

Testimony presented to the Committee indicated that the UAW's goon squad during the Kohler strike was manned by people who had been in the UAW for years, and that they were always on hand during the UAW's long series of violent strikes. The testimony referred especially to the background of violence of Ferrazza, Vinson, and Gunaca. In presenting his evidence, Representative Clare Hoffman, of Michigan, said of Ferrazza that "off and on for at least sixteen years he had a job of beating up people." (9388–89)

Chief Counsel Kennedy was probing for this process when he asked Hoffa why Frank Kierdorf, an ex-convict, had been hired as business agent for a Flint, Michigan, Teamsters local (the reader will remember Flint as the scene of some violent "organizing" from the top). Hoffa replied that "we needed an experienced man," and that "Kierdorf was recommended." The Chief Counsel then observed that the only relevant experience the Committee investigators could uncover was "armed robbery." (13511)

There is no stopping a professional criminal once he sees what he can get away with as a "labor leader." John Dioguardi had had an abortive career as a businessman; the "labor movement" proved to be more in his line. Once he learned all that Sam Zakman had to teach, he went in on his own, he and Anthony "Ducks" Corallo. It took almost a page in Part 10 of the Record to list the names, indictments, and convictions of the officials of the Dioguardi and Corallo locals (3634).

Thugs and racketeers may get their first jobs in the "movement" on special assignment from "respectable" officials who hire them in order to whip recalcitrant employers and employees into line. But once they see how easy it is to get away with violence, oppression, and economic coercion—all one need do is call himself a "labor leader"—there is no stopping them. If certain developments now afoot are allowed to continue unchecked, it will not be long before the "labor movement" becomes indistinguishable from the organized crime syndicates which are gnawing away at the vitals of this society.

The Committee scratched the surface of this subterranean confluence in its investigation of infiltration of trade unions by the Mafia, sometimes called the "Syndicate." In introducing the hearings on the "Syndicate," Chairman McClellan said that the Committee "has become convinced that the relationship of the national criminal syndicate with legitimate labor and business is far more critical than has heretofore been revealed. The ramifications of this problem present the gravest implications for the destiny of our national economy." (12192) A prodigious succession of invocations of the Fifth Amendment is mainly what the Committee got out of its witnesses, but there is no reason to doubt, on the basis of evidence presented by the Committee's own investigators, that the Chairman was correct in correlating "this illegal activity of the national crime syndicate and its infiltration and influence in labor-management relations." (12192)

Any number of the members of the "Syndicate" turned out to be officials of local unions (12282, 12289). They also, in the aggregate, covered the whole criminal spectrum, according to the testimony of Committee investigator George H. Martin. Martin had no idea of the total number of criminal offenses charged to the "Syndicate" members, but they added up, he thought, to fifty or sixty different crimes, ranging from "armed robbery, suspicion of murder, attempted murder, murder," to "extortion, extortion by threat, assault and battery, assault with intent to kill, felonious wounding," to "coercion, dynamiting, blackmailing, forgery, black marketing, smuggling, and indecency." They had also been guilty of or charged with "operating of unregistered stills, sale and possession of narcotics, violation of the alcohol tax laws," and any number of other such activities (12258).

There is no point, however, in detailing here the criminal activities of the "Syndicate." The McClellan Committee's job was to explore improper and corrupt practices in labor relations and to inquire into their causes, with a view to formulating corrective legislation. This job, Senator Curtis adhered to most rigorously. He sought tirelessly for the special features of labor law, policy, and practice which were responsible for attracting thugs, crooks, and racketeers into the "movement." Thus, when faced with the facts concerning the "Syndicate," he asked Martin F. Pera, an agent of the United States Bureau of Narcotics who had made a special study of the matter, for his opinion concerning the reasons underlying the drift of the Mafia toward labor unions:

SENATOR CURTIS. Mr. Pera, why has an organization such as the Mafia moved into the union business? That is the primary assignment of this committee to investigate labor and management. Now, why have they moved into union activities?

MR. PERA. Well, I think the answer could be very concise and very simple, that their activities and their background and the activities that they engaged in years ago indicated they were experts in extortion, and they are using the union as a front simply as another means of extorting.

SENATOR CURTIS. The fact that they are dealing oftentimes with a group that has compulsory membership; is that a factor?

MR. PERA. Oh, yes.

SENATOR CURTIS. Is it a fact that some labor leaders, even though they are not part of a criminal underworld, are using the element of fear on their membership—is that something that fits in with the Mafia characteristics?

MR. PERA. It is the pattern of extortion again.

SENATOR CURTIS. Now, the fact that unions enjoy certain immunities that other groups in the country do not have gives a group an opportunity for a base of operations; isn't that correct?

MR. PERA. Yes; I am certain that that was one of their considerations when they entered that field.

SENATOR CURTIS. This committee has found several instances where courts just wouldn't grant anybody any protection who had suffered at the hands of the union. One Philadelphia judge referred to it as a union brawl, and they didn't go into those things. Well, that gives a criminal group a very good place to hide; doesn't it?

MR. PERA. Yes; an excellent advantage for them. . . .

SENATOR CURTIS. . . . Now, do groups like the Mafia go into union business because it is revenue producing, too?

MR. PERA. Yes. Their primary consideration is the revenue-producing thing.

SENATOR CURTIS. The revenue from the workers, as well as the opportunity for illicit things, such as extortion?

MR. PERA. As well as the opportunity to control programs and entire industry. . . .

SENATOR CURTIS. I . . . think that the Congress cannot expect a cleanup in labor-management relations until we do something that we haven't done to date at all, and that is to deal with these powers and immunities and compulsion in the field of unionism, that invites the wrong kind of people to go into union leadership. (12256–57)

We have been the witnesses here of two kinds of corruption: the corruption of trade-union officials, and the corruption of trade unionism itself. The ultimate in corruption of trade unionism will come when the crooks, thugs, and racketeers, following Gresham's Law, chase out all the decent and honest union officials, just as bad money chases out good. This forced migration of decent men, while not directly investigated by the Committee, nevertheless appears in different parts of the Record, where fragments of evidence indicate that it is under way: an Ed Crumboch gets displaced by a Raymond Cohen; a Joe Kane is slugged by a James Cross (2806); two civilized local officers in Minneapolis are dynamited after refusing to cooperate in Gerald Connelly's vicious organizing methods (5392); Lester Washburn feels he has no alternative to quitting as president of the UAW-AFL when his executive board reverses his expulsion of John Dioguardi (3712–13). Thus the strong-arm men take over. Meanwhile the "legitimate" labor leaders preach Reuther's philosophy and follow Gibbons' and Reuther's and Hoffa's practice. They do not line their own pockets, but they will do whatever seems necessary in order to crush any worker, or any employer, who resists their hegemony. How many workers, how many employers, will resist? And if they do not, or cannot resist, will we not then know, in fact, corruption unlimited?

Industry

Horace Crouch's adventures with the Teamsters' pinball picketing of his Mount Hood Cafe were no more than the surface bubbles of a much deeper process. The pickets would have been removed, as we have seen in Chapter 2, had Crouch agreed to replace Stan Terry's pinball machines with those recommended by the Teamsters. But his relations with Terry had been good, and he wished them to continue. It was a matter, then, of Terry's getting approval from the Teamsters. Terry ultimately got that approval, but it took some doing.

The interested reader will never learn from Terry's testimony precisely how he got the Teamsters' approval, peruse the Record as carefully as he will, for Terry was obviously afraid to give any definite details (221, 230, 274, 293). He led the Committee a merry chase through devious investment proposals, middlemen, appointments which were made but never kept, long-distance calls planned but never placed. The story had to be pieced together by the Committee from the testimony of several other witnesses, mainly that of James B. Elkins. This witness was in a position to know as much as anyone about the underworld in Portland, Oregon, and Seattle and Spokane, Washington. He set forth a background which easily qualified him as perhaps the top man in that world. However, he was, the Committee said in its Interim Report, "a forthright and candid witness" whose "story stands corroborated before the committee by independent witnesses." (Report, 39)

Elkins gave a clear and coherent account of Terry's problem and the solution. He himself had had an arrangement with Teamster leaders to take over the entire pinball business, which was worth a quarter of a million dollars a year. Stan Terry was the biggest independent operator, and those high Teamster officials, John Sweeney and Frank Brewster, according to Elkins, "felt very strongly" about eliminating Terry. One Teamster agent had said to him, Elkins testified, that "he would crawl to Seattle on his knees if Stan Terry got in the union." (216) While Terry was still on the outside, Elkins said, he confessed to Elkins that he had been "a bad boy, and I am willing to pay for it." (216) It wasn't so easy. Terry had several disappointments in his efforts to buy his way back in, so that Teamsters would no longer picket saloons and restaurants which leased his machines. But finally, Elkins said, "he connived around and got in to Mr. Brewster and, I guess, gave him some money, and his troubles were over." Terry had told him, said Elkins, that he "maneuvered through various people to get acquainted, to get an introduction, to square it away with Frank Brewster." The final, fruitful contact was said to have been one Hy Goldbaum.

"What did you know or understand about Hy Goldbaum?" Chief Counsel Kennedy asked. To this Elkins sighed, "Oh, Lord." (217) Terry told him later, Elkins testified, that he had made his contact with Brewster through Goldbaum, and that he had had to pay "a chunk of money" in order to get back in to the union, so that his customers would no longer be picketed. When he asked the dimensions of the "chunk," Elkins said, "Terry told him $10,000 or more." (217-18)

This story is duplicated dozens of times in the Record and thousands of times in life. Strangely enough, at times some members of the Committee thought that the people in Terry's position, the businessmen, were more to blame than the union leaders who were shaking them down. Governments, state and federal, have made available to union leaders the unique privilege of seriously harming, if not exterminating, businesses which will not play ball. When, in order to avoid extermination, they do as Terry did—namely, pay off—a curious process of reasoning induces some to accuse them of bribery, rather than the union leaders of extortion.

Earl P. Bettendorf, a Texas manufacturer, had such an experience with Senators McNamara and Kennedy. Under contract with the United States government to supply pallets at the Tobyhanna Signal Corps Base, near Scranton, he found it impossible to deliver the pallets without paying an unforeseen fee of $13.12 for each truckload. This money was demanded by Teamsters Local 229, which claimed jurisdiction over all truck unloading in the Scranton area. According to the testimony of Mr. Paul Bradshaw, who had been a steward for Local 229 at the time, he and all other stewards were instructed to prevent any contractor's "getting away" with anything. He said:

> Well, I had orders when a contractor would come in on a job . . . to make it as rough for them as I could . . . and not to let them get away with a thing, and to keep pressing them all the time. So I would keep pressing them so when they complained to me, I had orders to tell them that they were wanted down at the business agent, to talk to them. (1744-45)

Bradshaw explained that trucks delivering anything within a 90-mile radius of Scranton had to be operated or unloaded by a member of Local 229. "If they were out of a 90-mile radius and they were out of our jurisdiction, we put a man on the truck." And this was true, Bradshaw affirmed, even if the driver was a member of another Teamster local (1745). To put it another way, Local 229 asserted a proprietary or governmental right over the Scranton area. Furthermore, this sovereignty was recognized by the United States government. Bettendorf got in touch with the government, told its contracting officer what he had run into at Tobyhanna, and secured an increase in the terms of payment reflecting this unforeseen cost. Instead of paying $13.12 for each truck, however, he made a flat deal of $175 per week with the business agent whom he went to see pursuant to Bradshaw's instructions, and he was then allowed to deliver and unload his pallets without further molestation from Local 229.

Senator Kennedy inferred that the money went into the pockets of the business agents, rather than into the pockets of Local 229 members. He was probably right, Bettendorf agreed. Thereupon, Senator Kennedy accused *Bettendorf*: "The fact is that you were paying them a bribe, then?" (1970) Bettendorf refused to be intimidated or to take the blame for doing something for which the United States government and the Teamsters were responsible. He said:

> Well, there was no bribe as far as I was concerned. [The Local 229 people] advised me that they had a contract, that the building of the Tobyhanna Depot was under the supervision of the United States engineer, and the United States engineers gave them the permission to take over the ground and charge $13.12 and that the United States Government paid it on all movements of Signal Corps supplies coming in as well as all of the other supplies. (1970)

If the United States had conceded the Teamsters' sovereignty in the Scranton sector, Bettendorf was scarcely in a position to rebel.

The distinction between bribery and extortion is important and must be clearly understood before one can properly evaluate the position of employers confronted with the overwhelming power which the unions have gained through default of government. The essential feature in bribery is a *giving* in order to corrupt the *recipient;* the essential feature in extortion is a *taking* from an unwilling giver through some improper or unlawful exercise of power. The person guilty of bribery is seeking a special privilege, to which he is not entitled, from a person who is in a position of authority, a person who is considered corrupt when he grants that privilege. The person guilty of extortion is seeking money through duress and under no color of legal right.

Had Senator Kennedy understood these matters, he would probably not have accused Bettendorf of bribery, for such an accusation would make sense only on the assumption that the Teamsters members *owned* or *controlled* Scranton and all the area around it *legally,* and that neither the United States government nor Bettendorf had a right to enter that area without paying the Teamster members for the special privilege. But of course neither the Teamsters nor its members have any such legal ownership and control. Bettendorf was clearly an extortion victim, as were all the employers whom some members of the Committee castigated for giving in to unions when the only alternative was serious damage to their businesses, if not annihilation. As Bettendorf said to Senator McNamara,

> Understand, Senator, I would like to add that we had no other option. Either we did not perform under our contract or we paid $13.12 [per truck]. There seemingly was no one in the Government to help us unload, and if we didn't pay the $13.12 nothing happened, we just sat there. So we were forced. (1977)

Bettendorf went on to say that since all his business at the time was with the government, he would have had to shut down his factory if he refused to make the payment demanded by Local 229 (1979). That added up to extortion, in Senator Mundt's opinion, but he thought the ultimate victim was the United States government (and the people who pay taxes), rather than Bettendorf (1979). Of course, the Senator was right. The people, as consumers, ultimately pay for all the extortion of which trade unions are guilty. Businessmen are only the intermediaries; they hand over the money, physically, and then present the bill to the public in the form of higher prices.

If unions have the power, through strikes, picketing, and boycotts, to prevent men from operating their lawful businesses, or to harass them in a thousand different, specially privileged ways, it is reasonable to expect that they will use such power as the leverage for extortion. Numerous heating contractors have sworn that they had to make payoffs to Arthur H. Cronin, a vice-president of the Sheet Metal Workers and president of its Chicago Local 73, if they wished to stay in business. Although the payoffs were described in great detail, Mr. Cronin swore that they were all lies.[2]

The modes of extortion from businessmen are many. Chairman McClellan called "labor peace put on the market for sale one of the most insidious of union practices,"[3] and one series of hearings delved deeply into the matter, when it considered the campaign of the World Wide Press for paid advertisements among businessmen. A publishing firm largely backed by Max Block of the Butchers (11818–19), World Wide Press did not reach the general public, and its advertisements were therefore of no use to the businessmen of whom ads were solicited. Its solicitors were an oily bunch, as reference to their sales pitch would reveal to anyone wishing to consult the Record (11841 ff.). Seven had penitentiary records as swindlers and confidence men (11842, 11953). Of a gross income of $710,000 in 1957, a substantial proportion came from Food Fair Stores, A & P, Grand Union, and certain other firms under collective agreement with Max Block's Butchers (11818–19).

The Record carries a similar story in connection with Benjamin Lapensohn's New York *Federationist*. A number of non-union firms made contributions to Lapensohn, to the great puzzlement of the Committee members, who wondered why they should be buying ads which were of no earthly use to them. International Business Machines, for example, contributed $22,-500 (10986–91), but was not sure just whose good will was being

---

[2] *The New York Times,* December 3, 1958, p. 30, col.3; December 4, 1958, p. 42, col. 5.
[3] *Ibid.*

purchased (10990). The puzzlement was not lessened when the Committee learned that 25 per cent of Lapensohn's income went to the New York Federation of Labor, which used that money in order to promote legislation that could scarcely be called friendly to business (10944 ff.).

The murky confusion in which the corruption was shrouded cleared up at times, as when Asa H. Farr, of the Kingston Trap Rock Company, told the Committee how he managed to induce a union steward to let his drivers unload at a construction job. Mr. Farr said he made a $1,000 contribution to a Lapensohn agent, presumably for an ad (which he never saw). The same trouble recurred, however, year after year, and only the payoff would remedy it. Chief Counsel Kennedy asked: "You were willing to make this . . . payoff in order to achieve . . . labor peace, is that right?" Mr. Farr's answer was "Yes." (10889)

But the leverage was not always so open to view. No doubt it was there, but well hidden. It had to be there, for it is impossible to believe that businessmen would buy otherwise useless ads, or invest in and join a country club operated by Max Block which they hardly ever visited (11552 ff.), or give Block inside information on forthcoming stock transactions (11598)—unless there was some compulsion. The Chairman asked Louis Stein, president of the Food Fair Stores, why he should want to do favors of that kind. Stein's answer was clearly understandable, though reserved:

> Because if anyone is in business, and you know that a person stands well in labor circles, you don't try to incur any ill will . . . not to get any benefits that you are not entitled to . . . but merely to be sure that you don't create ill will. (11138)

The "person" referred to was the shadowy Benjamin Lapensohn, whom the Committee could not interrogate, because he kept himself out of the country.

Mr. Lapensohn introduces a new subject and another phase in the corruption process—the go-between, the character who works both sides of the street, who has connections in unions which he peddles to managements who are having, or who might have, "labor troubles," unless, like Mr. Stein, they do what is necessary to avoid "ill will."

The Chicago Restaurant Association was formed, at least in part, to solve the vexatious "labor problems" which its members were experiencing. Abraham Teitelbaum seemed to be the solver. When Donald Strang was having the trouble which has been described in Chapter 3, Teitelbaum was recommended to him as an expert in labor relations, and Strang engaged his services (12573). After a while, the union, which never did represent any of Strang's employees, took its pickets away, and he received a bill from Teitelbaum for $2,240, which he promptly paid. Strang thought it unnecessary to look a gift horse in the mouth. He knew that the union had never been desired by his employees, and he thought that when the picket line was withdrawn his troubles were over. A year later, however, the same union approached him again, this time telling him that *the contract* was up for renewal. Since he had never signed a contract with the union, he was somewhat upset. The Record does not fill in all the steps, but it does show that Teitelbaum endorsed Strang's check for $2,240 over to the union. On the back was written: "in payment of 40 initiation fees at $20 a person, totaling $800, and one year's dues for $1,140." (12580) When Teitelbaum was sworn in as a witness, he took the Fifth Amendment, plus several other amendments, on every question—including whether he was an attorney and where and when he was born (12715).

Nathan Shefferman was the giant of the labor relations consultants, numbering among his four hundred clients some of the largest and most respectable of American businesses. The Committee's Interim Report found that "a source of a great deal of Shefferman's power was his close association with Dave Beck." The Report continues:

> The relationship was mutually profitable. Beck on a number of occasions received cash gifts from Shefferman. Beck's son was involved in a profitable business transaction with Shefferman's son. In addition, the Chicago labor consultant was used by Beck as a conduit through which he funnelled $85,000 of teamster union funds for the payment

of his personal bills. Shefferman, on the other hand, was
able to sell to employers his friendship with Beck and was
able to rely on Beck's teamsters for effective assistance in
efforts to defeat union organizing drives. (Report, 298)

According to the Report, Shefferman's Labor Relations Associates was thus a multipurpose organization, plying its various
trades among hundreds of corporations and many trade unions:
a payoff here, a deal preferring one union to another there, and
an all-out anti-union campaign in still other cases (Report, 298).

Insofar as the Shefferman firm engaged in coercive anti-
union practices it is of relatively little concern to this book.
The law strictly prohibits such practices, and it is equally rigorously enforced. If the law prohibiting anti-union coercion were
defective in any way, or if it were as defectively enforced as is
the law forbidding union violence and coercion, then the anti-
union phase of Shefferman's activities would call for more attention here. But the cases examined by the Committee were all
of the kind that the National Labor Relations Board is daily
prosecuting; indeed, for the most part the Committee covered
cases already passed upon by the NLRB. The Committee did
say that the law needed amendment in order to reach the activities of such organizations as Shefferman's (Report, 300). But
that is not really necessary. When any such firm is engaged by
an employer to conduct anti-union activities, the firm becomes
an agent of the employer, and as the agent of an employer it is
covered by the law equally with the employer. If the NLRB
has not yet issued an order against Shefferman's firm, either it
has not found that firm guilty of unfair practices or, having
found unfair practices, it has considered an order directed against
the employer sufficient. In any event the law covers the problem
as completely as law can.

The great significance of the middlemen to corruption in labor relations is of a different kind. Such men as Hy Goldbaum,
Benjamin Lapensohn, Abraham Teitelbaum, Nathan Shefferman, and John Dioguardi, too, though his career as a "labor
relations consultant" was as abortive as his career as a businessman, play an unhealthy but entirely logical and predictable role,
once the corruption of which they are a part is properly under-

stood. They are an inevitable development in the process which begins with vesting in trade unions a virtually unlimited power of coercion, violence, and compulsion. This process draws to trade unions unscrupulous men and forces from trade unions the decent men. The unscrupulous men are not satisfied with the power or the income to be derived from peacefully representing workers who want and need representation. There are not always sufficient numbers of such workers, in the first place; and in the second place, even when there are goodly numbers who want representation, the income is nothing special and no great power is available in a peaceable, voluntary setting. Besides, it is so easy to augment power and income, once one understands the special privileges which come with being a "labor leader." Strikes, picketing, boycotts, and violence always hurt and can often be fatal to a businessman. There is always a possibility, therefore, of one kind of a shakedown or another. Few businessmen—few people in any walk of life—will risk their all in defense of principle. The number becomes even smaller if the shakedown is not too extortionate, and if there may be some commercial advantage involved, as well. It becomes a business then, a shadowy and dirty business, and the go-between, the contact man, the person who can judge how much the market will bear, who has the experience and the know-how, who can size up the prospect and swing the deal—he becomes a very valuable man.

* * *

The go-between is a carrier. He carries the process of corruption from the shadow union to the business world, and he is thus an integral element in the process which leads to corruption unlimited.

Government and Society

While Max Chester's racket-picketing was going on outside (see Chapter 2), Paul Claude's employees, recent immigrants from Puerto Rico, stuck at their jobs inside his small machine shop. Noon came, and Claude went out to a worried lunch.

He returned, only to find his worries had increased—his employees were in the street. How did that happen, Chief Counsel Kennedy asked. According to Claude, the employees informed him that "the policeman had told them to go out there and picket." (3925) At an earlier point in this shakedown story, Claude testified before the Committee, a police captain had told him that he had to recognize Max Chester's racket local:

> You have got to make a deal with them. You have to make some kind of a deal with them because they are legitimate. (3923)

Donald Skaff went to the police when one of his drivers was viciously beaten and a murderous attempt made to run over him with a car. The license number was taken and turned over to the police, who reported back that it belonged to a car owned by Teamsters Local 332, in Flint, Michigan (6432). But nothing more was done, nobody arrested, and no prosecution. When asked why not, Skaff testified that:

> There was not enough evidence. Our man was struck from behind, and he could not identify anyone and there seemed to be a lack of enthusiasm to do anything. (6432)

Skaff said he had a three-hour session with the Flint chief of police. It was not productive. The police felt, according to Skaff, that "they could not get involved in a labor incident." They would be "glad to prosecute," however, if he dug up the evidence for them (6431).

The Record demonstrates a similar lack of enthusiasm on the part of the police dozens of times. The reader will no doubt recall many such incidents in the foregoing pages—how Strang had been told that the Illinois Governor's office had instructed the state police to stay out of his troubles with the Restaurant Union, on the theory that it was a "local affair," although the stoppage of his trucks on state highways was nothing of the kind; how Sheriff Mosch and Mayor Ploetz dragged their feet when it came to preventing and punishing the UAW's violence at Kohler and in Sheboygan; how in the reign of terror accompanying the Teamsters' organizing campaign in Tennessee there were few arrests and even fewer convictions. Senator Curtis, after seeing so much of it, began to call it the phenomenon of the "double standard," one standard of law and order for ordinary citizens, and another for union thugs and goons. Addressing David Cordivari, a conscientious detective on the Philadelphia police force, the Senator said:

> Well now, we seem to have a double standard in this country. I am not lecturing you on it but it is one of the problems the police have.

When Cordivari agreed, Senator Curtis continued with:

> Ordinary citizens are not only supposed to refrain from roughing up a policeman, but they are supposed to obey him. . . . But that is just winked at in connection with union activities. If one of our youths in our cities fights back at a police man, we call it resisting an officer, and he is in great danger of being branded as a juvenile delinquent and injured for life. But the public and judges pass over union violence and just say, "Well, that was a labor brawl." (10456–57)

The proper thing for police and judges to do, in the opinion of union leaders, is to treat union thugs very gently, far more gently than ordinary citizens are treated. The Record shows a good many union leaders prepared to compel such treatment by intimidation, or to induce it by outright bribery or a kind of concealed influence which comes worlds closer to true bribery than did Bettendorf's yielding to the Scranton Teamsters at the Tobyhanna Signal Corps base.

The career of a conspiracy indictment against thirteen officers and members of Chattanooga Teamsters Local 515 recapitulates most of what has been shown already in this book, and will help to bring understanding to a still higher level. One of the defendants charged with the conspiracy to dynamite was Glenn W. Smith. Chairman McClellan's summary of Mr. Smith's career in the Teamsters could scarcely be improved:

> Glenn W. Smith has served two penitentiary sentences for robbery and burglary; yet he was made the business agent of a teamster local in Paducah, Kentucky. While there, he was convicted of assault and battery and indicted

twice for malicious destruction of personal property, cases which have not yet been resolved. This apparently qualifies Smith for advancement. He goes to Chattanooga, Tennessee, where he becomes secretary-treasurer of a larger teamster local. There he is indicted on a conspiracy charge, including the slashing of truck tires, dynamitings, assault, and arson. With these admirable qualifications the international sends him back to Paducah, Kentucky, and places him in charge of his old local which has by then been put in trusteeship.

Smith is unwillingly extradited back to Tennessee, where the conspiracy charge against him is dismissed by Judge Raulston Schoolfield shortly after a fellow defendant, Chattanooga teamster official H. L. Boling, has boasted that the case has been fixed by a payoff of $18,500. This matter neatly disposed of, Smith is sent to Florida as an international organizer where, according to testimony before this committee, he is involved in a dynamiting and arson case. This seems to qualify him for even higher trust and he returns to Chattanooga as president of local 515. In the period he holds this office he is linked by testimony before this committee to dynamitings in Knoxville, Tennessee, and dynamitings and arson in Jackson, Mississippi, and other areas in the South.

These expressions of character by Smith qualified him for the top job in the teamsters union in the State of Tennessee, the presidency of joint council No. 87, the position he holds today. (7494)

The part of Smith's career which concerns us at present is the conspiracy indictment in which, ultimately, Judge Schoolfield took the case away from the jury and directed a verdict in favor of Smith and his associates.

The indictment itself had to be a good one, Thomas Crutchfield testified. Now since Crutchfield, as assistant district attorney in Chattanooga, had himself drafted the indictment, he might not have been entirely objective when he said he felt it to be "as strong an indictment as we could possibly have." (7447) However, the fact is that he had good reason for that belief, aside from pride of authorship. For one thing, he modeled the indictment on one which Judge Schoolfield himself had helped draft. Of course, the model, while successful, was against a Ku Klux Klan conspiracy, not a trade-union conspiracy; and that might have made a difference, in spite of the substantial similarities in the conduct of the two organizations. But Crutchfield didn't think that there was enough difference to matter; he was sure, he told the Committee, that the indictment against Smith and his associates in the "movement" was "just as good as it could possibly be." (7447) His faith was vindicated, at least temporarily, when the Tennessee Supreme Court refused to accept Judge School-field's first quashing of the indictment (7445). That ruling by the State Supreme Court meant that the indictment was solid, that it charged a real violation of law. It did not mean, however, that the defendants were guilty of the violation charged. Their guilt would have to be established by evidence at the trial Judge Schoolfield was compelled to conduct by order of the Supreme Court of Tennessee.

Crutchfield's confidence in his indictment would have been increased greatly had he but known Judge Schoolfield's original attitude toward it. To ascertain that original attitude we must refer to the testimony of James E. West, now an Internal Revenue investigator, but at the period in question a Chattanooga policeman assigned as Judge Schoolfield's court officer. According to West's account, Judge Schoolfield was at first enthusiastic about both the indictment and the evidence in support of it which West had uncovered. Suddenly, however, the judge's enthusiasm waned and, as West put it, "for some mysterious reason later these indictments were quashed." (7455)

As reference to the Committee's chronology of events will reveal, the waning of Judge Schoolfield's enthusiasm coincided with the issuance by Glenn W. Smith's Local 515 of an $18,500 check drawn to cash (7443–44). This check was drawn on July 2, 1951, and cashed by Smith on July 5. On July 6, Judge Schoolfield re-assigned the case, which had originally been set for trial on July 10, to some future and indefinite date. From then on, the case had a laggard and spasmodic career, stretching over many months. Then another check (for $1,500) was drawn to cash by Local 515, on March 17. On April 5, Judge School-field quashed the indictment. The Supreme Court reversed him in February, 1953, and sent the case back to him, ordering him to set it down for a trial. The case was tried. As soon as the prosecution presented its evidence, the judge directed a verdict for the defendants (7444).

The two checks, totalling $20,000, were identified on the union's books as having been used to pay attorney's fees. The only attorney engaged by the union at the time was H. G. B. King. He swore to the Committee that he had not received the money (7435). Where then did the money go?

Raymond Hixson, Deputy State Fire Marshal of Tennessee testified that H. L. Boling, secretary-treasurer of Local 515 at the time and a co-defendant with Smith, told him where the money went. Their conversation occurred on July 8, 1951, just two days before the date on which the case was originally set to be tried. It was a Sunday, and Hixson asked Boling whether "he was going to be ready for trial on Tuesday." Boling, apparently something of a blabbermouth, replied, according to Hixson, "that there was not going to be a trial." Hixson continues:

> I asked him how he knew. He said that there had been $18,500 passed to quash the indictments and there was not to be a trial. (7438)

Boling would not identify the recipient, but he seemed to get a big kick out of the fact that it had been passed, and was not at all reticent about that. In fact, Committee investigator LaVern J. Duffy testified that he found the same information, identified as coming from Boling, in the files of the Internal Revenue Service (7440).

Later, Boling proved to be of great assistance to an old schoolmate of his, Spence Galloway, who was in trouble, facing a three-year sentence from Judge Schoolfield. The Record indicates that by way of Boling a $1,000 campaign contribution went to Judge Schoolfield and that the next day Galloway got a new trial and was subsequently paroled (7461–88).

The Committee invited Judge Schoolfield to appear, and to set the Record straight, if it had gone wrong at any point. The judge did not accept the invitation. "On the basis of Judge Schoolfield's having declined . . . to testify," Chairman McClellan observed, "we must reluctantly let the record with its obvious implication speak for itself." (7495) The Chairman had other things to say about trade-union organizing techniques, as practiced in Tennessee:

> At the outset of these hearings, I announced that we were going to look into certain aspects of organized goon violence in the State of Tennessee, and in other States in that vicinity. Although fully prepared for some of the more serious aspects of the case, I do not think even the committee was prepared for the shocking pattern of viciousness, lawlessness, and disregard for the laws of the land to which the many witnesses have testified here.
>
> The hearings just completed . . . reveal a pattern of wanton disregard of the law to a degree never before revealed to this committee. (7493)

Circuit Judge F. H. Schlichting of Wisconsin was a different kind of judge, and because he was a different kind of judge he was the target of the vituperation of Emil Mazey, UAW vice-president. In a speech given at a union meeting and later broadcast to the Sheboygan radio audience, Mazey challenged Judge Schlichting's qualifications "to serve as a judge in this community." (8912) The provocation of this and other attacks upon Judge Schlichting was a two-year sentence imposed upon William Vinson for his unprovoked attack on Willard van Ouwerkerk (8980–85). Vinson, it will be remembered, was six feet three and a half, twenty-seven years old, and weighed 230 pounds; van Ouwerkerk was five feet six, over fifty, and weighed 125 pounds. The jury found Vinson guilty, as charged, with assault to commit great bodily harm. The maximum sentence possible in such a case was three years; Judge Schlichting sentenced Vinson to one to two years, of which Vinson actually served thirteen months. The UAW appealed the sentence for Vinson to the Supreme Court of Wisconsin, challenging both the ground upon which the case had been litigated and the sentence. The Wisconsin Supreme Court upheld Judge Schlichting in every respect. It said:

> The violence of Mr. Vinson's attack on Mr. van Ouwerkerk, the continuation of the attack of kicking while Mr. van Ouwerkerk lay helpless on the floor, the serious injuries which Vinson inflicted, the disproportion in the size and

age of the two men, which removed fear of personal danger
to Vinson from reprisal by van Ouwerkerk, are matters of
evidence which the jury was entitled to consider when reach-
ing a conclusion concerning Vinson's state of mind while
he carried on the assault. It is quite impossible to conclude
under such circumstances that in so doing, Vinson lacked
an intent to hurt van Ouwerkerk and hurt him badly.
Contrary to [Vinson's] contention, the evidence and the
inferences from which it was the province of the jury to
draw, established beyond a reasonable doubt that the assault
was made by Vinson with the intent to inflict great bodily
harm to van Ouwerkerk. (8871)

Notwithstanding this affirmance, Mazey thought the sentence
"extremely harsh" (8912); furthermore, he told the Committee,
Judge Schlichting should have disqualified himself, and the
failure to do so, said Mazey, justified his, Mazey's, challenge to
the judge's integrity (8913). Why should the judge have disqualified himself? According to Mazey, he should have disqualified himself because he had had the integrity to do that in certain
cases involving disputes between strikers and nonstrikers. Mazey
said that Judge Schlichting had, early in May of 1954, called
certain UAW people into his chambers "and said that he would
have to disqualify himself from a particular matter relating to the
union because he had an interest in a grocery store, and that he
sold groceries both to strikers and to nonstrikers." (8913)

Not knowing what he is talking about is no incumbrance to
Mazey. The fact that a judge might as well resign if, after
having the decency to disqualify himself in one case he must
disqualify himself in all, did not slow down Mazey at all. He
accused Judge Schlichting, at the hearings, of not presenting the
"charges to the jury properly"; yet the ultimate authority, the
Wisconsin Supreme Court, upheld Judge Schlichting on that.
He accused the judge, in sentencing Vinson to two years, of
passing the "stiffest sentence he could"; yet the statute permitted
the judge to impose a three-year sentence (8914). When faced
with this fact, Mazey accused the judge of trying Vinson under
the wrong statute: Vinson should have been tried for simple
assault and battery, according to Mazey.[4] Upon this magisterial

---

[4] Mazey did not know the facts, or, if he did, he was misleading the
Committee. The Record shows that Judge Schlichting himself suggested to

pronouncement, Senator Curtis asked Mazey: "Are you a law-yer?" Mazey replied: "No, but I know a great deal about the subject matter and I deal with lawyers all the time." (8914)

There is not the slightest doubt that Mazey knows a great deal about assault and battery, and it is quite probable that he has been accustomed, like his colleagues in the Teamsters and other unions, to little more than a slap on the wrist, if that, from law-enforcement authorities in some areas. It was therefore a shock to have the law applied to a union goon in the same way that it would have been applied to an ordinary citizen.

We have already seen, in Chapter 6, that campaign contributions had been made by the union to Sheriff Mosch and Mayor Ploetz. We have also seen that their "law enforcement" was directed more toward denying the rights of the Kohler Company and the nonstrikers than toward making the UAW and the strikers obey the law. That kind of law enforcement, undoubtedly, is what Mazey and the UAW feel that they have coming—not the kind served by Judge Schlichting.

The Governor of Michigan refused for years to do what the Constitution of the United States required him to do—namely extradite John Gunaca to Wisconsin, there to stand trial on a charge of brutal assault. This same John Gunaca, the Record shows, spent several weeks in 1953 working for the Wayne County (Michigan) CIO Council, in his words, "doing PAC work." (9101) Gunaca wasn't too sure of the offices up for election during his time with the CIO's Political Action Committee, but, he said, "I believe it was for judgeships." (9103) Senator Mundt expressed shock at hearing this:

> Are you sure this was an election for judgeships [Senator Mundt asked]? I listened to Mr. Mazey talk for two days about the fact that Judge Schlichting wasn't an unbiased and unprejudiced judge. Now you are telling

Vinson's attorneys that they move for inclusion of a simple-assault verdict. When they did so, the Judge submitted it to the jury. The jury, not Judge Schlichting, found Vinson guilty of the greater offense, for which the statutory minimum penalty was one year and the maximum, three. Judge Schlichting then sentenced Vinson to not less than one year and not more than two, of which Vinson served thirteen months. Such are the true facts which evoked Mazey's vituperation (8982–83).

me that the CIO is trying to elect its own judges in Detroit.
(9103)

Gunaca backed off at this point, saying he could not remember
just which offices were in issue. The Committee pressed him,
however, and he and his counsel, D. Charles Marston, some time
later produced additional information concerning the candidates
for whom Gunaca had campaigned in the spring of 1953. There
was a curious reluctance and generality in their testimony. Mr.
Marston told the Committee "there were a number of State
offices, county offices, and city offices up for election." (9134)
Addressing Gunaca, the Chairman asked: "Has your memory
been refreshed now? Do you remember whom you campaigned
for?" The rest of the colloquy is interesting:

> MR. GUNACA. Yes; I do, Mr. Chairman.
>
> THE CHAIRMAN. All right. Who?
>
> MR. GUNACA. For the regents of the University of
> Michigan, Miss Hatch and Mr. Robinson, and superin-
> tendent of public instruction was Mack Monroe.
>
> THE CHAIRMAN. Anyone else?
>
> MR. GUNACA. Well, the board of agriculture was Himes
> and Smith. (9134)

No judges, apparently—that is, until Senator Mundt himself
perused the list of candidates in the election. He found something else:

> I find that on the list that Mr. Gunaca was working for
> were . . . seventeen circuit court judges that he was sup-
> porting. He was supporting ten judges of recorder's courts,
> and he was supporting four judges of common pleas
> courts. (9136)

Every man has a right to campaign for the political candidates
of his choice. But when it is clear that a man or a union or any
other organization expects of its candidates special privileges in
the form of one-sided laws and corrupt law-enforcement, the
rest of the citizenry must be on guard. The Record indicates
with perfect clarity that the objective of the political action of
the trade unions is special privilege and corruption—in their
favor—of all government.

The Record is, unfortunately, very thin as regards the scope of the political action of the UAW and its president. It is much fuller on the Teamsters. Further disclosures in the Record indicated that Wallace Turner had rather understated the political accomplishments of the Teamsters when, on the first day of the McClellan hearings, he said:

> I think [other witnesses] can and will tell you exactly why no local authority can deal with the racketeers and hoodlums who have risen to prominence and power in the teamsters union. They tried to take over our city government. They attempted to ingratiate themselves with our State officials, and there is some evidence that they have succeeded to at least a limited degree. They plotted the overthrow of the attorney general of Oregon because he was violently opposed to organized prostitution. (8)

James B. Elkins—"the victim," according to Mr. Turner, "of one of the most thorough attempts at intimidation I have ever seen visited on any witness" (8)—was in a position to know at first hand the Teamsters' political ambitions. He had been intimately associated with the highest Teamster officials on the West Coast. "Practically every day," he told the Committee, the political power and ambitions of the Teamsters were the subjects of discussion in its highest circles (135). Frank Brewster, the West Coast Teamster chief had told him, Elkins testified:

> I make mayors and I break mayors, and I make chiefs of police and I break chiefs of police. I have been in jail and I have been out of jail. There is nothing scares me. (100)

These were no idle boasts. The Record confirms them in detail. Mayor Peterson of Portland described to the Committee how the Teamsters at first supported him and then, when he would not play ball, opposed and defeated him (551-53; see also 135). Elkins himself testified that the plan was to "take over the whole State of Oregon." (135) And it never occurred to the Teamsters, he later said, that a politician "might be honest or not go along with them." (550)

Elkins was regarded as a dependable witness by the Committee (Interim Report, 39), and his testimony was borne out

in all material points by the testimony of a number of other witnesses, including that of Howard Morgan, who had been Chairman of the Democratic Party in 1952–1956, the period covering
some of the Teamsters' most aggressive politicking. Morgan had
some reservations about the purity of Mayor Peterson (Record,
325-26), but his extensive experience with the Teamsters in all
other respects corroborated Elkins' testimony. According to Morgan, the Teamsters went after "both legitimate and illegitimate
advantage" from the growing strength of the Democratic Party
in Oregon (314). Seeing this at an early date, Morgan said, he
took "concrete action to attempt to stop improper control of government by those who should not come into such control." (314)

For reasons presently to be explained, a special target of the
Teamsters was the Oregon State Liquor Commission. At a large
dinner, Morgan testified, he was approached by Thomas A.
Maloney, who, incidentally, while a close associate of Frank
Brewster, had never been either a member or an official of the
Teamsters (730). This "gorilla," as Morgan described him,

> with no warning, walked up to me in the middle of the hall,
> with a cigar between his first two fingers, thumped me on
> the chest, scattering cigar ashes all over a dark blue suit
> I had on, and said, "You make [the State Attorney General]
> lay off that liquor commission investigation." (320)

Morgan said, while brushing the cigar ashes off his clothes, "that
sounds like an order." Maloney confirmed Morgan's judgment.
"That's an order," he said (320).

Morgan then asked Maloney what the great interest in the
Liquor Commission was, and why he did not want it investigated.
According to Morgan, Maloney replied: "You know damn well
what this means to us. Paul Patterson is our pigeon and we don't
want nobody shooting at him." (320) The Paul Patterson referred to was Governor of Oregon at the time. As Morgan explained, the State Liquor Commission was the Governor's
responsibility, and "any embarrassment to the Liquor commission
. . . is a tremendous handicap to the Governor." (320)

The more he saw of the Teamsters' actions the more anxious
he became for the future of his state, Morgan testified. "By the
fall of 1955," he said,

the situation looked worse and worse. There was no question in my mind that an attempt was being made to take over law enforcement in the State of Oregon from the local level in Multnomah County, in Portland, right up to and including the Governor's chair. (322)

The Teamsters hoped for many kinds of returns from their political control, but we need be concerned here with only one of their objectives. Morgan learned that the Teamsters wanted control of the Oregon State Liquor Commission because such control would help them to organize the employees of eastern distilleries literally "from the top." The Teamsters, Morgan told the Committee,

> were trying to sign up the employees of the distilleries in the East, and they wanted an arrangement whereby they could prevent liquor from certain distilleries being purchased and sold within a monopoly state like Oregon, not a drop within the boundaries, until a particular distillery signed up with the teamsters. (333)

* * *

We have upon occasion in this book noted a substantial identity in the conduct of all trade unions, those not investigated as well as those investigated by the Committee. The identity, despite vehement disavowals on both sides, is especially close between Reuther's UAW and Hoffa's Teamsters. The Teamsters have used much violence; so has the UAW. The Teamsters have engaged in extensive political activity; so has the UAW. The Teamsters regard politics, police, and judges as means of attaining special privileges for their violent and monopolistic conduct; so, it would seem, does the UAW.

In seeking to use the Oregon State Liquor Commission as a coercive organizing tool, the Teamsters did exactly what the UAW was doing, practically at the same time, when it induced several local governments to prohibit the use of Kohler plumbing fixtures in municipal construction projects. The one great difference between the Teamsters and the UAW is that the Teamsters have not—not yet, at any rate—attempted to disguise their corrupt conduct with an even more corrupt social philosophy.

There is, as we have seen, a great deal of crude braggadocio in the Teamsters. Besides the examples already encountered, the reader may be interested in a particularly choice one transmitted to the McClellan Committee by George Butler, a detective-lieutenant with the Dallas, Texas, police force. Butler was describing a discussion he had had with one Paul Ronald Jones, a man who had served time on murder and narcotics convictions (12520). Jones told him, Butler testified, of the "many different angles" involved in

> putting pressure on different companies and business. One of the things that he brought out, [Butler continued] was the fact that they were going to try to organize or unionize every truckdriver in the nation. He said, "When we do that, we can bring industry to its knees, and even the Government, if we have to." (12524)

The Record contains no such blatancies on the part of UAW officials and agents. Scurrility and misleading—though always pious—philosophizing are more in their vocal line. Yet, their acts speak for themselves. They will not tolerate any unorganized firms in what they consider to be their "jurisdiction"; if they have organized some plumbing manufacturers, they insist upon the right to organize all, even if violence is required.

When violence did not suffice to break Kohler, they attempted to get government on their side, thus adding another form of coercion to those which they had already exerted against Kohler and its nonstriking employees. Lucius P. Chase, Kohler's general counsel, gave the Committee an exhaustive account of the UAW's secondary boycotting of Kohler products (9750-9807). Besides noting that the UAW had attempted to induce the United States government to withdraw an artillery shell contract (9753), Chase described the UAW's successful and unsuccessful efforts to cause state and local governments all across the country to boycott Kohler products. Noting that "in most cases officials have been faithful to their public trust," Chase went on to say that it was a wrong and evil political principle for governments to take anything but a position of neutrality in labor disputes:

Neutrality is the only tenable position for public officials to take regarding a labor dispute. True neutrality consists of buying just what one would buy anyway without regard to a strike, not buying or refusing to buy a product simply because of it. (9755)

To this statement of principle, the UAW Washington lawyer, Joseph L. Rauh, took blusteringly vigorous exception—at first. When the Chairman showed indignation at the suggestion that government should not be neutral, Rauh back-pedaled. But the reader should not be misled by the back-pedaling. The Record indicates that Rauh had stated the UAW's position accurately in the first place. Referring to Chase's observation that neutrality is the only tenable position for public officials to take, Rauh said:

We challenge that, and we believe the whole history of the last twenty-five years is that governmental neutrality toward labor conditions is contrary to the way governmental policy has worked. (9808)

The reader will observe the Rauh has changed the subject. Chase did not say anything about "labor conditions," and much less did he purport to describe what government policy *had been* in the last twenty-five years. He said only that the *proper* position for government to take *during strikes* was neutrality. When the Chairman remarked that he, as a government official, "would be neutral" (9808), Rauh changed the subject still further. He instructed the Chairman on the UAW's efforts to induce governments to withhold all purchases and contracts from employers *guilty of unfair practices.* But Kohler was guilty of no unfair practices. It was the UAW which, according to all the evidence in the Record, had violated most of the National Labor Relations Act and several Wisconsin statutes as well during the Kohler strike. Hence his lecture about the UAW's efforts to get governments to cease dealing with employers guilty of unlawful conduct was at least doubly, and possibly triply, irrelevant. The colloquy rambled then to the question whether, if the UAW had the right to bring the pressure of outsiders on the Kohler Company, Kohler would have an equal right to bring outside pressures upon the UAW and the strikers. Rauh said that he had evidence of Kohler's preventing outside employment of strikers. When the Chairman asked whether he was charging that "the Kohler Company has actually been active in trying to prevent strikers from getting jobs," Rauh backed off again, saying "I don't have enough evidence to make such a charge." (9810)

The plain fact is that the UAW, like the Teamsters, *acts* to secure special privilege from governments and uses every kind of pressure available to reinforce its demands, resorting to vituperation against public officials who will not yield. Such action has been formulated into a philosophy by the UAW and its counsel. Neither its action nor its philosophy can be hidden by the kind of evasive performance we have just been observing.

* * *

Few historical instances of insolence and power-lust exceed those which the union officials continuously reveal. As this chapter was being written, the front page of *The New York Times* carried a story headed "Teamsters Plan to Picket Police in Campaign Here." [5] The story's source is identified as Henry Feinstein, president of the Teamsters' City Employees Union, Local 237, a man appointed by Hoffa, the story states, "as temporary head of a nation-wide campaign to bring all policemen, firemen, and other state, county, and municipal workers into his much-investigated union." The forty-man picket line was to be established, Feinstein said, in order to punish New York City Police Commissioner Stephen P. Kennedy for his ruling that policemen may not join unions. The story reports Feinstein as saying: "We are going to give the Commissioner a taste of the economic force and pressure of the teamster union." There are undoubtedly some who believe that the title of this chapter, "Corruption Unlimited," is strained and extravagant. Let those who so feel, consider carefully the response of New York Deputy Police Commissioner Walter Arm to the news. The Teamster picketing would not be restricted, he is reported to have said,

[5] December 30, 1958, p. 1, col. 1.

and if pickets are sent to Police Headquarters, the Police
Department will provide police officers to see that the pickets
are not interfered with, and to preserve order.

Feinstein expected that as a result of the picketing "the Police
Commissioner will freeze in his office." He was not sure whether
policemen would themselves refuse to cross the picket line, although "more than 3,000 had secretly joined his organization,"
but he felt confident that other teamsters would refuse to make
pickups and deliveries at the picketed Police Headquarters.

*   *   *

On the editorial page of the Hartford *Times* of August 25,
1958, there is a cartoon which was perhaps intended to be
humorous. It shows a leering Hoffa seated next to a window, and
in the distance, not too far, appears the Capitol dome. The
caption is "Maybe Next Year I'll Organize the Senate."

*   *   *

The corruption of a society is not yet complete merely because
violence and lawlessness occur, even if they occur frequently; for
these can be checked and quelled. Corruption is not yet unlimited
while the institutions and principles of society are in the process
of subversion; for courage and will may still eradicate subversion. Corruption prevails when a society has no longer the
sensitivity to detect it, the judgment to weigh it, or the will to
fight it.

Part II

THE ANATOMY
OF POWER

Some perspective may be had by imagining an application of the techniques of the labor market in some other field. If A is bargaining with B over the sale of his house, and if A were given the privileges of a modern labor union, he would be able (1) to conspire with all other owners of houses not to make any alternative offer to B, using violence or the threat of violence if necessary to prevent them, (2) to deprive B himself of access to any alternative offers, (3) to surround the house of B and cut off all deliveries, including food, (4) to stop all movement from B's house, so that if he were for instance a doctor he could not sell his services and make a living, and (5) to institute a boycott of B's business. All of these privileges, if he were capable of carrying them out, would no doubt strengthen A's position. But they would not be regarded by anyone as a part of "bargaining" —unless A were a labor union.

—Edward H. Chamberlin

Chapter 8

HIDDEN RELATIONSHIPS

Compulsion as a policy inevitably brings to the top men who understand the use of that weapon to get quick and easy results. Such men have only contempt for the harder, slower, and surer method of responsible service to the membership—the only source of true "union security."

—Joseph H. Ball

* * *

A hasty view of the phenomena described in the foregoing pages might suggest that they are largely disparate events, related only in that they are all parts of one Record. The annihilation of the independent Barbers Guild by the stranger-picketing of the affiliated Journeymen Barbers; the Sheet Metal Workers' attempt to destroy the Burt Manufacturing Company; the compulsory membership of A & P's grocery clerks in the Butchers Union; the Teamsters' reign of terror in the Tennessee organizing campaign; the UAW's violence, obstruction, and riots at Kohler and Perfect Circle; the abusive dictatorships of the Bakery Workers, the Operating Engineers, and the Teamsters; the manipulations of the mighty through paper locals and packed conventions; the beating of a member who wanted to put in his two cents at union meetings; the shameful crawling of another union member who had mistakenly believed that Raymond Cohen was stealing from Local 107's treasury; William Young's dogged persistence in continuing despite a savage beating to deliver supplies to Horn & Hardart because he had "faith in that company"; Stan Terry's merry-go-round evasion when asked to describe precisely how he managed to get Teamster approval of his pinball machines; the friendly relations between the Food Fair Stores and Max Block and Benjamin Lapensohn; the unyielding resistance of the Kohler Company to the taking of its property and the invasion of its rights by unions; the Teamsters' efforts to boycott the eastern distilleries through control of the Oregon State Liquor Commission; the UAW's efforts to boycott Kohler products through state and local governments; the infiltration of criminals and of organized crime syndicates into the "labor" movement; faint-hearted law enforcement; the bribery, the shakedowns, the pay-offs, the financial contributions to some government officials and the excoriation of others; the view that a man who chooses to work during a strike is an outlaw, an enemy, and a traitor against whom the arm of the righteous should be raised—all these, to repeat, will seem to the superficial observer to be no more inherently related than the succession of horrors in a nightmare.

It is the function of this and the next two chapters to demonstrate that the foregoing events and all the others disclosed in the McClellan Record are as tightly and organically related as the incidents in the most perfectly conceived dramatic plot.

The Key

Some men who go into business make a great deal of money. When they do, it is because they have managed to figure out what consumers want and how to get it produced cheaper and better than their less successful competitors. Their large incomes are the result of the voluntary purchases of the consumers. When they no longer serve the consumers as well as or better than their competitors do, they lose money, their fortunes diminish, and, unless they repair their mistakes, they find themselves impoverished and out of business. For no businessman can compel a consumer to purchase his product; and when a consumer prefers another, whether because of quality or price, he is free to shift his patronage and will usually do so.

Some men who go into politics achieve success in *their* line. The talents and efforts requisite to political success are vastly different from those requisite to success in business. Yet, there is one surpassingly important feature common to both business and politics. Although men in politics have a larger proportion of "captive voters"—as a consequence of our patronage traditions—than businessmen have captive customers, the success of the political figure, like that of the businessman, depends ultimately on his ability to attract more votes from an uncoerced citizenry than his competitors.

The businessman acquires economic power—command over material resources—strictly in proportion to his ability to serve consumers. The politician acquires political power—command over men and, through the taxing power, over resources, too—strictly in proportion to his ability to convince the voters that he will best serve their interests. Neither the businessman nor the politician may force the consumer or the voter to accept what he is offering.

The disclosures of the McClellan Record—"the rascality, the thievery, the very scum of union behavior," the violence, the monopolistic coercion, and all the rest—are the surface expression of a deep lust on the part of men who have achieved position in trade unions for more power, money, or both than their positions as union officials can legitimately bring. They seek, and some have already attained, economic power greater than that of any businessman. They seek also, and this many union officials have attained, a power over men of a kind and to a degree not available to any politician in a free representative government. While seeking such power, however, the union leaders are not willing to operate within the framework of peaceable and voluntary action which controls in the case of businessmen and politicians.

Acting on behalf of workers who seek representation when they have grievances against their employers is a job from which a decent human being can take a great deal of satisfaction. But it is not one from which a great deal of either power or money can be derived, legitimately. The job of representing workers is modest, though honorable in the highest degree, basically because most workers do not, in the long run, either want or need outside representation.

The production function of the businessman and the govern-ernmental function of the politician are here to stay—they are permanent categories of human action. But representing work-ers in disputes with their employers is a fluctuating and frictional operation. Highly valuable as it is when needed, it is a temporary function for the most part, and its work is done as soon as the backward employer is made to see that he is only hurting him-self when he treats his employees as less than human beings.

The point is that no person in the world has a greater interest in a happy, well-paid working staff than the employer of that staff. The tremendous development and unceasing interest of business managements in the arts and sciences of personnel rela-tions demonstrate this point. Some employers beyond much question will not of their own motion ever give due attention to employee relations problems. They are the ones who will have to deal with unions continuously over long periods, even if unions are completely voluntary associations which the em-ployees can shed when and as they wish, without fear of physi-cal force or economic reprisal. But in a competitive economy, such employers will most probably constitute only a small number. The larger number of employers who survive in com-petition will be able and farseeing men. They will be as at-tentive to employee relations problems as they are to other aspects of their business. Probably more so, since employee re-lations are among the basic and most important features of any business.

When all is said and done, when the marvels of technology, the pyrotechnics of salesmanship and advertising, and the im-posing charts of management organization are duly saluted—the immutable fact remains that a business firm is no more and no less than the human beings of which it is composed. The tech-nologists are men, too, as are the salesmen, the advertising copy writers, and the people who draw up the organization charts. Moreover, nothing they do has any meaning until it is trans-lated into production for the consumers by the working staff.

Due regard for the working staff is therefore a built-in re-quirement which cannot be mishandled in any business without the severest consequences. It takes its place of primacy among those other basic concerns of any business management: the stockholders and the customers. These three—the customers, the employees, and the owners—are the body and soul of business.

Considering the interests of employees when basic business decisions must be made is thus inherent in the management function. The heads of the giant organizations which call themselves trade unions would have us believe that the interests of employees will always be neglected unless they, the trade-union leaders, are in control. That contention is simply silly, when it is not a deliberate misrepresentation. In the first place, no trade-union leader knows as much about the business and the problems of *all* the personnel as the management does. More often than not the union leader represents only a fraction, sometimes but a small fraction, of the total personnel. At best he seeks advantage for that fraction at the expense of the rest; at worst, he is not even interested in that fraction, for itself, but only in the dues and the power he derives from it. In all instances, the leadership of the big trade unions is engaged in a struggle to suppress and exploit the legitimate interests of the two other major components of any business—the consuming public and the owners.

In the second and far more important place, no management, in this country, whether or not it deals with a union, is in a position to exploit employees, even if it should be stupid enough to wish to do so. An employer who fails to pay fair market wages and to provide working conditions as favorable as those prevailing generally will find himself before too long either with no employees at all or with decidedly inferior ones. People have long taken it for granted that unions are entitled to the credit for the improvements we have known in the real wages of *all* workers. But this careless assumption can no longer be accepted. Careful thinking and extensive researches by the most competent economists in the nation have produced a contrary conclusion: that the big unions we know today are in fact the most viciously self-centered pressure groups in the country.

Professor Edward H. Chamberlin of Harvard has made the basic point. He has noted, for one thing, that the unions are not, as they so continuously proclaim, the defenders of the public at all. Emil Mazey attempted to justify his vilification of anyone in the community who did not actively assist the UAW's violent conduct by preaching that the UAW was the universal savior. "It helps the butcher and the baker and candlestick maker and it helps everybody." (9009) But Professor Chamberlin exposes this fakery. As a general rule, he begins with, "trade-union members today fall within the middle-income rather than the low-income sector of our society." [1] When unions do raise the real wages of their own members above the level they would reach without unions, he continues, the unions do so at the expense of those less well able to defend themselves against the great power that the unions have amassed:

> Indeed there can be no doubt that one effect of trade union policy, with respect both to wages and to non-wage benefits, working rules, etc., which raise costs and thus prices, is to diminish still further the real income of the really low-income groups, including not only low-income wage receivers, but also such other elements of society as "self-employed" and small businessmen, students, old people and other unemployables, insurance beneficiaries, pensioners, etc., etc.[2]

The unions do nothing for anyone but their own members; those members are but a small minority, less than one-fourth, of the working force; and as we shall soon see, there is reason to doubt that they do something beneficial even for *all* their members. For the present, however, let us note carefully Chamberlin's basic point—namely, that the person interested in the downtrodden should not expend his sympathy on the unions:

> Those who are *really* concerned with the lot of the under-privileged in our economy will hardly be impressed by the

[1] "The Economic Analysis of Labor Union Power," in *Labor Unions and Public Policy* (Washington, D.C.: American Enterprise Association, 1958), p. 4.
[2] *Ibid.*, pp. 4–5.

claims of the trade union sector. Today's underprivileged
are to be found elsewhere.[3]

When it comes to the question of the effect of union action
on the real wages of *all* workers, the unanimous answer is that
unions have not altered the pattern of income distribution which
prevailed in this country before there were any unions to speak
of. Professor Arthur Ross of California has said that "the spread
of collective bargaining in recent years has not created any
tendency for labor's share of the national income to increase."[4]
Professor Milton Friedman of the University of Chicago agrees,
and goes on to the more important point. He says that the effect
of the most monopolistic and violent trade-union conduct has
only been to exploit the defenseless members of society by re-
distributing income from the weaker to the stronger: "roughly
. . . we might assess the order of magnitude of unions' effect on
the structure of wages by saying that perhaps 10 per cent of the
labor force has had its wages raised by some 15 per cent, im-
plying that the remainder of the labor force had its wage rates
reduced by some 1 to 4 per cent."[5] In a brilliant article summing up all the researches and conclusions of economists in
recent years on this issue, Professor Philip D. Bradley of the
University of Virginia stated flatly these two propositions:

1. Unions have not raised the general level of real wages
   in the United States.
2. Unions have not increased labor's share in the national
   income.[6]

The recent researches of these economists are of the greatest
possible significance. They confirm the existence of facts which
should have long been evident to all. The best wages and work-

[3] *Ibid.*, p. 5. One of the first and still the best short account of the true
role of trade unions in America is Henry Hazlitt's *Economics in One Lesson*
(New York: Harper & Bros., 1946), pp. 143–58.
[4] "Collective Bargaining and Common Sense," 2 *Labor Law Journal* 435
(1951).
[5] In David McCord Wright (ed.), *The Impact of the Union* (New York:
Harcourt, Brace & Co., Inc., 1951), p. 216.
[6] "Involuntary Participation in Unionism," in *Labor Unions and Public
Policy* (Washington, D.C.: American Enterprise Association, 1958), pp. 60–61.

ing conditions in the country are by no means confined to organized firms, and never have been. Wages have risen steadily
in all industries in this country; very frequently they have risen
faster and farther in nonunionized firms than they have in the
organized ones. The difference, as Bradley points out, is that
a great deal more hoopla accompanies wage rises negotiated by
unions than those steadily and quietly granted by nonunion
firms:

> Under a system of individual bargaining, rates of pay are not
> frozen for any stated period [as they are in collective bargain-
> ing agreements] and therefore may be adjusted momentarily
> to even small changes in supply and demand conditions.
> Small adjustments, even though repeatedly made and
> adding up ultimately to the large change which might be
> made under collective bargaining, attract less attention than
> large adjustments. There is, moreover, no one whose liveli-
> hood depends upon promptly publicizing and claiming credit
> for them.[7]

When unions raise real wages over what they would be in the
absence of union action, the result is always—without exception
—at the expense of the general public, of Professor Chamberlin's "underprivileged," and of some of the members of the ex-
ploiting union itself. John Lewis, Walter Reuther, and James
Hoffa have all probably managed to secure higher wages
than would otherwise have prevailed in the industries in
which they have found it necessary to rule continuously with
an iron hand of violence and monopolistic coercion. But such
wage structures produce prices higher than they would otherwise be; the artificially increased prices put the product out of
reach of some consumers; production must therefore be de-
creased; with the result that fewer workers are employed than
would otherwise be the case. In each such industry, unemployment is a constant problem. In the bituminous coal industry, for example, there are 200,000 fewer miners employed, according to most estimates, than there would be but for the
violent and extortionate "collective bargaining" which has gone
on there for many years. Many newspapers have been forced to

[7] *Ibid.,* p. 56.

go out of business, most of them giving labor costs as the primary reason. In January, 1959, hundreds of thousands of auto workers were not employed or not fully employed.

Professor Bradley illustrates the process by reference to the International Photo Engravers' Union. By rigid control of access to its field of employment, that union has been successful in securing monopoly wages. Its minimum period of apprenticeship is six years, "a longer period," Bradley notes, "than is needed for the professional training of a doctor, lawyer, or atomic scientist." [8] During the worst of the depression of the thirties, the union's restrictive policies enabled it to push up wages. But the result was that most of its members were either fully or partly unemployed. Bradley's statistical research established that "in the worst years of the period only 16 per cent of the membership could find full time employment, 46 per cent found part time employment while the remaining 38 per cent was unemployed." [9]

The key to the McClellan Record lies in these hidden relationships. Pure and legitimate trade-union representation of workers is not normally and naturally a source of either substantial material wealth or power over men. It is a natural source of neither kind of power, political or economic, because the welfare and well-being of employees is something with which the deepest self-interest of employers requires them to be concerned. As regards those employers who do not immediately perceive where their self-interest lies, the freedom of workers to cast their lot with the more enlightened employers, or to go into business for themselves, is a good teacher; it forces the backward employers to emulate their betters. Trade unions have a temporary function to perform in the teaching of that lesson. They have a more permanent function to perform only in respect of those employers who never learn. And in a competitive economy, the latter will be at a minimum, for they are not likely to be stupid in regard to only their employee relations. They are likely to be stupid generally, and if that is true they will not be in business long. Thus trade unions are a source of big power and big money only when they are socially abusive. If they are given

[8] *Ibid.,* p. 75.
[9] *Ibid.,* p. 76.

the privilege to be socially abusive, they will present their society with the appalling and disgraceful series of events collected in the McClellan Record.

Compulsion

Trade unions can secure for a part of their members wages and working conditions better and higher than those prevailing on the free market *only if they destroy the free market*. That much is perfectly self evident. They must in the first place compel all employees to join the union; they must in the second place compel all the employees to participate in their strikes, picketing, and boycotts; and they must in the third place, after their monopolistic conduct has created unemployment by pushing wages above the free-market level, use violence and coercion to keep the unemployed from bidding for jobs at lower rates than the unions have fixed.

Compulsion is the essence of every stage of this process, as it is the key and the explanation of the McClellan Record. Stranger-picketing, secondary boycotts, and compulsory-unionism contracts—the variety of trade-union tactics set forth in Chapter 2 of this book—are designed to carry out the first stage of the compulsion process, the compelling of all workers in an industry to join the union, whether or not they wish to do so, in order that the union may supplant the free market with its rigid control. Donald Skaff's experience with the Teamsters' stranger-picketing and violence is thus to be understood. So too are the Teamsters' successive reigns of terror and campaigns of stranger-picketing all over the country to be understood—as the basis of establishing a monopoly control, through the destruction of free markets, so that monopoly wages may be extorted.

The violence and the coercion are called for because of a very simple and earthy reason—not all employees wish to join unions. If they did, there would be no problem, for the law protects their right to join unions and the unions' right to represent them in collective bargaining. The picketing, the boycotts, the compulsory-unionism agreements, and the violence are all—beyond the possibility of any doubt—an expression of the determination of union leaders to shove their unions down the throats of unwilling employees.

The UAW's Kohler strike is in this sense a museum-piece, or perhaps it might better be called a textbook case, since it illustrates so many points. For one thing, evidence in the Record which has not yet been considered here indicates that the Kohler strike was designed in part to perform the same function as the Sheet Metal Workers' boycott of the Burt Manufacturing Company. Some Kohler competitors in the plumbing equipment industry had already been organized by the UAW, with the inevitable result that they were saddled with inflated wage costs, the usual UAW restrictive practices, and other interferences; they were therefore made uncomfortable by Kohler's freer competition (9018; but see also 9529 ff.). William Vinson, the man who broke Willard Van Ouwerkerk's ribs and punctured one of his lungs, was actually employed by a Kohler competitor, and he explained to the Committee that he had participated in the Kohler strike, among other reasons, in order to help eliminate the "sweatshop" conditions there (8874). He did not mention that hundreds of the Kohler employees were highly satisfied with their jobs at Kohler; that Kohler has always had a waiting list of job applicants; and that he and other UAW people had to engage in the most outrageous violence in order to keep people from flocking in for jobs at the Kohler "sweatshop." These people may have been outlaws, traitors, and enemies—from the UAW point of view. But, as we have seen in Chapter 6, from a more disinterested point of view they would appear to be normal, intelligent persons, distinctive only in that they did not choose to have their decisions made for them by the UAW.

The Kohler case illustrates, too, the fundamental reason for the frequent occurrence of violence in disputes over wages and hours. Violence in labor disputes is always a sign that the strikers and their leaders have been arrogant or stupid or both—that they have called a strike when the conditions necessary for a successful strike do not exist. Calling a strike is a sound move when an employer arbitrarily refuses to meet the economically justified demands of his employees. Two circumstances must exist: first, the employer must be insisting upon substandard wages and working conditions; second, his employees themselves must be definitely dissatisfied with those wages and working conditions. When these circumstances obtain, a simple work stoppage—unaccompanied by picketing, violence, or threats of violence—will make the employer see the light. But when these two conditions do not exist, a strike cannot be successful unless the union uses the violence or the monopolistic methods which we have observed the UAW using in the Kohler strike. And even then, as the Kohler strike illustrates, the strikers and their union may fail to achieve their ends, despite the universal havoc they have wreaked by their antisocial conduct.[10]

For if the employer is not insisting upon substandard conditions, some of his employees will not be in sympathy with the strike; and other workers, previously employed at less attractive terms, or unemployed, will seek the jobs vacated by the strikers. Both phenomena, it will be remembered, occurred during the Kohler strike, once the UAW's blockade was lifted pursuant to the court injunction. Moreover, when nonstrikers and striker-replacements start working, the strikers themselves will reconsider their decision to participate in the strike and will, unless forcibly restrained, go back to their jobs—again a phenomenon of the Kohler strike, where 700 of the strikers went back to their jobs (8380). The mass picketing, the personal assaults, all the violence and vandalism of the Kohler strike were designed to intimidate, coerce, and restrain—not only the nonstrikers and the striker-replacements—but the strikers as well.

Each and every time that a union establishes a picket line during a wage dispute in an attempt to obstruct access to employment premises, or uses other coercive, intimidatory, and violent means, the observer may be sure that the leaders of that union have made one or another kind of error in judgment growing out of their overweening lust for power. They have misjudged conditions on the labor market or the temper of their own members or both.

[10] Cf. Hazlitt, *Economics in One Lesson*, pp. 145–47; see also S. Petro, *The Labor Policy of the Free Society* (New York: The Ronald Press Co., 1957), pp. 114–15.

The businessman who thinks that the price of his product is too low attempts to correct the situation by the peaceful, civilized method of simply raising the price. If the product does not move at the new price, he has to reduce it. Using violence against his purchasers, to force them to pay the higher price, is simply unthinkable.

The union leader is not satisfied to proceed in this manner; he is determined to force his arrogant and misguided programs upon all workers, all employers, and ultimately on the consuming public which pays all the bills. Only thus can he gain the power over society which he so deeply craves, but which cannot be gained through peaceful, normal, and sensible representation of those employees who want and ask for union membership.

The quest of union leaders for unlimited and illegitimate power is endless. The Kohler Company insists today that the UAW does not represent anywhere near a majority of the presently employed Kohler workers, and it therefore will not bargain with the UAW without proof, in a secret-ballot election, that the UAW does in fact represent a majority. In such an election, under present law, only persons currently employed at Kohler will be able to vote; for the law declares that strikers who have been permanently replaced are not eligible to vote upon questions of representation in bargaining units in which they are no longer employed.

It ought to be clear to all that this law is perfectly sound. Replaced strikers, men who have voluntarily left their jobs and whose jobs have been permanently filled by others, have no business at all telling those others who should represent them. People not employed at Kohler have no more right to tell Kohler employees which union they should have, if any, than residents of Chicago have a right to tell residents of New York City who their mayor should be. In the queer and distorted ethical system of the UAW officials, however, it is "unjust" to preclude nonemployees of Kohler from choosing a representative for the employees. Emil Mazey, for example, using the usual misleading language and symbolism of the "movement," had the following to say about the law.

The provision of Taft-Hartley law is where a strike-breaker replaces a striker, he can vote, but the striker can't vote, and I say that is unjust. (9005)

Plainly uninformed on the full truth of the situation, Senator Mundt agreed that "if what you say is a statement of fact, it sounds unjust to me, if you say a strikebreaker can vote and a striker can't vote." (9005) What Senator Mundt did not know —and what of course Mazey failed to explain—is that strikers may not vote only when they have been permanently replaced— only, that is, when they have no more interest in the bargaining unit in question than Michigan residents would have in the election of the Senator from South Dakota. If he were fully apprised of these facts, there could be no doubt of Senator Mundt's reaction. He would have thought Mazey's position on this point as specious and deceptive as he so plainly thought Mazey's other concepts of ethics, law, and morality were (9000 ff.).

The Sheet Metal Workers' destructive boycott against the Burt Manufacturing Company was similarly designed to demolish the representation rights of the Burt employees. Those employees had voluntarily chosen representation by the United Steel Workers of America, not the Sheet Metal Workers. Therefore their jobs had to be destroyed.

How can anyone credit the contention—so unceasingly proclaimed—that trade unions serve *all* the people? How can one take seriously the constant refrain of the trade-union leaders that they are selfless servants of the general interest, with no special interest of their own to serve? The selfless public service of the trade unions and their officials is a myth, and more than that, a deliberate fraud. They are engaged in a blunt pursuit of power and will trample upon anyone who stands in their way, not only unorganized workers but members of other unions, and affiliated unions at that. Jurisdictional disputes and strikes, some of them as bloody and violent as the Perfect Circle strike, have been a constant feature of the "movement," and there is no indication of any end to these battles between unions for power and control of men and jobs. Even the widely publicized "no-raiding" pact of the AFL-CIO, which must in any accurate analysis be viewed as a worker-exploiting cartel arrangement, has not eliminated jurisdictional disputes. The "pact" is an agreement, and as such, within the precepts of common morality, ought to be honored. But an old saying holds that "there is no honor among thieves." The saying needs an amendment, the addition of "or among union leaders," when it comes to a question of controlling large numbers of men or jobs.

The lust for power, served through the virtual privilege to engage in violence and monopolistic coercion of the picketing and boycotting variety, lies at the bottom of all the McClellan Committee disclosures. That lust, served by those instruments, establishes a far-flung hegemony over workers and industries. Reinforced by the further special privilege of imposing upon employers "agreements" under which union membership is made a condition of employment, it ties together in a completely coherent and unified pattern every single improper and corrupt practice found in the Record.

Corruption Within Unions

Once union leaders and their apologists have managed to deceive the public and the policy makers into believing that (1) unions serve best the interests of workingmen and the general public, and (2) that the obvious virtue of the unions merits the special favoritism of law and public policy, all the rest follows. Special privileges are accorded them, formally in laws which grant them the power to do things allowed to no one else in society, informally through winking at their violence, and illegetimately by interpreting away laws plainly designed to reduce the power of unions to wreak havoc upon the economy. There is available in print a demonstration, which no one has been able to refute, that the National Labor Relations Board has construed into an innocuous toothlessness all the Taft-Hartley provisions which were designed to curb the very violence and monopolistic picketing and boycotts which fill the McClellan

Record.[11] It is entirely possible that no McClellan investigation would have been needed had the NLRB enforced the Taft-Hartley Act rather than repealing it. But that is another matter, and the situation is what it is.

As we have seen in Chapter 7, the fact that unions retain the power to compel and coerce draws to unions men who excel in compulsion and coercion. At first they are called in to do particular jobs calling for their specialties. Once they see that their specialties are an acceptable way of life in the "movement," they feel that they would be fools to stay out of it. Viewed in this realistic light, the theory of the "legitimate labor leaders" that they can keep the thugs from getting "on the inside of the organization" (3702) seems incredibly naive, and the revelations of corruption within unions and among high union officials which so absolutely stunned Mr. George Meany—all those things would seem to follow as a matter of course. For the thugs and racketeers have no interest at all in the workers they are supposed to represent; instead they actually exploit the members in a fantastic variety of ways and on a scale hitherto unknown in any free society. Union treasuries are robbed, and union members who object are silenced in one or another way. Businessmen are bullied and terrorized; the shakedown, in all its devious varieties, the sweetheart contracts, and the oily confidence-man methods of inducing businessmen to guard against incurring the ill-will of any person "who stands well in labor circles" (11138)—these become the American way of life. There is a steady two-way procession in the "movement": the good and decent men, who would be satisfied with the modest power and income to be derived from honest representation of the grievances of workingmen, are on the way out; while the thugs, the racketeers, and the power hungry, who have no scruples against the use of violence and other coercive and corrupt practices, the men who are out after big power and big money—these men are marching in, and if they are already in, they make their positions

[11] S. Petro, *How the NLRB Repealed Taft-Hartley: A Study of Congressional Intent and NLRB Interpretation* (Washington, D.C.: Labor Policy Association, Inc., 1958).

stronger by the various maneuvers which we have called, in Chapter 6, the "manipulations of the mighty."

Society and the Power-Lust

Society knows no way of keeping men from lusting after great power, and it knows no way of keeping men who have acquired unlimited power from abusing it. The lust for great power is born in some men, and the most profound students of genetics have not the slightest idea of the mechanism involved, beyond certain question-begging generalities which label the unknown as "genes" and "chromosomes." But even if a great deal were known about the spiritual and biological processes involved, it would be a tragic error to tamper with them, in an effort to eradicate the lust for great power. That lust, directed away from abusive modes of conduct and toward creative action, probably accounts for some of the greatest achievements of mankind. Walter Reuther modestly told the McClellan Committee that he could have made a "whole lot more money in private industry" than he has made in the "movement" (10043). With his drive and his talents, he might not have been just bragging. Maybe he was right. But if he was, then society and Reuther have both been losers in tolerating a legal and social framework in which so much of his effort has been directed toward interference with rather than participation in private industry.

It is no more advisable to accept great power with the hope that it will fall into the "right hands" than it is to attempt to eradicate the power drive. Unlimited power is bad in itself. It will corrupt the best of men. Moreover, it involves a special privilege to one at the expense of the rights of all others. One man's privilege to coerce means the deprivation of another man's right to be free of coercion. The Teamsters' power to throttle the New York metropolitan area, which Chief Counsel Kennedy seemed to consider dangerous only if it fell into the "wrong hands" (3597), is intolerable in any hands. More than that, such power is an irresistible lure to the power hungry. If it is left dangling out there, the avid power-seekers will snatch it sooner or later. There is a fateful symbolism in the fact that the New York Joint Council of Teamsters is today, despite the fact that close to one-half of the McClellan Record is directed to the misconduct of the Teamsters and Hoffa, in the hands of Hoffa men. Martin Lacey and "Honest Tom" Hickey, both opponents of Hoffa, are both out.[12]

If society can neither eliminate the power drive nor have a reasonable hope that power will fall into the "right hands," there is only one thing left to do. It must take such steps as are necessary to prevent the exercise of any power that is socially dangerous. This will direct the power drive of able and useful men into socially desirable channels, and will put the men who have nothing to offer but a power-lust in a position where they can do no harm.

The socially dangerous powers now available to unions and their officials are violence and economic, monopolistic coercion. These must be extirpated. But before considering the possible methods of extirpation it is best to examine the evils more closely, so that the remedies may be tailored to them as precisely as possible.

[12] *The New York Times*, December 14, 1958, p. 1, col. 4.

Chapter 9

PLANNED VIOLENCE

We cannot have peaceful communities invaded by lawless mobs led by imported hoodlums, law enforcement nullified, and the citizens subjected to a lawless reign of terror.

—Lyman C. Conger (9506)

* * *

The purpose of this chapter is to analyze the methods and the causes of violence in labor relations, and to inquire into the legal deficiencies which account for the existence of violence in labor relations to a degree overwhelmingly greater than that which prevails in any other area of society. The hard fact presented by the McClellan Record is that violence is a way of life in labor relations. Of all the private associations known to our society, only trade unions use violence frequently and on a large scale. Why?

Strategy and Tactics

"Mr. Reuther," Senator Curtis said at one point in the Kohler hearings, "the UAW record is written day to day by the people that carry it out. Their record is not changed by what somebody comes before a senatorial committee and presents as his individual views." (10139) These remarks were provoked by the UAW president's protestations of a strong personal distaste for violence, his disclaimer of responsibility for what went on at Kohler, and his repudiation of Emil Mazey's attack upon Judge Schlichting.

The view that labor violence is a kind of spontaneous outburst resulting from personal animosities or, as the Supreme Court once said, from "animal exuberance," will not stand examination. Violence is encountered in three areas of union activity: in organizing, in collective bargaining, and in the internal affairs of unions. In all three it is carefully and deliberately planned, with malice aforethought; it is cold and impersonal in the planning and more often than not in the execution as well.

Direct evidence of this cold deliberation while sometimes available is not really needed; the external facts speak for themselves. Blowing up trucks, freezing internal combustion engines, and setting fire to buildings and garages during organizing campaigns are not activities which occur on the spur of the moment. The materials with which these acts are accomplished —the dynamite, the shellac, the sugar and syrup, the phosphorous crystals—need to be acquired in advance, and bought and paid for. They may be used by simple union members upon rare occasions; but not in a single instance did such an occasion appear in the Record. The bombings, the arson, and the beatings, too, were always by thugs with long criminal records who were on the union payroll as business agents, stewards, or in some other such capacity. Chief Counsel Kennedy remarked, for example, that practically everybody on Raymond Cohen's payroll in Philadelphia Teamsters Local 107 had had "major difficulties with the law." (10435) It has already been observed herein that a full book would be needed in order to give an adequate account of the criminal careers of the relatively few union agents investigated by the Committee.

The Committee was not always able to pin down the actual purchases of bombing and arson materials with union funds. But upon occasion it had some luck. The books of Teamsters Local 821 in Knoxville, Tennessee, were particularly revealing. They showed extensive purchases of sugar and syrup. Mrs. Lola Freels, the conscientious bookkeeper of Local 821 confirmed the Committee's suspicion that those commodities had not been used for tea parties (1955-1956). They were part of the propaganda and persuasion equipment which the Teamsters used in their organizing in Tennessee—in a campaign which was as destructive and violent as it was coldly and deliberately planned.

The same is true of the large-scale violence so frequently associated with "collective-bargaining" strikes. The Record contains full documentation of only two instances of that kind of violence, that which occurred in connection with the Kohler and Perfect Circle strikes. But Representative Clare Hoffman, whose House Committee did pioneering work in investigating strike violence, and whose help was acknowledged by Chief Counsel Kennedy (9385), showed that the UAW had been developing the techniques of the Kohler and Perfect Circle violence ever since it was formed in the thirties (9365–9400). Moreover, there is no reason to doubt that the UAW's Kohler program is fairly representative of the strategy and tactics of the numerous violent strikes by other unions, such as the Electrical Workers, the Mine Workers, and the Packinghouse Workers—although these were not investigated by the Committee.

We have already covered the gross facts of the Kohler violence, but it will be well at this point to attend more carefully to the timing and sequence of the events, and the relationship of the parent UAW to what went on. Consider the fact that within an hour of the strike-call something like 2,000 persons assembled in front of the plant (9492). That this instant massing could have been spontaneous seems unbelievable, and the incredibility grows when one learns that the massing of pickets was turned on and off like a faucet at various points in the bargaining and in accordance with the progress of certain legal proceedings (9496–97). The common—and arrogant— union practices of issuing passes and of *permitting* management and office personnel to get through are also highly revealing (8428–32, 9492). They suggest a carefully planned strategy, the objective of which is to keep out only the workers over whom the union wishes to exert control. A spontaneous group boiling with passion is not likely to be so selective.

The International UAW protested, as we have seen, that the local people were in full control, but a brief review of the evidence will demonstrate the falseness of that contention. Two nonstrikers who had worked at Kohler for many years recognized none of the activists in the ranks of the massed pickets.

They thought there were at least 100 outsiders (8401). UAW vice-president Mazey and a dozen other international representatives were identified on the picket line or in positions of authority elsewhere (8491, 8540, 9194). The evidence shows clearly that outsiders, nonresidents of Wisconsin, came to Kohler at Mazey's order or request (8956, 8986, 10370). Strike bulletins issued by union headquarters regularly identified the people who returned to work, and were followed closely by reprisals against those people (9501). Then there was the shallowy disguised incitement by International agent Robert Burkhart, with which we have dealt fully in Chapter 4, followed by further incidents of vandalism. The NLRB trial examiner specifically found union responsibility for the home demonstrations (10230). Finally, as we have also seen, the outsiders were directly involved not only by way of inciting violent conduct; they were actually guilty themselves of brutal individual assaults.

It is impossible to credit Reuther's disavowal of UAW responsibility in the face of these facts. Moreover, it is impossible to view these facts without seeing behind them careful and deliberate planning. None of the International representatives in charge of the violent tactics, none even of those who were guilty of violent assaults, were either punished or dismissed by the UAW, although its top officers admittedly knew of them. Mazey, when confronted with the fact that the UAW had defended William Vinson in the action arising out of the assault on Willard Van Ouwerkerk, and that he had continued Vinson's salary, indeed asserted that he "would do it again under the same circumstances." (9060) Chief Counsel Kennedy interposed with "if that is not condoning that kind of operation—" only to be interrupted by Mazey's fantastic "it isn't condoning at all, and I did not like what he did, and I raised the dickens with him about it." (9060) But Mazey did not punish Vinson, or fire him, or even repudiate him publicly. Indeed, Donald Rand was promoted by the UAW after his role in the Kohler strike (10117). Such action by the UAW may perhaps be appreciated more fully by those who know that under the common law a principal is himself considered guilty who keeps in his employment an agent who has committed an unlawful act, if the principal knows of it, and certainly if it has been committed in the normal course of the agent's employment.

The Record reveals beyond any doubt that the violence which occurs in labor disputes is carefully planned and executed. More than that, it reveals such care in the planning and execution as to make the job of dealing with it one of the most difficult ones that society and the law have ever faced.

The Mob and the Police

Sorting out the varieties of violent tactics and methods is the necessary first step. The obstructive type illustrated by the massed picket lines and the clay-boat riot at Kohler falls into one category. The personal assaults and the vandalism at Kohler and the bombing, the arson, the tire-slashing, and other such conduct associated with the Teamsters' organizing all fall into a second category. The individual assaults by thugs upon union members in rebellion against the exploitation and thievery of union officials also fit into this second category.

The police have one kind of problem in dealing with mob action, and for present purposes the mass picketing and the riot of the clay-boat incident may both be regarded as presenting but two varieties of that one problem. It is a problem, basically, of sheer numbers. Both Kohler police chief Capelle and Sheboygan County sheriff Mosch agreed that they and their deputies were simply not numerous enough to "open up" the picket line. It may come as a shock to some that there are still those who would challenge the very basis of civilization by refusing to obey the lawful orders of duly constituted authorities. Yet that is exactly what the UAW, its agents, and its members did during the Kohler strike. All the police authorities testified to that effect—the Kohler Village chief of police, the Sheboygan sheriff, his undersheriff, the Sheboygan mayor, and the Sheboygan chief of police.

Undersheriff Lawrence Schmitz showed at the hearings a complete understanding of what his duty was. He knew it was his job to prevent violent obstruction of the right of nonstrikers to access to the plant. But his testimony makes it clear that he was helpless to perform his duty. He frequently conducted non-strikers to the picket line and commanded the pickets to permit passage, but was never in a single instance obeyed. "We gave orders," he testified, "both myself and the chief of police, to open the line; but they were not obeyed." (8469) The Chairman asked whether he had been given orders "to use bayonets to open them up"; to which Schmitz responded: "My orders were not to use any violence." (8469)

The uniform opinion of the authorities was that they would have needed at least 500 men to overpower the defiant pickets (8536). Schmitz thought that "if you were going to open that line, it would have required several hundred men. And, after you had the line open, in my estimation, it would have taken several hundred more men to keep it open." (8470)

Kohler Village police chief Waldemar Capelle's most conscientious efforts both to prepare his police force for the kind of thing that happened and to contend with it once it did happen proved similarly unavailing (8508). Chief Counsel Kennedy seemed to suspect a deep dark plot between Capelle and the Kohler Company. He virtually accused the police chief of being a tool of the Company, questioning Capelle's decision to increase the police force shortly after the UAW became bargaining representative, and even the training he gave the new men in the use of tear-gas guns and machine guns (8501-13). The Chairman and Senators Goldwater, Mundt, and Ervin, however, set the record straight by questions which elicited from Capelle the information that it is sound and universal practice to train police personnel in the use of all available weapons, including tear gas guns (8513); that the decision to increase the police force when the UAW got in was the only sensible thing to do in view of the UAW's history of violent strikes, and that if the actual events proved anything they proved only that Capelle had not added a sufficient number of new men (8514). Indignant at the implications of the Chief Counsel's line of questioning, Senator Mundt observed:

> I don't know what the purpose of all the questioning is, but I can tell you that in South Dakota you wouldn't

stay chief of police fifteen minutes if you didn't train your
men in the use of tear-gas shells, and target practice, and
to be a good marksman, because we want law-enforcement
officers to have a background who can take care of violence when it develops. . . . And so I think you are to be
commended rather than criticized in the training of your
men to handle firearms. That is part of the job of a good
police officer. (8511)

The Chief Counsel's attitude becomes the more peculiar when
one realizes that he was perfectly well aware of the intransigently
obstructionist policies of the top UAW leadership, and had in a
hundred instances in the Record run across evidence that trade-
union unlawfulness was abetted by the failure of police and other
local authorities to do their plain duty. When the Chief Counsel
asked UAW vice-president Mazey whether he believed that the
massed pickets had "a right to protect their jobs by physically
stopping those who want to go to their jobs," Mazey replied: "I
do." (9058) The Chief Counsel was present, too, when Senator Mundt summed up Mazey's position and secured Mazey's
agreement to the restatement: "that mass picketing of the type
that was engaged in at Kohler by the union is in your opinion
legal and proper, and defensible, even though it physically pre-
vents a nonstriker from entering the plant to earn a living for
his family." (9074)

*   *   *

The problem thus begins to emerge in clearer focus. Unions
believe that they have a right during strikes to obstruct access
to the struck premises. They plan deliberately the congrega-
tion of overwhelming numbers and deliberately incite them to
mob action of a clearly unlawful obstructionist kind. Local police are ordinarily unable to secure respect for the law and the
rights of others from such mobs, without using armed force
leading to bloodshed. The alternatives are equally clear. Society must accept the power of unions through mob action to
deprive others of their rights; or it must overpower the mob
with riot guns, tear gas, and bayonets; or it must take such
steps as are necessary to prevent the gathering of resentful
crowds.

Furtive Crime and Reluctant Witnesses

Individual acts of violence and vandalism—personal assaults, tire-slashings, dynamiting, arson, the paint-bomb and acid treatments associated with the Kohler strike—raise different problems. For one thing, unlike the Kohler mass picketing, they pose the problem of detection. Then, too, they pose the additional problems of prosecution by the legal authorities and of conviction in the courts.

As to detection, the McClellan Record tells a sorry tale. Of almost 900 acts of vandalism in Sheboygan County, almost all of them went undetected. Sheboygan chief of police Steen W. Heimke saw a clear pattern running through all the vandalism, and he thought it had a professional finish; but he was never able to apprehend the small professional group whose existence he suspected (9343). The Kohler Company engaged private detectives to do the job which the police were unable to do; but all it got for its efforts were sneering innuendoes from Senator Kennedy and Chief Counsel Kennedy about what they called "spying" (8847-59).

We have seen the same incapacity of the police to detect the guilty parties in numerous instances of violence and vandalism reported in the Record. Donald Skaff reported to the Committee that the Flint police would be willing to act if he produced the parties guilty of the assaults against his employees and his property (6431 ff.). The reign of terror in the Tennessee organizing campaign went largely undetected (7053-65). Donald Strang was told that the state police could not help him because of the direct orders it had received from the "Governor's office" (12577). The Record is full of similar instances of such conduct by the police, but perhaps the most startling instance of all was what happened to Miss Helen Canfield, a Teamster member who ingeniously uncovered evidence in a dynamiting case which the police had never been able to solve. When she presented her evidence she was arrested and charged with "obstructing justice." (1838, 1844)

Miss Canfield seemed to be quite a girl. Other phases of her experience and at least one of her observations are relevant in the present inquiry. Her local had been taken over by a Robert Malloy, whom she described as a dictatorial bully (1843), and she did not like what was going on at all. The men, however, would not stand up for their rights:

> nobody has backbone enough to get up and do anything about it. . . . And men, they call themselves men, how can they sleep at night and call themselves men when they sit back and let a woman get up and do their fighting for them? (1844)

If all employers and employees showed the courage of Miss Canfield, of the Kohler management, and of some Kohler nonstrikers, a part of the present problem would be solved. At least in those instances where the legal authorities were willing to do their share, some results might be secured. But as the Record repeatedly demonstrated, the police frequently found it impossible to secure convictions because witnesses—and very often the victims themselves—would refuse to come forward, would refuse to prosecute or give testimony. David Cordivari, a Philadelphia police detective who took his job seriously, told the Committee that witnesses in cases of labor violence were often reluctant to testify, even if "we can get them as far as a court." (10457)

Law and the Welfare State

If in regard to crime associated with labor disputes the police will not act vigorously to uncover the evidence, if witnesses will not come forward as men should, if the state will not prosecute with determination, and if the courts will not apply the law firmly to the persons involved in labor violence—then, some might think, the situation is hopeless. Or they may think, with Senator Ives, that the situation has nothing to do particularly with labor relations, but relates to the general problem of law enforcement. "I think we have to bear in mind in dealing with this question," Senator Ives said, "that some of these matters cannot be solved by law and cannot be solved by legislation. If you do not have law enforcement, there is nothing you can do by way of law that will solve them." (7459)

Those interested in the survival of their society cannot take the position that the task of keeping crime within narrow limits, especially crime associated with labor disputes, is hopeless. At least they may not rationally take that position until it is shown that all possible and acceptable methods of combating labor crime have been utilized. If, after the resources of law and society have seriously and intelligently been directed to the suppression of crime associated with trade unions, such crime continues in the magnitude indicated by the McClellan Record—then it will be time for us to turn away from the grandeur of civilization and to reflect somberly upon our chances of survival in the jungle. But not until then.

As for Senator Ives's view, there is something to be said for it, but not much. It is true that there is a general problem of law enforcement in this country—that crime prevails generally on a greater scale than it should, that the police protection available to the citizenry is something less than it should be. Full consideration of that problem would go beyond the scope of this book. For it is not essentially a problem associated with the special privileges which trade unions have acquired and which have led to the corruption disclosed in the McClellan Record. It is a problem arising instead out of the welfare-state ideology.

Yet it is intimately associated with the proper concern of this book in at least one sense: the same thinking which is producing the welfare state has also been largely responsible for the special privileges accorded trade unions. Furthermore, the welfare-state ideology has given the state so many diverse jobs to perform that it can no longer properly perform the basic job for which it was designed. That job was to insure domestic tranquillity by protecting honest citizens against thugs and criminals. Proper performance of that basic function requires, obviously, a primary and predominant preoccupation by government with the police force and the administration of justice.

While we expend our substance in granting special privileges and subsidies to the strong pressure groups, encouraging idleness and unproductiveness, we underman our police forces and pay them poorly, so that they have neither the numbers nor the quality of men necessary to do what is, after all, the basic job of civilization: keeping the peace. And even such police as we have are directed in greater numbers to harassing motorists under vexatious traffic rules and regulations than to the prevention of crime and the protection of honest citizens.

While recognizing, then, that Senator Ives had hold of a piece of the truth in observing that the crime disclosed in the McClellan Record is a part of the larger problem of law enforcement created by the welfare-state distortion of the role of government, his view is not on the whole accurate. At least it is not the whole truth if he means to say that there are no independent causes for the prevalence of crime and corruption in trade unions. *It is not the whole truth because it fails to explain why, among all the other private associations of society— the business firms, the bar associations, the medical associations, and the thousands of other private associations in this country— violence, crime, and corruption do not prevail as they do among trade unions.*

The Job of the Law

Violence, crime, and corruption prevail among trade unions to a degree unmatched in any other private association because trade unions have acquired from society and the law special privileges allowed to no other private association. There is every reason to believe that any other private association accorded the same privileges would manifest the same characteristics which the McClellan Record discloses in trade unions.

If, for example, businessmen were allowed to compel the purchases of their customers, to assault them when they showed any intention of removing their patronage, and to block access to competitors—there is very little reason to believe that such conduct would not become common business practice, leading to more and more of the same as the selective process wore on in business in the way that it has in trade unions: with the productive and the ingenious giving ground before the thugs, the bullies, and the master strategists of large-scale organized violence.

Businesses compete in a civilized way partly because the law compels them to do so and partly because the law's compulsion has created a selection process which grinds out the thugs and the lawless and advances the able and the industrious. Among trade unions, precisely the contrary process of selection has been going on, with, as might be expected, precisely the contrary results.

As we shall see in the next chapter, trade unions can compel membership and tie up industries in cartels which enhance the compulsory powers which trade unions alone are permitted to possess. These powers make trade unions more attractive to thugs and racketeers than they would otherwise be, for they insure a privileged and guaranteed source of income to those who would not be able to earn the big money after which they lust, in honest industry. Once they have been attracted into the unions, the rest follows: the hiring of thugs to quell rebellion among the membership, of confidence men to oil the extortion and shakedown machinery, and of wily operators to reinforce their control in the larger political affairs of their unions.

The degree to which crime is associated with trade unions is explained, then, by two facts: (1) the special privileges of trade unions attract the criminal type; (2) the criminal type acts criminally when allowed to do so and does what it can, by way of bribery and other forms of corruption of public officials, to increase its immunities.

This analysis, it should be emphasized, explains much more than the prevalence of crime among trade unions; it also shows why trade unions *particularly* are infected. And it explains still more than that. It shows why law enforcement is uniquely difficult as regards the crimes—the personal assaults, the dynamiting, and the arson—associated characteristically with trade-union affairs of both the internal and the organizing variety.

Trade-union members do not act the manly role which Helen Canfield would have them play because they are cowed by the thugs whom special privilege has attracted to trade unions; they do not rebel against abuse, they do not make good witnesses in court, because the thugs have taught them to expect brutal and even deadly reprisals—and, on the other hand, experience has taught them not to expect much protection from the law. They do not *read* about these things; they see them happen; and they know that society cannot and will not provide them with perpetual police protection.

As to law-enforcement officials, they are to a great degree ineffective for closely related reasons. The thugs attracted to the trade unions by the special privileges they enjoy as union officials have no scruples against bribery and other forms of corruption of the law authorities. The special privileges are therefore accountable for corruptly ineffective law enforcement. Furthermore, they are accountable only a little more indirectly for an important part of the other signal phase of ineffective law enforcement, namely, the sheer incapacity of the police—even when willing—to cope with carefully planned and large-scale violence and vandalism. Deliberately planned, large-scale violence is a feature of labor disputes because of the kind of men who have risen to positions of power in trade unions as a result of the process of selection controlling there, and that process of selection is a result of the special privileges which trade unions alone enjoy.

It is important to understand these things clearly if measures appropriate to the true evil are to be fashioned. It would do little good, for example, to prohibit the employment of ex-convicts by trade unions. On the one hand, ex-convicts must live, too, and there is a possibility of useful and legitimate work for them in trade unions. On the other hand, a good many of the men guilty of the strong-arm tactics disclosed in the Record, for example William Vinson, had had no previous criminal records. The better part of wisdom and humanity is to eschew such simple-minded solutions of what is a much more complicated problem. The true task is to eliminate the conditions which attract bad men to trade unions as a source of easy money *and* as an area in which they may "legitimately" continue their criminal ways. Society should not add to ex-convicts a penalty beyond that already assessed against them in their sentences. To do so would be both unjust and unwise. And it would miss the mark completely.

The remedy for the criminal conduct associated with internal union affairs and organizing drives lies in eradicating the special privileges described in the next chapter—the special privileges which, for lack of a better term, are here called "monopolistic compulsion." Removing those special privileges will not by itself insure aggressive, vigorous, and effective law enforcement. But it will reduce the overwhelming size of the problem with which law-enforcement authorities now must cope in labor matters; moreover, it will cut down the potential of bribery and corruption; and it will, finally, in reducing the attractiveness of unions to crooks, racketeers, and their bully-boy henchmen, serve to diminish the fears which now cause union members to decline to cooperate with the police in detecting crime and in convicting criminals.

* * *

There is, as we shall see, a point at which the remedies for large-scale violence of the Kohler variety converge with those for the types of criminal conduct with which we have thus far been concerned. In both cases the law must be designed to select out for socially minded and moderate union leadership. But there are differences too in the problems posed by large-scale, deliberately planned strike-violence.

An important part of the problem lies in the habit of trade-union officials, as we have observed in Chapters 4 and 5, of promoting the false and antisocial notion that all rights lie with the strikers, that nonstrikers and striker-replacements are outlaws against whom any kind of reprisal is permissible. There is a natural tendency on the part of strikers to resent those who chose to work during a strike. Yet all the evidence suggests that such resentment does not by itself produce the range and quantity of violence and vandalism associated with the Kohler strike. Deliberate planning by the union leadership is needed. The union leaders establish the mass picket lines. They incite the strikers to threats and hard feelings against the nonstrikers. Their agitation and propaganda machinery creates the mobs and whips them up into a fury. They print names and addresses of nonstrikers in their "bulletins" and blatantly induce strikers to engage in menacing home demonstrations. Only after such carefully planned incitements does the mob rule which characterized the Kohler strike prevail.

Union agents engage in all sorts of attempts to rationalize such conduct. They say that mass picketing is necessary in order to display to employers the unity of worker sentiment; yet they admit when pressed that such picketing is really designed to block access of nonstrikers to the struck premises. When confronted with particular instances of harassment and violence, they insist that the strikers are only defending themselves against violence instigated by the employer; yet against a pitifully few unverified instances of violence against strikers, the Record shows hundreds of verified instances of violence against nonstrikers. And no rationalization can possibly explain away the fact that massed picket lines are designed to, and do in fact, prevent nonstrikers from entering the struck premises. No amount of specious evasion can make employers or nonstriking workers responsible for such blocking of access.

The basic rights are clear, and no one—not even union leaders—disputes them. Workers have a right to work or not to work, a right to join in a strike or to refuse to join in it; they have a right to continue working during a strike, and they have an equal right to seek the jobs which strikers have voluntarily vacated. The public and its representatives would not for a moment agree to a law requiring the shutting down of every business establishment merely because some, or even all, of its employees had decided to strike. Everywhere in the United States the law on the point is clear: *obstruction of the right to work or not to work is illegal.*

The fundamental social problem is to translate this common understanding and common sentiment into a binding rule of the game. Union leaders and union members need to learn that the rules of the game, which they abstractly understand and accept, apply to them as well as to all others. They must have brought home to them vividly that their right to strike is not superior to the right of equally free men to choose to work during the strike. All wish to live in a free and well-ordered society. The same man who is anxious to strike or to leave his job would bridle if he were told that he had to remain at work, in spite of his wishes to the contrary. He would consider it intolerable if he had to buy a Ford simply because a majority of his neighbors chose to purchase that automobile.

The man who prefers not to strike has no right to attempt to force others to continue working. But his right to pursue his own inclination in regard to working or not working is as basic and as powerful as his right to purchase or not to purchase any particular commodity, regardless of the buying habits of his friends and neighbors. Unless this is universally understood and accepted we shall continue to suffer the vicious evils associated now with so many strikes. It is a mockery to call a country free in which law-abiding citizens are made to cower under the mob-rule and lynch-law conditions so blatantly evident in the Kohler, the Perfect Circle, and any number of other strikes of recent times.

There are no easy solutions to problems of this kind, because in some ways they require the eradication of passion and prejudice—and fear. Yet a number of promising and workable legal remedies suggest themselves. Much of the savagery incident to mob rule is a consequence simply of the numbers of persons involved. A statute prohibiting during strikes all picketing by more than one or two persons at a time would help a great deal. Under such a statute it would be possible for the police to act swiftly, and it would be easier for courts to issue injunctions immediately upon proof of the assembly of greater numbers than that. It would not be necessary to wait until hard feelings had been engendered and had erupted in violence, sabotage, intimidation, vandalism, and all the other sad consequences of mob action. Once things have been allowed to reach that

point, the harm to the peaceful life of communities is virtually ir-
remediable, as was brought out in the Kohler hearing, where the
whole life of the community was disrupted for years and where,
it is probable, the wounds have not yet healed.

More rigorous application of the common-law rules of responsibility would also help a great deal. No change in the law
is needed here, except in those states where trade unions are
not suable entities. In those states, statutes are needed which
make union treasuries as vulnerable to suit as corporate treasuries already are. In the others it is necessary only for the courts
to apply the law as rigorously to unions as they do to all other
persons and entities whose agents violate the law. There cannot
be the slightest doubt that if the courts were to assess sizable
judgments against union treasuries, the union officials would quit
planning and inciting large-scale violence. Indeed, no effort at
all would be required on their part. They would only need to
cease and desist from their past practices.

The National Labor Relations Board is also in a position to
induce union officials to refrain from violence and coercion.
That Board already has the power to make unions pay for the
violence which occurs in connection with strikes.[1] Although it
has not seen fit to use that power, the time has come for it to
begin. If it does not, the McClellan Committee would be well
advised to make the Board's decisions the next subject of its investigation. It would find, if it looked carefully, much to concern it.

Functional Checks

The foregoing steps, as promising as they are, do not exhaust
the law's potentiality for eradicating strike violence. There will
always be hard feelings in any strike which is not backed by all
or almost all of the present and potential employees of the
struck employer. The objective of well-designed law will be
to do whatever law can do in order to insure that strikes will

[1] See S. Petro, *How the NLRB Can Prevent Union Violence* (Washington,
D.C.: Labor Policy Association, Inc., 1958).

be called only when all or almost all of the workers are united in sentiment. For only then will the basic cause of strike violence and animosity disappear.

Sound union leaders even today will usually wait for such conditions before they suggest or call strikes. The problem becomes one, then, of conceiving the legal structure best designed to produce such leadership. There is, of course, no simple and direct means to that end; it is beyond the power of law alone, however well conceived and enforced, to insure that union members will always elect sound, socially minded, and intelligent leaders—any more than citizens always elect the best political candidates. Still, the law can apply in union affairs the same rules applicable in all other vital areas of society. On the theory that union leadership, like any other leadership—in business, in government, or anywhere else—will be better the more it is required to maintain its position by competitive excellence, the problem for the law becomes one of creating conditions in which union leaders are the agents and servants of employees, not their masters, and in which union leaders have to make serious payment for their mistakes and their arrogant intransigence.

The principle of free employee choice is the key here. The current rule declaring that permanently replaced strikers are not eligible to vote in representation elections must be retained. It exposes union leadership to the same kinds of risks that business leaders face when they abuse their position. Any businessman who persists in charging a price which the public will not pay faces losses of profits and eventual bankruptcy. There is no good reason for shielding union leaders from that risk; on the contrary, the Record discloses all the reasons in the world for exposing them to it.

Chapter 10

PRIVILEGED MONOPOLY

The course of decision in this Court has now created a situation in which, by concerted action, unions may set up a wall around a municipality of millions of inhabitants against importation of any goods . . . notwithstanding the fact that the purpose and inevitable result is the stifling of competition . . . and the creation of a monopoly. . . . The only answer I find in the opinion of the Court is that Congress has so provided. I think it has not provided any such thing. . . .

—Mr. Justice Owen Roberts [1]

* * *

With this decision, the labor movement has come full circle. . . . This Court now sustains the claim of a union to the right to deny participation in the economic world to an employer simply because the union dislikes him. This Court permits to employees the same arbitrary dominance over the economic sphere which they control that labor so long, so bitterly and so rightly asserted should belong to no man.

—Mr. Justice Robert Jackson [2]

* * *

The business managements of this country are comprehensively regulated by laws designed to prevent all monopolistic practices and restraints of trade. Yet trade unions are specially privileged to tie up the country in the very types of monopolies and restraints of trade which the antitrust laws prohibit to busi-

---

[1] Dissenting from the reasoning of the majority in Allen Bradley v. Local No. 3, Int. Brotherhood of Electrical Workers, 325 U.S. 797 (1945).

[2] Dissenting, with Chief Justice Stone and Justices Roberts and Frankfurter, from the decision of a bare majority of the Court in Hunt v. Crumboch, 325 U.S. 821 (1945).

ness. While the antitrust laws were being amended to prohibit even industrial mergers aimed at increasing efficiency, the chief political leaders of the nation were sending laudatory telegrams to trade-union leaders on the occasion of the merger of the American Federation of Labor and the Congress of Industrial Organizations. Under the antitrust laws, any tampering with the price structure by businessmen is held to be unlawful; still, under the labor laws, as they have been construed, trade unions are privileged to establish monopoly control of all workers, to regiment industries, and to impose pricing practices which abuse and exploit consumers.

The McClellan Committee was vastly disturbed when it discovered the monopolistic privileges which trade unions have acquired, especially since it soon became apparent that those privileges lie at the bottom of much of the compulsion and corruption so rampant in trade unions. The origins of the special privileges which trade unions enjoy are so complex that, if they are to be removed, careful attention must be directed to understanding and unraveling their sources. The objective of this chapter is therefore twofold: first to set forth in connected fashion the special privileges of monopolistic compulsion which trade unions uniquely possess, together with the total power position which has resulted; and second, to demonstrate as precisely as possible which branch or agency of government has been responsible for the creation or extension of those special privileges.

The Power

Trade unions have the power and the privilege to compel union membership and to regiment employers by economic measures which are in many instances as irresistible and overpowering as the mass picket line which the UAW established during the Kohler strike. The method utilized by the Journeymen Barbers to force the members of the Barbers Guild to forsake their own union, that is, stranger-picketing, is one which the Teamsters have used in hundreds of cases in recent years to increase their membership. As we have seen, a stranger picket line established at a place of business which depends upon pickups and deliveries for its survival will naturally throttle that business if it induces a stoppage of the pickups and deliveries.

No other method of monopolistic coercion has accounted for as much forced union membership as this one, and none has been as specially privileged. The Waldorf-Astoria barbers did not wish to join the Journeymen Barbers. At first, neither the Waldorf-Astoria management nor the management of the Terminal Barber Shops, Inc., the employer of the barbers, was inclined to pressure them into changing their affiliation. But after the Teamsters Union compelled its members to respect the Journeyman Barbers' picket line by refusing to make pickups and deliveries at the Waldorf (Tr. 82), both managements began to crack. For the Waldorf, the blockade meant disaster, even though it had no dispute at all with any of its own employees or with the Teamsters, or even with the picketing Journeymen Barbers. For the management of Terminal Barber Shops, Inc., loss of its lease at the Waldorf seemed imminent. As Jay S. Bauman, the president of Terminal Barber Shops, described the situation to the Committee, "we were being squeezed, and we in turn turned pressure on [our employees to join the Journeyman Barbers]." (Tr. 62)

A point of the utmost importance must be emphasized here. What the Journeymen Barbers wanted was control over the Waldorf barbers, and it secured that control through the pressure which its picketing exerted on their employer. It did not matter whether the stranger-picketing was called "organizational" or "recognition." The question whether the design was to "organize" the Waldorf barbers or to secure "recognition" from their employer had in this case, as it has in all cases, as much significance as tweedledum and tweedledee.

The two expressions are interchangeable ways of referring to the quest of unions for control over employees through one compulsive and coercive device, stranger-picketing. Whatever it may be called, this picketing has one objective, control over employees; one modus operandi, economic pressure on the employer; and one result, compulsory membership. Many state courts, recognizing this point, have held all stranger-picketing unlawful and coercive, whatever it may be called.[3] Their realism is of small utility, however, because the Supreme Court has ruled that the state courts may not exercise jurisdiction in labor cases involving interstate commerce.[4] The interstate-commerce area, the area which covers most organizational picketing, belongs exclusively to the NLRB, according to the Supreme Court. That holding serves to privilege stranger-picketing. For the NLRB holds stranger "organizational" picketing privileged; moreover, as regards the "recognition" picketing which the NLRB does hold unlawful, the remedy it offers is of small utility, if any.[5]

The Teamsters owe a very substantial part of their vast membership to the skill with which they have exploited the special privileges accorded them by the NLRB and the Supreme Court. They have made a highly polished and effective science of stranger-picketing. When they cannot picket directly against the employer and the employees over whom they wish to exercise control, which usually happens when the employer has no fixed location, they engage in roving-picketing. They follow the trucks to every point at which those trucks stop to make pickups and deliveries. When the truck has stopped, the Teamsters proceed to picket it. Since many such stops are made at warehouses which the Teamsters have already "organized" through one or another form of coercive pressure, the picketing there is sufficient to induce the warehouse employees to refuse to handle the merchandise involved. Thus another employer, and another group of employees, are subjected to the hegemony of the Teamsters (Tr. 669-70).

[3] For a collection of the cases, see S. Petro, *The Labor Policy of the Free Society* (New York: The Ronald Press Co., 1957), pp. 237-38, especially notes 3-5.

[4] Garner v. Teamsters, 346 U.S. 485 (1953). For a review of the Supreme Court's pre-emption decisions, see 32 *New York University Law Review* 267-91 (1957).

[5] See S. Petro, *How the NLRB Repealed Taft-Hartley* (Washington, D.C.: Labor Policy Association, Inc., 1958), pp. 59-66, 123. Hereinafter referred to as *NLRB&TH*.

The point to remember here is that such "roving-picketing," too, is privileged by an NLRB interpretation of the Taft-Hartley Act—not by the terms of the Taft-Hartley Act.[6]

The "hot-cargo" contract is another carefully tooled machine of oppression for which the Teamsters have managed to secure a privilege from the NLRB, although Congress intended to outlaw it.[7] This contract device is an indispensable phase of the "leap-frog" organizing method of which Hoffa is so proud—as well he may be since it has proved so efficient in dragooning thousands of employees who wanted no part of Hoffa or his Teamsters Union. On long-distance hauls, trucking companies often interline freight. A Pennsylvania company may haul freight to Ohio, at which point the same freight is transferred to the equipment of an Ohio company, which then proceeds with it to, say, Indiana, and so on. Now, if the Pennsylvania and the Indiana companies are already "organized" by the Teamsters, the probability is that they have "agreed" (upon threat of a strike or some other form of coercion) to a "hot cargo" contract. If they have, the Ohio company with which they interline freight will probably be doomed to the same subjection to the Teamsters that they have already suffered. For under a hot-cargo contract, the employer agrees either that he himself will not do business with any firm which resists the Teamsters or that he will not require his employees to handle the merchandise of such a firm. Thus the Ohio company will be squeezed in the middle by the refusal of both the Pennsylvania and the Ohio companies to deal with him (Tr. 5–6).

Desmond A. Barry, president of the Galveston Truck Lines, suffered such an experience. He told the Committee that a Teamsters' agent slammed a contract down on his desk one day, instructing him to sign it. When Barry asked whether the Teamsters represented his employees, the agent said, "That doesn't make any difference. We are organizing you from the top." (Tr. 565) Barry then invited the Teamsters' agent to talk

[6] See *Teamsters and Schultz Refrigerated Service, Inc.*, 87 N.L.R.B. 502 (1949), and the discussion of that case in *NLRB&TH* at pp. 94–101.

[7] See Petro, *NLRB&TH*, pp. 103–8.

to the employees, but the agent replied, according to Barry: "I don't want to do that." (Tr. 566) Later, the agent did actually attend a meeting of Barry's employees, but he told them that the Teamsters "didn't care what they wanted, that [the Teamsters] were signing a contract with [Barry], not with them." (Tr. 567) Regimentation of an industry, not representation of workers, was obviously the Teamsters' objective.

Barry's evidence tended further to disclose that the Teamsters' regimentation was either encouraged or acquiesced in by other trucking companies, especially competitors of Barry. Subject to the Teamsters' hot-cargo contracts, they joined their employees in obeying them "voluntarily." (Tr. 570 ff.) What businessmen cannot do by themselves under the antitrust laws —namely, squeeze out a competitor—they apparently may do with the cooperation of a union.

That is one of the two important conclusions to be drawn from Barry's experience. The other arises from the fact that, even though Barry ultimately secured a decision in his favor from the Interstate Commerce Commission, he was never able to secure such a decision from the NLRB (Tr. 577–82). As Barry pointed out to the Committee, a formal decision by the Interstate Commerce Commission in a trucker's favor is of very little utility. He will be bankrupt by the time the decision is handed down (Tr. 595). The second important conclusion, therefore, is that *immediate injunctive relief is an absolute necessity if businesses are not to be destroyed by unlawful, industry-regimenting boycotts.*

The NLRB alone is empowered to seek injunctive relief against violations of the Taft-Hartley Act. While it has refused to hold that hot-cargo contracts are in themselves unlawful, it would be a mistake to assume that the threat of unlawful destruction of businesses will be removed simply by a statutory amendment reversing the NLRB. If real protection is to be afforded, Congress must not only reverse the NLRB's stand on hot-cargo contracts but must also give the injured party the right to go directly to court for immediate injunctive relief. Otherwise the prohibition of the unlawful boycott is of no use.

This point is vividly documented in the Record by the testimony of Tom Coffey, former owner of Coffey's Transfer Company. He is identified as the "former owner" because the unavailability to him of immediate injunctive relief against a vicious Teamster boycott resulted in the destruction of his business (Tr. 627 ff.).

Like Mr. Barry, Coffey had a form contract thrown at him by Teamsters agents who indicated that they were not going to be bothered with trying to organize the employees. Coffey described the situation to the Committee:

> They were going to [organize the men] from the top down and they didn't have time to fool with the little companies such as mine and I suggested then that we ask the NLRB for an election. They said they weren't interested in an election and I said that I would insist on an election.
> They informed me that if I did, that they would stall any election that I might insist on until I was bankrupt anyhow. (Tr. 630)

True to its word, the Teamsters drove Coffey out of business. They instituted a strangling boycott, supplemented with liberal use of violence; delayed the election; made and broke a promise to the NLRB to desist from the boycott while the endless election complexities dragged on; and, although Coffey ultimately came out on top legally in every way—he was still forced out of business (Tr. 631–63). Coffey put it succinctly:

> I never lost a case before a Federal Court or before the NLRB, but I lost my business. (Tr. 663)

The Committee was of the opinion that the NLRB's dilatory election processes were fundamentally responsible for Coffey's sad experience. NLRB Chairman Boyd Leedom was therefore summoned to give testimony on that issue. Briefly summarized, Leedom's testimony was that the Board's election procedures, like all legal procedures, can always be abused by parties intent upon delaying decision. In exigent cases this delay may hurt the injured party irreparably, but the requirement of due process will not permit the waiving of otherwise valid rules (Tr. 778). "It looks like red tape to a union or an employer which feels frustrated by the delays," he pointed out, "but what is one man's red tape is sometimes the other man's due process." (Tr. 784) Leedom could think of no way to help the Committee in its solicitude for small businessmen who are destroyed by vicious union conduct occurring in the interim of legal proceedings. He thought that there were "no glaring defects in our own procedures." (Tr. 795)

The obvious answer of course is for Congress to close up the loopholes which the NLRB has created in the secondary-boycott prohibitions of the Taft-Hartley Act, *and then* to give back to injured persons the right that it has taken away from them to go to court directly and immediately, not through the NLRB, for injunctive relief. Equity courts developed the temporary restraining order precisely to guard against the kind of disaster Coffey suffered. If Congress gets down to business and gives back the rights it has taken away, the NLRB's dilatory election proceedings may be allowed to drag out forever. Of course if unions learn that their destructive and unlawful practices must be terminated while election proceedings are pending, they will no longer avail themselves of all the opportunities for delay afforded by the NLRB's election rules. Permitting employers direct access to the courts would therefore secure two worthwhile results: it would prevent the destruction and regimentation of business, and it would tend to speed up the Board's election processes.

NLRB Solicitor James V. Constantine instructed the Committee on other features of the Board's rules on secondary boycotts. He told the Committee that under the "common situs" rule, where two or more employers share a common location for their businesses, a union may engage in "primary" stranger-picketing of the employer whose employees it is trying to "organize" without violating the boycott proscriptions of the Taft-Hartley Act, even though the business of the other employers at the same premises is drastically harmed by the picketing. In order to get away with such harm to all the employers and employees involved, it is necessary for the picketing union only to say that it is "organizing" and that its dispute is with the one employer whose employees it seeks to control (Tr. 20).

Again, under the Board's interpretation of Taft-Hartley, a union may extend its pressures to neutral third parties if those third parties may somehow be considered "allies" of the employer with whom the union is primarily disputing. For example, if a struck employer sends out work to another firm for completion, the striking union may, under the Board's rules, extend its pressures to that other firm, inducing a strike by its employees even if there is no labor dispute between them and their employer (Tr. 47). Senator McClellan, it will be remembered, could see little justice in this rule when discussing it with UAW attorney Joseph Rauh during the Kohler hearings. The Senator observed then that if strikers may seek work elsewhere without fear of the struck employer's inducing other employers to refuse to hire them, it is only fair to permit the struck employer equal access to alternative methods of production during the strike (9810).

* * *

The foregoing powers of economic compulsion and immunities to equitable relief have all accrued to trade unions as special privileges to dominate employees and to control industries in a manner specifically prohibited to employers. But one vital special privilege of monopolistic compulsion has as yet not been mentioned here, the special privilege to impose upon employers contracts which make union membership a condition of employment. Like all the rest of the special privileges, this one too conflicts with fundamental principle in that it constitutes an exception to the rule that employees may not be coerced in their free choice to join or not join unions. Moreover, it is a strong link in the chain of control which unions have wrapped around industries and by means of which the abuse of union members is facilitated. Mr. Justice Roberts pointed out in the dissenting opinion quoted in part at the head of this chapter that the control of employment which unions acquire through industry-wide closed-shop and union-shop agreements is indispensable to monopolistic trade-union action. Without it, trade-union barriers to free trade and free competition are more easily hurdled.

In summary, then, trade unions are privileged by law to engage in economically oppressive methods which organize employees "from the top," regardless of their own wishes; employers are unable to resist such pressures because in most instances they are held lawful; and where they are not lawful, effective resistance is still impossible because the only real remedy, immediate injunctive relief, is unavailable. Compulsory-unionism agreements of the closed-shop or the union-shop variety are then clamped upon the employees, helping to reduce them to a captive condition. From this process emerges the status of serfdom described in Chapter 6, the widespread corruption considered in Chapter 7, and the enviornment in which the furtive crime and violence discussed in Chapter 9 may flourish.

If effective remedies are to be forthcoming, it is necessary to eradicate these special privileges. But before they may be cleanly eradicated they and their sources must be understood as completely as possible. This is a complicated matter, for the responsibility is distributed widely.

The Responsibility

The sources of the special privileges which trade unions enjoy are to be found in the policies and conduct of the federal government over the past thirty years, beginning in 1930 and continuing to this date. The responsibility is nonpartisan, with Republicans and Democrats sharing it, although not in equal proportions. It is distributed in another way. Rather than being confined to one or another of the three branches of the federal government, it is shared, instead, by all three: the legislative branch, the executive branch, and the judicial branch.

Unwise laws have been made worse by the administration and interpretation they have had, while socially beneficial laws have been reduced to impotency by reluctant administration, on the one hand, and dubious interpretation, on the other. Without exonerating Congress from its share of the responsibility, one still must acknowledge in the interests of accuracy that its record is not as defective as that of the other parties: the National

Labor Relations Board, representing the executive branch; and the United States Supreme Court, representing the judicial branch.

Accuracy calls for further qualification. There have at all times been on the Supreme Court some justices who resisted valiantly and with great legal ability the errors and excesses of that court.[8] Again, some of the justices who earlier participated in the most dubious decisions of the Court have shown since then that theirs were good-faith errors; and, as all good and learned men will do upon finding themselves in error, they have taken steps toward correction.

It should also be noted that at frequent intervals between 1935 and 1953 there were some members of the NLRB who recognized and dissented from improper decisions of the Board. Moreover, the majority of the Board since 1953 has been guilty of nothing comparable to the outrageous misinterpretations of the Taft-Hartley Act handed down by the majority which prevailed from 1949 to 1953, although the more recent majority has been very slow to correct some and has failed completely to reverse the most serious of its predecessor's misinterpretations.[9]

Whereas the NLRB and the Supreme Court have preponderantly contributed decisions heightening the abusive powers of trade unions and negating the efforts of Congress to reduce such powers, the record of the Federal Circuit Courts of Appeals has been one, preponderantly, of the kind of excellence in legal scholarship, fair-mindedness, and fidelity to law and precedent which is to be expected of all judges. The Circuit Judges, with some exceptions, have neither tried to give trade unions and their officials more privileges than the laws of Congress intended, nor have they negated, except by direct mandate of the Supreme Court, the laws of Congress which were intended to limit abusive and monopolistic trade-union conduct.[10]

Ensuing sections of this chapter will elaborate this summary, but only to the degree necessary in order to clarify the problem of legislative correction. Exhaustive documentation of the fore-

[8] See footnote 2, page 221.
[9] See Petro, *NLRB&TH*, p. 52.
[10] *Ibid.*, pp. 84–88.

going allocation of responsibility would require several technical books, and such books are already available in print. Dean Roscoe Pound has brought his unsurpassed legal learning to a survey of the "Legal Immunities of Labor Unions," and how those immunities came into existence.[11] Professor Charles O. Gregory's *Labor and the Law* [12] contains an execcellent account of the decisions in which the Supreme Court negated the anti-trust laws as controls upon monopolistic union action; it also demonstrates the defects in the Supreme Court's theory of picketing as a specially privileged form of freedom of speech—a theory which for many years gave complete protection to the coercive and monopolistic organizing campaigns out of which the present vast powers of trade unions have grown. My own book, *The Labor Policy of the Free Society*,[13] covers the statutory provisions and the NLRB and Supreme Court decisions which have denied to victimized employers and employees any effective protection against the most vicious and abusive conduct of trade unions. My monograph, *How the NLRB Repealed Taft-Hartley: A Study of Congressional Intent and NLRB Interpretation*,[14] demonstrates from an exhaustive analysis of the Taft-Hartley Act and its legislative history how the NLRB, between 1949 and 1953, grossly misinterpreted the obvious and plain meaning of the Act; and how, by engaging in impermissible methods of statutory construction and improper use of the legislative history, it permitted trade unions to continue the very abuses of employers and employees which the Congress intended to eliminate—and which have led to the infinite corruption exposed by the McClellan investigation.

In preparation for its hearings on picketing and boycott abuses, the McClellan Committee invited NLRB Solicitor James V. Constantine to describe the rules applied by the NLRB under the Taft-Hartley Act to such union activities (Tr. 7-50).

[11] Roscoe Pound, "Legal Immunities of Labor Unions," reprinted in *Labor Unions and Public Policy* (Washington, D.C.: American Enterprise Association, 1958), p. 122. See also, in the same volume, Gerard D. Reilly's comprehensive analysis of the pre-emption problem, p. 93.

[12] (New York: W. W. Norton & Co., Inc. 3d rev.; 1958).

[13] See footnote 3, page 224.

[14] See footnote 5, page 224.

These rules, both in fact and as described by Mr. Constantine, are so confusing, so conflicting, so inconsistent with each other, and so generally nonsensical and unrealistic that they dismayed at least some of the Committee members. Senator Ervin, seeking a ray of light, asked whether anyone had written a treatise on the Taft-Hartley law. But Mr. Constantine could not think of any, not right offhand, anyway (Tr. 43).

In these enlightened days it would be most unrealistic to expect the NLRB Solicitor to refer Senator Ervin to a monograph entitled *How the NLRB Repealed Taft-Hartley*, even though that monograph constitutes beyond any question the most exhaustive and complete review in print of the Taft-Hartley Act, its legislative history, and the leading NLRB picketing and boycott decisions. The incident is worth a moment's consideration because it bears upon another form of corruption in the labor law field.

A curious feature of this field is that neither the Supreme Court nor the NLRB has ever bothered to acknowledge the existence of legal analysis, however carefully documented, which challenges their reasoning and conclusions. The great liberal tradition holds that persons in positions of authority, especially judicial officers, should engage in analysis and evaluation of at least the principal rational arguments and opinions on all sides of every issue. Only thus, the tradition insists, may error be exposed and truth and accuracy prevail. By their unbending refusal even to notice, let alone demonstrate the error of, challenges to their decisions, the Supreme Court and the NLRB may be motivated either by scorn of those challenges or by reluctance to expose their own conclusions to the arguments to the contrary. They have never bothered to inform the legal profession on either.

This too is a form of corruption in the field of labor law. It is a part of the failure of those who make, administer, and interpret the labor laws to formulate them wisely, to understand them accurately, and to apply them vigorously, honestly, and straightforwardly to trade-union conduct. As we proceed in this chapter it will become evident how Congress, the Supreme

Court, and the NLRB share responsibility for the monopolistic special privileges from which the evils described herein have grown.

Of Congress

The principal responsibility of Congress for the conditions disclosed in the McClellan Record lies in its violation of one of the fundamental principles of a free society—the principle that every man who feels himself aggrieved by unlawful conduct has a right to a day in court and to immediate relief from that Court when irreparable injury is threatened. This right, Congress has taken away from employers and employees injured by even the most viciously unlawful trade-union conduct. In doing so, Congress has also insured the weakening of employer resistance to the most antisocial and corrupt trade-union demands.

Upon frequent occasion during the hearings, Chief Counsel Kennedy and some members of the Committee heaped scorn as well as direct accusations of impropriety upon employers who had yielded to shakedowns or who had accepted unions before they acquired voluntary majority status among the employees. In all such instances the employers were not fundamentally to blame. The blame belonged, in any proper analysis, to the federal government and to the Congress which made it impossible for the victims of trade-union wrongdoing to secure any help from the law.

The means whereby Congress has denied direct access to the courts for immediate injunctive relief are two: [15] *First*, the Norris-LaGuardia Act expressly prohibits the federal courts from issuing injunctive relief in any labor case except one involving violence which reaches the level of civil insurrection. To be more precise, no employer can go to federal court and get an immediate injunction against the most damaging picketing or secondary boycott, even if it violates the Taft-Hartley Act. Moreover, he cannot secure injunctive relief against violent union action unless he can prove that the local authorities are

---

[15] For extended discussion of both, see Petro, *The Labor Policy,* chap. xix.

unwilling or unable to control the violence. That means, of course, that injunctive relief may be secured only after the damage has been done, in violence cases; and not at all in the stranger-picketing and secondary-boycott cases which have been described in this chapter and in Chapter 2. As Tom Coffey's case demonstrates, the result is often destruction of the resisting business; and, that being true, an employer can scarcely be blamed for yielding to a shakedown or accepting a union's hegemony in preference to destruction.

Second, in respect to union conduct charged as a violation of the Taft-Hartley Act, the NLRB and its General Counsel, by express Congressional provision, have exclusive jurisdiction.[16] If the NLRB and its General Counsel refuse to prosecute the case, the standing rule has been that the party who feels himself injured must simply grin and bear it, or, again, yield to the unlawful union pressures. With the best will in the world, the NLRB and the General Counsel could not afford injured employers and employees, especially small employers, a remedy swift enough to protect them from irreparable injury. The administrative process, though it was sold to a credulous Congress and an inexperienced nation as a cure for all the defects of traditional legal procedures, makes all those defects seem like virtues in comparison to the evils and delays built into administrative law.[17] A vastly greater appropriation in the federal budget would be required in order to provide the necessary personnel. Moreover, it would obviously be an unwise principle, encouraging needless litigation and other abuses, to compel the General Counsel to take court action whenever a charge of a Taft-Hartley violation was filed. Finally, there is no point in creating such a bottleneck; it can only bring delay and other evils.

Some may wonder why those unable to secure relief in the federal system do not go to state courts for immediate injunctive relief. The answer is that this avenue of relief was explored and utilized frequently—until the Supreme Court barred it by accepting the fallacious theory that the enactment of the Taft-

[16] *Ibid.,* pp. 265–69.
[17] *Ibid.,* pp. 284–88.

Hartley Act evidenced an intent on the part of Congress to oust the states of jurisdiction. With this "pre-emption" theory we shall deal in a little more detail presently.

If Congress wishes to repair the damage done by its abandonment of the fundamental principle that every man has a right to a day in court, it must either repeal the Norris-LaGuardia Act or amend it to permit persons to secure immediate injunctive relief from conduct which violates the Taft-Hartley Act and which threatens irreparable injury. Congress must also provide —at the very least—that the power of the NLRB and its General Counsel to prosecute and adjudicate violations of the Taft-Hartley Act is no longer exclusive.

Such legislative action will do more than all other suggested measures combined to reduce the abuses and the corruption disclosed in the McClellan Record. It will stiffen the backs of employers, and it will put adjudication back in the courts, where, under our Constitution, it belongs. It will also effectively and definitively erase the pre-emption theory of the Supreme Court which, so far as it has any basis at all, rests upon the present exclusive jurisdiction of the NLRB and its General Counsel.

Congress must be charged with responsibility also for at least some of the corruption and coercion traceable to the continued prevalence of compulsory unionism agreements. Here too the evils flow from a violation of fundamental principle. The fundamental principle of the Taft-Hartley Act is the principle of free employee choice. Employees are expressly declared to have the right to join or not to join unions, free of economic or physical coercion by either employers or trade unions. Naturally, all forms of compulsory unionism are inconsistent with that principle. If a man must join a union in order to hold his job, he is being subjected to the kind of economic coercion which the Act generally makes an unfair practice. Yet, compromising this fundamental principle, Congress explicitly permitted unions to impose union-shop contracts upon employers and employees, at least in states where such contracts were not prohibited. From that compromise, together with the denial of direct access to the courts, the lethargy of the NLRB, and the Supreme Court's pre-emption theory, all the abuses associated with the nationwide prevalence of compulsory-unionism conditions have developed.

Since the union shop was permitted, unions could see little reason to stop there. So they insisted on strictly closed shops, rather than union shops. Most employers felt that they could not resist such demands, even though they were unlawful, because they could not go to court directly for relief; and the NLRB, although it was empowered to do so, would not except in rare and exceptional cases seek injunctive relief.[18] For a while, employers went to state courts for relief from union action aimed at compulsory-unionism contracts. But, as already seen, the pre-emption doctrine barred that avenue of relief. Indeed, that doctrine has recently been extended to states which have right-to-work laws under which all forms of compulsory unionism are prohibited—in spite of the fact that in Section 14(b) of the Taft-Hartley Act Congress specifically empowered the states to prohibit all forms of compulsory unionism, including the form permitted by the Taft-Hartley Act.[19] The state courts are embittered about these rulings, but they feel bound, by the Supreme Court's ruling, to deny relief to people who are being seriously harmed by conduct which violates both federal and state law. The North Carolina Supreme Court has recently said, for example:

> It seems patent to us that Congress did not authorize a State to enact a statute and at the same moment prohibit it from enforcing the statute.[20]

*　*　*

Congress inherits a responsibility too from the failure of the NLRB and the Supreme Court to interpret the Taft-Hartley Act as it was intended and to enforce it vigorously. This means that even though it has already prohibited the types of picketing and boycotts which the NLRB and the Supreme Court have held privileged, Congress must amend its legislation to make the

[18] See Petro, *NLRB&TH,* pp. 123–24.

[19] Int. Brotherhood of Electrical Workers v. Farnsworth & Chambers Co., 353 U.S. 969 (1957).

[20] Douglas Aircraft v. Electrical Workers, 247 No. Car. 620, 34 CCH Labor Cases ¶ 71352, p. 96234 (1958).

prohibition unmistakable. Specifically, it must write legislation which expressly covers all stranger-picketing and all other secondary boycotts, overruling the NLRB's hot-cargo, roving-situs, common-situs, and allies doctrines—all of which, as can be shown, constitute illegitimate amendments of the Taft-Hartley Act.

Of the NLRB

The literal language of the Taft-Hartley Act covers all stranger-picketing and all secondary boycotts. Moreover, the explanations of the sponsors of the Taft-Hartley Act on the floor of the House and the Senate, prior to passage of the Act, confirm the literal meaning of the Act's language. Nevertheless, contrary to both the language of the Act and its legislative history, the NLRB has held that the Act falls short in the ways already suggested and here to be described in more detail.[21]

Consider, first, the subject of stranger-picketing, whether for "organizing" or "recognition" purposes. The language of the Act prohibits, without qualification, every form of trade-union coercion of the right of employees to join or not to join unions.[22] As the Ninth Circuit Court of Appeals has held, that language naturally covers all stranger-picketing because the effect of such picketing, by placing pressure on the employer, is to make employees accept unionization as the only alternative to loss of their jobs.[23] Besides this definitive reason for holding all stranger-picketing violative of the Act, the principal sponsors of the legislation, Senators Taft and Ball, specifically declared on the floor of the Senate that stranger-picketing was one of the forms of coercion that the Act was intended to prohibit.[24] There is a great deal of additional evidence of the same kind which the interested reader may find in the source cited in the foregoing footnote. Notwithstanding this mountain of evidence, the NLRB held until late in 1957 that *all* stranger-picketing was privi-

[21] See generally the analysis of the Act, its legislative history, and the NLRB decisions in Petro, *NLRB&TH*.

[22] *Ibid.*, pp. 2, 11–34.

[23] NLRB v. Capital Service, Inc., 204 F.2d 848 (9th Cir. 1953).

[24] Petro, *NLRB&TH*, pp. 26–33.

leged;[25] since 1957 it has been holding that only "recognition" picketing is prohibited while "organizational" picketing continues privileged (Tr. 20, 35); and, what is much more important, it continues to decline to seek injunctive relief against even "recognition" picketing, although that is the only kind of relief which is really of any value to the employer and employees subject to a picketing blockade.

Consider, second, the refusal of the NLRB to hold that all hot-cargo contracts in themselves violate the Act. The language of the Act, in Section 8(b)(4), specifically makes it an unfair practice for a union to call a strike, or to induce any kind of work stoppage, where an object is to force one employer to cease doing business with any other person. Under a hot-cargo contract, the employer agrees not to require his employees to handle the so-called hot cargo of some other employer.

One critical question must be addressed to the means by which unions secure such agreements. The answer is that they secure such agreements in the same way that they secure all other agreements—namely, through the threat of a strike against the employer of whom the concession is sought. Now a strike of that kind is precisely what the Act prohibits in Section 8(b)(4); for it is a strike to compel an employer to agree to cease doing business with some other employer. The NLRB Solicitor took the position at the Hearings that the Act prohibits only strikes, not threats of strikes. Therefore, he contended, the Board was correct in holding that the refusal to deal occasioned by a hot-cargo contract secured by only a strike threat does not fall within the Act's prohibition (Tr. 17-25).

That is an excellent example of the reasoning by which the Board has reduced the Taft-Hartley Act to impotency. In submitting the legislation to Congress, Senator Taft declared that it was designed to prohibit *all* secondary boycotts,[26] and the hot-cargo agreement is one of the most widely used boycott instruments. Yet by a specious course of reasoning, the Board has managed to provide it with immunity. Constantine's and the Board's reasoning is specious because there is no reasonable

[25] *Ibid.*, pp. 59–66.
[26] *Ibid.*, p. 46.

basis for holding that a hot-cargo agreement secured through a strike threat does not fall naturally within both the spirit and the language of the Act.[27] Consider in this connection the position taken by the NLRB when a similar question arose under the Act's prohibition of coercive employer conduct. The Act makes it an unfair practice for an employer to interfere with, restrain, or coerce employees in the exercise of their right to join unions. From the very beginning, to the present, the NLRB has held that employers violate this prohibition even when they engage in conduct—for example, spying on union meetings—about which the employees are completely unaware. No actual coercive effect needs to be shown when it comes to employer unfair practices; according to the Board, it is the employer's intentions and the probable consequences of his conduct which count.

If the same approach is applied to the question whether a hot-cargo contract secured by a strike threat violates the Act, the conclusion that it does becomes inescapable. But the Board's position is subject to even further criticism. The Board would not hold a hot-cargo contract unlawful in itself even if the employer agreed to it after and because of an actual strike. Its position is really, at bottom, that such contracts are not in themselves unlawful no matter how secured. Yet the Board holds that a union violates the Act if it takes any action to induce the employees of the contracting employer to cease work in accordance with a hot-cargo contract (Tr. 25). Here we reach the ultimate absurdity—the rule that a contract is valid but that a party to it may not take the very action which the contract permits. Indeed, the Board has held that a union official may not even tell an employee to "let your conscience be your guide." [28] The Supreme Court has approved this anomalous approach.[29]

The only rational construction possible is that any work stoppage pursuant to a hot-cargo contract violates the Act. A hot-cargo contract secured through a strike is a literal violation

[27] *Ibid.,* pp. 103–8.
[28] Local 511, Carpenters, 120 N.L.R.B. No. 211 (1958).
[29] Local 1976, Carpenters v. NLRB, 35 CCH Labor Cases ¶ 71599, 78 Sup. Ct. Reports 1011 (1958).

of the Act, and one secured through the threat of a strike falls within the same ban. In either case a secondary work stoppage of precisely the kind that the Act was designed to eliminate is brought about. Naturally, there is no basis for a complaint under the Act until an actual work stoppage pursuant to the contract occurs or is threatened. But this fact should not obscure the ultimately important point that the hot-cargo contract is in itself the very kind of inducement or encouragement of a work stoppage which the Act specifically prohibits.

The problem reduces, finally, to whether a work stoppage induced by a hot-cargo contract falls within the statutory language which prohibits *all* inducements or encouragements of secondary work stoppages. To this there can be only one answer. The statute does not except work stoppages induced or encouraged by contracts; it prohibits all secondary work stoppages, no matter how induced. Even if the inducement were by way of a cryptic code in a newspaper advertisement it would still be an inducement prohibited by the Act. That it is imbedded instead in a contract which might itself be called an anticipatory violation of the Act does not legitimately afford it the shelter which the old Board gave it and which the new Board has failed to remove.

The story is the same with all the other NLRB amendments of the boycott prohibition of the Act. The "allies" doctrine is a pure piece of judicial legislation. The Act does not make any exception in favor of "struck-work" boycotts, and neither equity nor justice requires any such exception. So long as employers are prohibited from blacklisting strikers by inducing others to quit dealing with or hiring them during a strike, it is only equitable to prohibit unions from blacklisting and otherwise boycotting employers during strikes. The exception embodied in the "allies" doctrine is not only an illegitimate amendment of the Act;[30] it is not only an inequitable amendment; it also flies in the face of the legislative history of the Act, for it was specifically and expressly recognized that "struck-work" boycotts would become unlawful if the Act were passed.[31]

[30] See Petro, NLRB&TH, pp. 73–77.
[31] *Ibid.*, see especially p. 48.

Similarly with the "roving-situs" doctrine. Here we encounter multiple, illegitimate amendments of the Act. In the first place, stranger-picketing is illegal under the Act even when confined to the premises of the victimized employer;[32] in the second place, it violates the rights of a neutral party when it is removed from those premises and occurs at the premises of some other employer;[33] in the third place it more often than not combines a request for recognition with insistence upon a closed- or union-shop contract, a request which no union may legally make unless it already possesses majority status. The more unlawful union action is, it would appear, the more privileged it becomes.

The "common-situs" doctrine is of a piece with these others. It is true that a difficult question arises when a majority union calls a strike against an employer who shares common premises with another. The Act privileges such strikes and accepts the right of the striking union to engage in peaceful picketing of the struck premises.[34] But the cases are rare in which the "common-situs" doctrine is used in order to hold privileged picketing in connection with a majority strike. The normal "common-situs" case involves stranger-picketing. Once one realizes that such picketing is unlawful even in connection with the picketing of the employer with whom the union is primarily disputing, it follows as a matter of course that it is unlawful insofar as it embarrasses the operations of the secondary employer, who is the innocent victim of a dispute in which he has no interest and about which neither he nor his suffering employees and victimized customers can do absolutely anything.[35]

Judge Harold Medina once referred to the NLRB's esoteric amendments of the Taft-Hartley Act as "ascending into the empyrean where the atmosphere is too thin" for ordinary mortals to breathe.[36] The plain fact is that these ramified and labyrinthine complexities have been vehicles of power for unions and of

[32] *Ibid.*, pp. 54–66.
[33] *Ibid.*, pp. 94–101.
[34] *Ibid.*, pp. 77–84.
[35] *Ibid.*, pp. 101–3.
[36] NLRB v. Teamsters, 219 F.2d 394, 396 (2d Cir. 1955).

exploitation of employers and employees. Take the case of the Waldorf-Astoria barbers, for example. They were compelled into a union to which they were definitely opposed, because of the pressure which that union exerted against the Waldorf management and their immediate employer, the Terminal Barber Shops. At the hearings, NLRB Solicitor Constantine could not see how the NLRB might afford any relief to either the Waldorf or the beleaguered barbers. In his opinion this was one of those difficult "common-situs" cases (Tr. 30).

Obviously the difficulty exists only in the minds of the NLRB and its staff. The case is not a difficult one at all. The Journeymen Barbers' picketing was unlawful as addressed to the Waldorf barbers, and it was doubly unlawful inasmuch as it harmed the Waldorf-Astoria Hotel itself, a secondary employer. Furthermore, the Teamsters' refusal to cross the picket line, a refusal directed by Teamster officials, was an independent violation of the Act. It amounted to inducement of a work stoppage by a union in an attempt to make one employer, the trucking company employing the Teamsters, cease dealing with another, the Waldorf-Astoria Hotel. Indeed, but for the fact that this analysis would become too complex and too lengthy, it could be demonstrated that a number of other Taft-Hartley violations occurred in the Journeymen Barbers' picketing, the accompanying boycott, and the ultimate result.

*   *   *

To the NLRB's impermissible negation of the Taft-Hartley Act must go a major share of the responsibility for the vicious conditions discovered by the McClellan investigation. By a thoroughly disingenuous emasculation of the Act, the Board provided trade unions with precisely the powers of compulsion which Congress had hoped to eradicate. With those powers, unions have abused countless numbers of employees, extorted from employers, and exploited the public. That the Board should be abolished and its functions given to the courts seems perfectly plain to the present writer, even though, as already noted, the present members of the Board are guilty of only passive acquiescence in the wrongdoing of its predecessor.

The case for abolishing the NLRB rests ultimately on two grounds. *First,* it and all other quasi-judicial agencies are unconstitutional. The Constitution demands that judicial functions be performed only by persons who have permanent tenure in office and irreducible salaries, while the Board is composed of short-term political appointees.[37] *Second,* the political influences upon the Board, the very influences which the Constitution sought to avoid in insisting upon permanent tenure in office, render it unfit for reliable judicial interpretation. Such interpretation calls for fidelity to law, not for the preoccupation with politics and "policy" which has been the essential characteristic of the dominant majorities of the NLRB from the day of its creation till the present, and which must always characterize the personnel of every administrative agency manned by short-term political appointees.[38]

Complete abolition of the NLRB would call for far-reaching changes in the national labor policy, changes going far beyond the subjects of the McClellan investigation. The whole election machinery of the current legislation would have to be dismantled and the duty of employers to bargain with majority unions repealed. In the present writer's opinion, the desirability of these changes far outweighs such inconveniences as might temporarily accompany them. Yet, since the McClellan investigation and its findings are the basis of the recommendations to be made in this book, and since those findings are not addressed to the more far-reaching question of total abolition of the NLRB, proposals falling short of that are more appropriate here. It is sufficient for the present, finally, if we deal with those evils which *must be corrected now.*

The McClellan Record establishes a strong need for withdrawing all judicial powers from the NLRB *now,* and turning over those powers to the state and federal courts. Such a change is not only called for but demanded by the Record, and it would unquestionably bring with it a multitude of benefits in terms of both speed and quality of adjudication.

[37] For further discussion of this matter, see Petro, *The Labor Policy,* pp. 267–69.

[38] *Ibid.,* pp. 284–88.

The minimum change compelled by the McClellan dis-closures is amendment of the Taft-Hartley Act to override the NLRB's exclusive jurisdiction and its misinterpretations: ex-plicit outlawry of all stranger-picketing and of all compulsory unionism, and removal of the esoteric doctrines with which the Board has emasculated the Act's boycott proscriptions and privi-leged the most viciously monopolistic trade-union aggression. Proposals to these ends are made in Chapter 12.

Of the Supreme Court

During the past twenty years—the period coinciding with the tremendous growth of trade unions in numbers, power, and corruption—the Supreme Court of the United States has pro-vided a succession of privileges for aggressive, coercive union action. This succession began with a sharply contested series of decisions releasing unions from the controls of the antitrust laws. It continued with the Court's identification of a coercive economic weapon—picketing—with the freedom of speech which the Constitution protects. And today the Court provides a practical privilege for monopolistic trade-union practices by hold-ing that no injunctive relief may be granted by state courts to employers and employees injured by those practices. Since such relief is by federal law not available in the federal courts, and since the NLRB has proved either unwilling or unable to pro-vide sufficient protection, employers and employees thus have nowhere to go.

No wonder violence, corruption, and universal abuse are associated with trade unions—no wonder employees are dragooned by the hundreds of thousands, and employers of all kinds and all sizes have been shakedown victims! The law has failed miserably; all branches of government—federal, state, and local; legislative, judicial, and executive—have joined, in turning the other way when it comes to protecting the injured, and in going forward to provide additional weapons when it comes to the ex-ploiting trade unions. The *London Times* editorial writer of 1845 anticipated the United States of 1930-1958 when he wrote of "powerless men oppressed with impunity and overbearing men tolerated with complacence."

Whether or not the majority of the Supreme Court (there were vigorous dissents in most instances) was "evilly motivated" in granting trade unions this succession of privileges is irrelevant to our present inquiry. Even the question whether the majority had a sound legal or constitutional basis for granting the privileges is irrelevant. The present writer's opinion is that in each of the three instances the Court erred—in some more indefensibly than in others. But these technical matters are dealt with adequately elsewhere, and it would only unduly extend and complicate this book, without contributing anything substantial, to review those analyses here.[39]

Our problem is to fix as precisely as possible the sources and the current status of the privileges which have made it possible for trade unions to abuse the nation. Only in that manner may adequate remedies be conceived. The important inquiry at this point, then, is to determine the degree to which Supreme Court decisions are currently significant in the structure of trade-unionism's special privileges.

Addressing ourselves to this inquiry, we find that the Court's antitrust decisions are of no great significance today; that its picketing–free-speech decisions, while of somewhat greater significance, still do not, any more, provide a substantial arsenal of special privilege; but that the decisions pre-empting the power of the state courts to issue immediate injunctive relief create a great problem.

The antitrust decisions are of no great importance because the Taft-Hartley Act was specifically designed, and well designed, to outlaw all the kinds of monopolistic strikes and secondary boycotts which the antitrust laws had been prohibiting before the Supreme Court ruled them inapplicable to trade unions. If all else fails, it may one day become necessary again to revive the antitrust principle in order to break up the power aggregations of trade unions. But the vagueness and the unpredictability of the antitrust laws make them inferior methods

[39] See generally the works by Dean Pound (footnote 11, p. 232), and Charles O. Gregory (footnote 12, p. 232).

of dealing with the problems posed by trade-union power. It is better to approach those problems in the specific manner of the Taft-Hartley Act. Therefore, the Supreme Court's antitrust decisions may well be disregarded, for Congress has shown itself capable once of getting around them; and, although it was not successful the first time, because of the failure of the NLRB to enforce the Taft-Hartley Act as written, it should have learned by now how to handle the NLRB.

The new majority of the Supreme Court, over the bitter dissents of the reactionary old guard (Justices Black, Douglas, and Warren), have repaired most of the damage done by the picketing–free-speech decisions. They have gone so far as to hold, in a solid and clean-cut opinion by Mr. Justice Frankfurter, that stranger-organizational picketing may constitutionally be enjoined because of its coercive character.[40] Moreover, there is no reason to believe that the Court would strike down a statute limiting the number of pickets established during strikes —the kind of statute so critically needed in every state as well as in the federal system. Only one problem remains. The Court has recently held that a state court may not enjoin all picketing even when violence and name-calling have been associated with it, if the picketing is in connection with a strike (not to be confused with stranger-picketing, where there is no strike).[41] The Court ought not to interfere with the judgment of state courts in such cases. Those courts are in the best position to decide whether, in view of past threats, any picketing at all would, if permitted to continue, represent a source of fear to the non-strikers. This is the kind of problem which cannot be solved by legislation. Only the Supreme Court can solve it. And it can do so only by a sensible appreciation of its own limitations.

The Supreme Court's pre-emption decisions cannot be dismissed so lightly.[42] Indeed, the harm that they are doing every

---

[40] Teamsters v. Vogt, Inc., 354 U.S. 284 (1957).

[41] Teamsters v. Newell, 34 CCH Labor Cases ¶ 71468 (1958).

[42] The principal pre-emption decisions are Garner v. Teamsters Union, 346 U.S. 485 (1953), and Guss v. Utah Labor Relations Board, 353 U.S. 1 (1957). There have been a great many others, and they are difficult to reconcile. For detailed analysis of them all, see 32 *New York University Law Review* 267–97 (1957) and 33 *New York University Law Review* 691–98 (1958).

day all over the country cannot be exaggerated. In order to judge the dimensions of this evil, one must bear in mind the kinds of pressure which unions have been exerting against employers, the shakedowns, the extortion, the organizing from the top; and one must realize that these pressures are in the main doubly unlawful, under both state and federal law. Only then do the true dimensions of the pre-emption doctrine emerge clearly. The employers and employees victimized by extortionate and monopolistic union conduct are prevented by the Norris Act from going to the federal courts for relief and by the pre-emption doctrine from going to the state courts for relief. Their only hope for relief lies with the NLRB, and that agency's procedures are so excruciatingly dilatory, its rulings so unpredictable, and its remedies so meager, that even if the injured party finally secures action from the NLRB it will be too little, too late.

But that is by no means all. For some employers, the pre-emption doctrine means no relief at all—in any circumstances. This is the situation which confronts all small employers, the ones who need help the most, who have the least power of resistance to the trade-union juggernaut. These are the people in the no-man's-land. Their businesses are not large enough to come within the NLRB's jurisdictional standards. Those standards therefore mean that all small employers are not entitled to the protection of the law. Even as to them, the Supreme Court has held, the pre-emption theory applies. They may not go to state courts for relief in spite of the fact that the NLRB will undoubtedly refuse to act upon their charges, no matter how seriously they are being harmed by trade-union aggression, and no matter how flagrantly unlawful that aggression is.[43] If the Committee is seriously seeking the cause of the corruption, the extortion, the shakedowns, the sweetheart contracts, and all the other evils disclosed in the Record, it need only look at its own laws and the administration of those laws. The corruption exists in the trade unions all over the country, but the source lies in Washington, D.C.

[43] *Ibid.*, and see San Diego Building Trades Council v. Garmon, 353 U.S. 26 (1957).

Practically all the state courts have submitted to the pre-emption theory and have thus denied relief in a multitude of the most egregious cases imaginable of union oppression. Once in a while, however, a state judge straightforwardly challenges the doctrine and refuses to decline jurisdiction. Judge Smith of Michigan is such a man. The case involved a secondary boycott designed to drive out of business a nonunion contractor and out of employment his nonunion employees. The business was too small for the NLRB to bother with, even though the boycott was a plain violation of the Taft-Hartley Act. Pre-emption or not, said Judge Smith, he was going to take the case and give the aggrieved contractor and his employees the relief which they were entitled to expect from any decent legal system. To accept pre-emption in a case of this kind, the judge said, would involve

> a total deprivation of due process or of any process. To limit access to any forum to persons who do a stated amount of interstate business is to make resort to law a privilege instead of a right. This court is firmly of the opinion that no such power rests with Congress and consequently no act of Congress should be construed to this end . . . Pre-emption without occupation is pure anarchy. The mandate of the Constitution is plain. No court can change it and this court certainly has no such disposition.[44]

* * *

Conditions of this kind cannot be permitted to continue. The Supreme Court will not reverse itself where the due process denied is only that to which businessmen and nonunion employees are entitled. It continues to feel that the most ruthlessly powerful self-interest groups in the country today—the big trade unions—are underdogs entitled to special favors and special privileges. The decent citizens of this country must therefore band together and insist to Congress that it proceed expeditiously to an effective overruling of the pre-emption theory. This is something that should have been done more than five years ago, when the Supreme Court first indicated that it in-

[44] Johnson v. Grand Rapids Building Trades Council, 35 CCH Labor Cases ¶71816 (Mich. Cir. Ct. 1958).

tended to wipe out the only effective avenue of relief remaining after the Norris-LaGuardia Act and the exclusive jurisdiction of the NLRB denied the sure protection of the federal government to employers and nonunion employees.

No further delay from Congress is tolerable. Manly resentment by Congress to the way the NLRB and the Supreme Court have pushed it around, negativing its laws and foisting upon it the denial of due process which stirred Judge Smith to rebellion, should be sufficient to induce a remedy. If that is not strong enough, surely the overwhelming social dangers revealed by the McClellan Record should move it to action. And if the present members of Congress will not act even under that impetus, then they must be removed by a citizenry which refuses to sit idly by, watching its most precious institutions destroyed by default of its elected representatives.

* * *

The job of Congress is to defend society, to preserve it, to protect it—not to cower before vicious self-interest groups which have too long arrogated to themselves unearned and undeserved power and privilege. The citizenry must demonstrate that it will be satisfied with nothing less than a Congress which sees its true job clearly. The alternative is the kind of society and the ultimate degradation which no one wants.

Part III

TOWARD SURVIVAL

Society is an organism, and its laws are an expression of the conditions which it considers necessary for its own preservation.

—Mandell Creighton

Chapter 11

HYDARNES,
HADST THOU BUT KNOWN
WHAT FREEDOM IS...

... this country could become a jungle so far as civiliza-
tion is concerned, racketeers, gangsters, thieves, thugs,
crooks taking over this country. You couldn't do anything
about it through law and order. We would all have to
resort to the bullet and to the dynamite and to the
knives that cut tires. We would all be forced to take
that measure of defense for our own lives and for the
protection of our property and our loved ones.
                    —Senator McClellan (7490)

                    *   *   *

This is the summing up. The Record is before us, with
all its tangled incident the overlay and product of a lust for power
licensed to express itself at will. One sentence will serve as summary—*Intent upon securing a position in the world which simple*
representation of employee grievances cannot afford, union lead-
ers seem bent upon destroying the free society which will not
voluntarily yield to them.

The Record in Review

The leaders of the big unions produce nothing, they contribute nothing to society, and a society left free rewards generously only those who produce and contribute generously. In
order to gain their ends, of big power, of big money, or of both,

the union bosses must therefore extort; for extortion is the sole means of extracting that which will not be given voluntarily. But extortion is possible only with some leverage with which to pry the object of desire from its owner. A gun, a letter, a careless conversation overheard, a compromising photograph—any one of these will serve the furtive extortionist, satisfied to slink quietly from one victim to the next, always hiding from the law. But union leaders have sought and found an infinitely superior leverage. Not quite legal, not quite overt, it approaches both and sometimes reaches them. It is compounded of the special privileges to coerce, to compel, and to monopolize.

These privileges make up the formal power base. With and upon them, union leaders build material power. First comes control of workers, for they provide the leverage without which all else must fail. Workers contribute to society, and he who controls their labor has, therefore, the means of exacting power and treasure which would otherwise be withheld. Violence, picketing, boycotts, compulsory unionism, and all the other specially privileged forms of monopolistic compulsion which we have encountered are the instruments with which the union leaders establish control over the vast numbers of workers who, whether willing or unwilling to serve, are necessary if the leverage is to be effective. Once organized from the top or beaten into submission, the outlaws are transformed into serfs. The status of serfdom may be formalized in union constitutions and bylaws passed by majority votes at union conventions. But that is only the outer suit; there is that within which passeth show.

There is in print an article entitled "Why They Cheer for Hoffa," which suggests that Hoffa is a hero to Teamster members.[1] No doubt he is—to some—and well he may be, for although his memory is defective at times, his two-fisted hardness and raw courage cannot help winning admirers. Moreover, as he once said to the members of his own Local 299: "we are out to sell your labor at the highest buck we can get." But to suggest that all who pay dues to Hoffa cheer him is impermissible in the light of the Record. The Teamsters Union has secured a substantial

[1] A. H. Raskin, "Why They Cheer for Hoffa," *The New York Times Magazine* (Nov. 9, 1958), p. 77.

part of its membership by pure terror and by a campaign of monopolistic secondary boycotts unapproached in American history. It binds the members to it with a prescription of vicious brutality and, through compulsory-unionism contracts, the alternatives of outlawry or serfdom for all who would rebel.

And yet, even with all this, Hoffa could not be elected president of the Teamsters without chicanery and blatant rigging of the Teamsters convention. Such was not only the charge made by Senator McClellan on the basis of evidence in his possession; it was also the finding of the court, in the suit prosecuted by Godfrey P. Schmidt, which imposed a court-appointed board of monitors to keep its eye upon the Teamsters' treasury. Apparently they do not all cheer for Hoffa.

A great many opportunities open up for the union leader once he has command of hundreds of thousands of workers and the fortune in dues which they turn over monthly. Here in themselves are power and treasure of substantial proportion. But not enough. And more than that, union leaders learn the terrible lesson which all have learned who seek power and treasure through the use of force. One must go on and on if only to maintain what one has already mastered. For power built upon compulsion requires more compulsion in the keeping. A moment's relaxation, a brief interval of peace and freedom, and the structure begins to crumble.

* * *

The second stage is, therefore, more of the same: violence and monopolistic coercion pressed into service in order to justify continued power by gaining economic victories impossible on a free market. This is the true meaning of the Kohler and Perfect Circle strike-violence—if those strikes are construed as having had better wages and working conditions as their objective. If they were really designed to impose unionization upon unwilling employees, as the Kohler and Perfect Circle managements testified, then they should be classified as first-stage phenomena. But it makes no real difference. In either event, the method is extortionate. The gain in any case is exacted from the employer and eventually from the public; it is not yielded voluntarily, for nothing is offered in return. The union and its members do not offer more work or fewer obstacles to production in return for the concession they seek, whatever that may be. They are out to get—not to give. That is what union leaders have always preached, and they mean it.

The same is true of the nonviolent monopolistic techniques which are habitually used, not only by the unions the McClellan Committee investigated, *but by practically every large union in the United States today.* The secondary boycotts of the UAW against Kohler, the Sheet Metal Workers against the Burt Company, the garbage collectors against the Safeway Stores, the Barbers against the Terminal Barber Shops, Inc., the Teamsters against everyone—these represent the thinnest possible sampling of the thousands of secondary boycotts which are known to any informed student of labor law, for the law reports are filled with them. The basic pattern of extortion is the same in secondary boycotts as it is in strike-violence. They are in fact alternative methods of extortion, used interchangeably depending upon the lie of the land, and often supplementing each other. Precisely like strike and organizing violence, the secondary boycott is designed to destroy the free market and in doing so to extort from employees in some cases, the employer in other cases, and the public ultimately in all cases. The Sheet Metal Workers case is definitive. The union was out to get all it could. If it had to monopolize an industry, drive a firm out of business, and take away the jobs of men belonging to an affiliated union in order to maintain a manifestly unjustified and consumer-gouging wage scale, the Sheet Metal Workers was prepared to do so—and to proclaim its righteousness in the process.

* * *

Classical extortion and union extortion merged in the Record when Earl Bettendorf told the Committee about his payoff of $200 a week to the Scranton Teamsters. That money, if it had actually gone to Teamster members, would have been extorted money, for it was taken under duress from an unwilling giver, and the union had nothing legitimate to offer in return. But it would have been extortion of the kind which trade unions practice each time they use violence or monopolistic pressure in order to gain wage increases. It did not become classical extortion —or pseudo-union extortion—until the Bettendorf shakedown went to the Teamster officials, rather than to Teamster members for doing no work. At that point the transfer of money from the taxpayers, to the United States Government, to Bettendorf, to the Scranton Teamster officials was as purely extortionate as the classical blackmail or protection rackets.

From the same power base of special privilege grow the more devious forms of extortion with which the Record is filled: the sweetheart contracts, the unused memberships in country clubs, the inside information on stock-market transactions, the worthless but costly advertisements in union newspapers, the pinball machine rackets, and all the rest. A union membership reduced to serfdom by the special privileges of violence and compulsory-unionism contracts will do as it is told. When a picket is stationed before the Mount Hood Cafe, and the Teamster members are told to "respect" that picket, they blindly do so. That the Cafe has no dispute with its unionized employees makes no difference. The owner is using Stan Terry's pinball machines, and Stan Terry has been a bad boy. Until he makes his peace with the Teamster leaders, his machines are contraband.

* * *

As this business grows, it becomes more complicated, and jobbers and brokers are needed. The raw power base tends to recede from consciousness, as does the dynamo powering the lamps which give light at a finger touch in your home. But the Sheffermans and Teitelbaums would be as meaningless without the violence and other monopolistic coercion which power them as the bulbs would be should the dynamos go dead. They have no power of their own. Workers and society have power. This power is delivered to union leaders, and they wire it to the jobbers, who are then in a position to press the buttons. When they press the button either a businessman pays, his employees become union members, or other union members swing into action. In any event, the power is destructive of the most important social interests.

This power can do many things. It can kill a business, or it can put that business into a specially favored competitive position. In those industries where the power is perfected, and the trucking industry is not the one, surprising as it may seem, in which the current peak of perfection has been mostly nearly realized, the businesses which survive do so on sufferance of the union overlord. Opinion may vary as to which union has come closest to perfection. My judgment would give this accolade to the International Ladies Garment Workers' Union. In New York City and in Los Angeles its hegemony is solid. Its prestige and the accuracy of its bookkeeping are unquestioned. The wife of the Governor of the State of New York considers it an honor to sew on the ILGWU label, its own particular boycotting technique.[2] The McClellan Committee has not investigated the ILGWU, it is true, but the greatest power is that which goes unnoticed. In this sense, power unlimited is like corruption unlimited. Both exist when they are so pervasive as to seem to be laws of nature, as compelling and as ineluctable.

* * *

I do not mean to shock anyone or to be facetious when I say that the single occasion for optimism provided by the McClellan Record is that it contains so much evidence of violence and of corruption of public officials. These are genuinely impressive indications that neither power nor corruption has as yet become unlimited. If trade unions had perfected their monopolistic control of industry, they would not need to use violence in order to gain their ends. Those areas where trade unions do not need mass pickets during their strikes are the ones in the worst trouble. Those in which they need but are not allowed to have mass picket lines are in the best shape. Those in which they both need and are allowed to have mass picket lines and other forms of violence, and these predominate, are swinging in the balance. Although the latter are also the areas in which unions find it necessary to corrupt public officials, from that necessity, too, some encouragement may be drawn. For it means that the last stage

[2] *The New York Times,* January 10, 1959, p. 18, cols. 1-4.

of the pattern suggested by the McClellan Record is not yet complete.

That pattern will be complete when the basic moral structure upon which all decent civilization is built has been subverted; when virtue becomes vice, and vice virtue; when civil order becomes the disguised anarchy of the rule of brute force; when industry responds primarily to the wishes of the unions rather than to the consumers; when government protects the assaulting thug rather than his victim.

So long as all people agree that it is still the job of the public authorities to protect the innocent against aggression, there is hope. The central problem then becomes one of discovering the truth, of figuring out who is the aggressor and who the victim, who the exploiter and who the exploited. This is not an easy task, for there is much confusion as to the occupants of these roles. Some union leaders and their apologists have played so fast and loose with language, truth, and reason that the utility of even the most carefully compiled dictionaries is brought into serious question. One must make a determined effort to hold fast to basic truths and the commonly understood meanings of words if he is not to be lost completely in the infinitely regressive fallacies which union leaders and their apologists have attempted to establish as the basic premises of public policy. If these fallacies are exposed, the widespread confusion may diminish. The public may acquire a clearer view of the identity of the exploiter and of the exploited. With such a view it may be less inclined than it now is to perpetuate the special privileges which unions have enjoyed.

A Glossary of Fallacy

COLLECTIVE BARGAINING

Union version: Negotiation between unions and employers in which they jointly arrive at "just" wages and working conditions with due regard for interests of business owners, public, and workers. *Truth:* A diverse activity. Sometimes as described in union version, if no violence or monopolistic boycotts exerted. Often directed mainly to compel union membership, as in Kohler. Often utilized also to mislead public into believing that union leaders have large responsibilities for running businesses about which they know little or nothing. When prolonged more than a few hours, a cover-up for union mistakes and mainly preoccupied with frantic searches for methods of saving face of union leader who has promised more than he can secure. Always, without exception, verbal phase of continuous union effort to get something for nothing or more for less—more money for less work. See also "Mediation."

INDUSTRIAL DEMOCRACY

Union version: Democratic participation by workers through unions in operating business in accordance with standards of "fairness," "justice," and "equity." *Truth:* Most often involves increase in number of bosses from one—owner of business—to three: owner, union, and third-party arbitrator. Latter frequently knows little or nothing about complexity of operating business enterprise, yet is called upon to make decisions of the utmost consequence. Defies basic common-sense principle that those upon whom responsibility rests must have commensurate authority; confuses and obstructs progress in development of socially desirable personnel policies; accounts for such arrogance as UAW official Paul Carper's declaring a one-day holiday at the Chrysler plant where he was employed in order to participate in morale-building during Perfect Circle strike violence (10364).

JUNGLE LAW AND GOVERNMENT BY INJUNCTION

Union version: Conditions existing when common law gave special privileges to anti-union employers, enabling them to prevent unionization by force and to secure court injunctions against peacefully conducted strikes; at same time holding unions guilty of criminal conspiracies in going about their legitimate business in a peaceful way. *Truth:* Above conditions never existed. Employers could at one time refuse to hire or could fire workers for belonging to a union; they could also refuse to bargain with unions. But they could never use force legally, to resist unionization; when they did use force it was in circumstances such as those presented in Kohler and Perfect Circle strikes or Teamsters' reign of terror in Tennessee. *Further truth:* Common law held that unions had right to pursue legitimate objectives in peaceful and uncoercive way. *Still further truth:* Jungle law conditions may accurately be said to exist when under guise of "human rights" some persons are given special privilege of violently assaulting person and destroying property of other human beings and when, as under present conditions, employers and nonunion employees have no legal protection against destructive and monopolistic boycotts.

LABOR OF A HUMAN BEING IS NOT A COMMODITY

Union version: Wages must not be established in accordance with laws of supply and demand on a free market. Human beings are involved. Rules of competition applicable to purchase and sale of inanimate commodities are, therefore, inappropriate. *Truth:* Foregoing confuses labor of human being with human beings. In free society human beings are not commodities, may not be bought and sold, but their labor must be bought and sold on free market if they are to be free. Only alternative is quasi-serfdom, with wages of labor fixed, without regard to wishes of all workers, by violent and monopolistic action, as in Kohler dispute. *Further truth:* All true union leaders, like Hoffa, recognize duplicity of present entry; all are out to "sell labor at the highest buck they can get." *Final truth:* Present entry is designed by unions mainly to hide from public fact that unions are bent upon exploiting and extorting from defenseless members of society.

LABOR MOVEMENT

Union version: Spontaneous reaction of workers to exploitation by employers; also selfless, public-serving, courageous, and dedicated leadership of trade unions. *Truth:* Rigged imposition of membership in large monopolistic combines known as trade unions upon all employees, willing or not, under carefully deliberated and coercively implemented plans of union leaders determined to secure power or money, or both, not available to those who represent only workers who positively wish representation; not to be confused with small, independent unions, such as Barbers Guild, which actually arise because of wishes of employees and disappear when function of making employers respect interests of workers has been served. *Further truth:* Institutionalized power aggregates concerned essentially with self-perpetuation and self-aggrandizement and bent upon achieving those goals even if all free institutions must be destroyed in process. See also next entry.

Labor Solidarity

Union version: Manifestation of identity of interests of all members of working force as against ineradicably conflicting interest of employers; therefore, by implication, of society-serving character of labor unions, since they are protectors of workers and since workers and their families constitute vast majority of members of society. *Truth:* Reflects one of cardinal Marxian fallacies, fallacy that there are permanent and sharply distinguishable class interests in private-property societies. *Further truth:* There are no material class distinctions at all in private-property societies, let alone permanent and sharply distinguishable class conflicts. Confuses free, private-property societies with feudal or slave societies, in which birth defines future status in society. In free, private-property society, interests of workingmen, a category which covers all who work and produce, including owners of capital and employers, are in a ceaseless flux of formation, revision and dissolution, with employers and employees more frequently having interests in common than in conflict. *Still further truth:* Employee interests conflict as frequently as interests of all human beings do, as in case of members of Sheet Metal Workers against members of United Steelworkers in Burt situation. *Final truth:* Present entry designed by union leaders to disguise fact that much of their power is based upon monopolistic restraints of trade designed to compel a "solidarity" which does

not naturally exist, such as Teamsters helping Journeymen Barbers
to destroy Barbers Guild by suffocating the Waldorf-Astoria.

MEDIATION

Union version: Participation by government officials in collective bargaining; required because of reactionary intransigence
of businessmen who refuse to make moderate and socially beneficial concessions requested by unions. *Truth:* A practice which
reached substantial proportions when federal government was a
stooge for big unions. Growth of mediation encouraged by union
leaders as an additional pressure to secure from employers concessions not otherwise attainable, as when UAW asked government to withhold contracts from Kohler or to help prevent unloading of clay boat. *Example of mediation in action:* Airline
dispute arose when Flight Engineers objected to airline plan to
require pilot licenses of engineers as well as of two pilots in new
jet planes. Engineers' union objected on ground that this plan
would force it to go out of business, since Pilots' union would
naturally serve interests of engineer-pilots. Federal board solved
dispute by conceiving another "bold new idea," namely that of
adding fourth man to control cabin of new jets, three with pilot
licenses and fourth an engineer without pilot license.[3] *Prediction:*
When federal government begins performing its duty to public
in labor disputes, and ceases to aid unions in extorting from
business and public, mediation by government agencies will find
oblivion it richly deserves, from point of view of public interest.

PRODUCTIVITY

Union version: A magical quality which always increases;
though of mysterious origin, probably attributable to unions and
workers; therefore, its material fruits should go preponderantly,
if not exclusively, into pay envelopes of workers represented by
unions, in form of automatic increases, year after year. *Truth:*
Productivity is a function associated with all factors of production
—land, plant, machinery, capital, management, workers. A

[3] *Ibid.,* p. 18, col. 5.

productivity index might be formulated in terms of the ratio of total production of goods and services to any one or more of those factors of production, but in no case would such an index reveal which factor was responsible for the increase, if any (for productivity may and does decrease also). Man-hour (or labor) productivity is the index used because of its arithmetical simplicity —not because all productivity increases are brought about through more and harder work by wage earners. *Further truth:* Common sense would suggest (1) that since worker effort, skill, or devotion to work has not increased notably in last fifty years, general productivity increases are result of capital growth and increasingly rational management and combination of firms; (2) that union action has on the whole brought about productivity decreases since it is usually directed to reducing effort of workers and interfering with management plans for increasing efficiency; and (3) that unless unions desist from such conduct they will universally overcome even the best efforts of management and capital to increase productivity, as they have done in a good many firms where their obstructive conduct has been responsible for bankruptcies. *Still further truth:* A free market, where laws of supply and demand are allowed to work without interference of violence and monopolistic coercion, distributes fruits of increased productivity equitably in accordance with public interest—to all consumers, in form of lower prices; to those who provide capital, in accordance with supply of and demand for capital; to employees, both as consumers and as wage earners, in form of lower prices and higher wages when growth in capital and in purchasing power of public creates additional demand for labor. *Final truth:* Union labor, except that part thrown into unemployment, has in all cases of wage increases secured through violence and monopolistic coercion taken for itself the shares in increased productivity to which consumers and investors are equitably entitled.

PURCHASING POWER

Union version: The key to national prosperity for everyone lies in permitting unions to increase the wages of their members by whatever means are necessary; by such increases, the purchasing power of those members is put to work creating a greater demand for all products, and thus prosperity is spread all round. *Truth:* It does not work that way at all. Professor Chamberlin has put the matter briefly and definitively:

> Whoever receives a higher money income gains relative to others who do not, and there is nothing in the argument to indicate why union laborers any more than anyone else should . . . have the agreeable privilege of mysteriously spreading prosperity in this way. The plain truth is . . . that when any group of laborers receives higher money wages it is thus enabled to buy more goods, so that its real income is increased. Its own higher wages raise the cost and hence the price of the goods it produces, and thus others are able to buy fewer goods, so that the real incomes of others are diminished.[4]

SWEATSHOPS

Union version: Starvation wages and deplorable working conditions would be the permanent condition of workers without unions; they have been ameliorated by trade unions in spite of the resistance of employers. *Truth:* Wages and working conditions are relative concepts, relative to time, place, and wealth. A materially progressive society involves progressive improvement in wages and working conditions, in precisely the same way that it involves progress in all other material respects. Wages in a materially poor society will be relatively inferior to wages in a materially rich society at the same time or to wages in the same society at a later date, if it has progressed in the meanwhile. Wages and working conditions in the United States have been better than elsewhere for a period beginning long before unions achieved any power in this country. This has not been a workers' paradise beginning only in 1930 or even in 1890. Millions upon millions of immigrants came here beginning early in the nineteenth century (when, according to the union version, trade

[4] "The Economic Analysis of Labor Union Power," in *Labor Unions and Public Policy* (Washington, D.C.: American Enterprise Association, 1958), pp. 8–9.

unions were outlawed); they came because, among other things, wages and working conditions were better here. *Further truth:* Wages, hours, and working conditions have been improving steadily in the United States, at about the same rate, since the earliest recorded times. *Still further truth:* If unions were responsible for eliminating sweatshops and low wages, European trade unions, many of them stronger than American trade unions, would have secured for European workers better conditions than prevail here. But the conditions of most European workers, including those in countries with the strongest trade unions, are not much better than those which existed here in the early 1900's. *Final truth:* Unions may no more accurately claim credit for improving working conditions than they may for anything else of general social utility or benefit. Ludwig von Mises has explained the true state of affairs: "The fact that the standard of living of the average American worker is incomparably more satisfactory than that of the average Chinese worker, that in the United States hours of work are shorter and that the children are sent to school and not to the factories is . . . the outcome of the fact that the capital invested per head of the employees is much greater than in China and that consequently the marginal productivity of labor is much higher.[5]

The Truth About Unions

The truth about the big unions is that they have done great social harm in the past and that they constitute at present a threat to our survival as a good and strong nation. Unions have a function to perform, a decidedly useful one; and some unions, especially small unions which have been formed voluntarily by employees, are doing this job ably and well. But the big affiliated unions are not doing the job which there is for unions to do in an enterprise economy. They are not doing that job because their leaders have been intent on other things. In giving union leaders powers and privileges to which no one is entitled, government has caused conditions in the big industry-wide unions which not

[5] *Human Action* (New Haven: Yale University Press, 1949), p. 749.

only critically imperil society, but also drag union leaders farther and farther away from any hope that they will be able to do the job properly, even if they set their minds to it. Everyone is being hurt in the process—nonunion workers, union members, union leaders, unionism itself, businessmen, and finally government and society.

Nonunion workers, as we have seen, have come to be viewed as a kind of fair game; there is always open season on them for union organizers. If they resist union membership, it is shoved down their throats. If they happen to work in a plant where substantial union membership exists, they are told that they have no right to make their own decisions. The law has already taken from them their right to bargain for themselves. Now unions insist that, because they cannot bargain for themselves, they must not exercise any independent judgment at all, not even in respect to one of the most important decisions a workingman makes—that is, whether or not to strike.

Union members are worse off. Those who join unions voluntarily are worse off in only some ways; those who have been forced into unions, in every way. If they have not been reduced to the state of serfdom which prevails in some unions, they are likely to have been exposed in others to a thoroughly antisocial, ruthless philosophy. Self-interest is a law of nature which no amount of socialistic nonsense can eliminate, and it accounts for all the progress mankind has made. But the self-interest preached by most trade unions is a vicious thing. It has gone far toward changing a great many decent American men into brutes. That they are out to get all they can for their labor is not bad in itself. The bad thing is that they are beginning to feel, with their leaders, that the world owes them a living, and that any means necessary to securing that living, however hallucinatorily they conceive it, are appropriate. Fortunately, this development has not gone far as yet. The union leaders still need goons in most areas, because the morals and values of the working union members have not been corrupted totally. But of all the tendencies created by the current pattern of trade-union power, this one ranks among the most ominous.

The development of industry-wide unions under the special privileges which now prevail is making the job of the top union leadership a hopeless one. Concurrently, the operation of Gresham's law is complicating things still further. Left to develop naturally, there will be a considerable variety in the productivity and hence in the wages and working conditions from one firm to another and from one industry to another. Such variety can never be eliminated in a market economy, because a market economy is nothing but the free action of the various participants in economic activity, and the variety in economic activity will reflect the inborn variety in men. But industry-wide unionism attempts to fix upon this living thing an iron rigidity, and the results are foul and unnatural. Unions not only expect all firms in the same industry to provide closely similar wages and working conditions; the tendency under industry-wide unionism is to pit the leader of one industry-wide union against the leaders of all the others. This is a sure way to encourage union leaders to make fools of themselves, to ask for more and more special privilege, and to corrupt government still further and on still higher levels. If General Motors has had a good year, Chrysler may have had a bad year; if General Electric has had a good year, Westinghouse may have had a bad one. If all the auto companies have had a bad year, the steel companies may have had a good one. Yet, the pressure of prominence makes it necessary for top union leaders to strive for equal concessions from all. This can only result in violence, wasteful strikes, and what may be even worse—large-scale unemployment in industries which have been forced to make wage concessions which not all firms can afford. The United Mine Workers secured a tremendous wage increase in 1958, but at a tremendous cost. It has created still more unemployment in mining, still more misery, and still more ghost towns in the coal mining country.[6]

The special privileges which trade unions have acquired are at work, as we have seen, inviting bad and antisocial men into the unions and driving out the decent men. This development, together with the one just sketched, is transmogrifying trade unionism from the socially useful form of voluntary association

[6] *The New York Times,* January 11, 1959, p. 1, col. 2.

that it might have been, had unions been subject to the same rules of civilization which apply to all other voluntary associations, into a vast, multi-faceted engine of antisocial destruction. Today's trade-unionism covers almost the whole spectrum of subversion: from purely criminal racketeering, to the habitual use of violence, to the regimentation of industry, to the propagation of theories and doctrines which would substitute the laughable fallacies of Marxism for the grand truths in the discovery of which Western civilization has achieved its greatest glory.

If current trends in trade unionism are allowed to continue, precisely the same total corruption will infect American industry. The beginnings are already apparent. The strength of unions is already such in many industries that they may decide who is to remain in business and who is to be expunged. Shakedowns have long been a widespread practice in some industries; the next step in those industries involves taking over the businesses instead of shaking them down. This process is already in motion in a good many industries. As it spreads, thugs and racketeers will infest industry as they now infest the trade unions. When that happens, the material progress which has been one of America's two greatest contributions to civilization will come to an end.

The second major American contribution, its Constitution, will come to an end at the same time. For thoroughgoing corruption of business can come about only as a result of the complete failure of government to do its duty. So long as government does its job of preventing vicious aggression by trade unions, there will be a sufficient number of stouthearted businessmen to resist the pressures and the monopolistic blandishments of trade-union leaders or of any other subversive influences. There are fools and subversives among businessmen, too. But take them by and large, and man for man, they are the best, most intelligent, and most productive citizens in the country. They are selected out for those qualities. They have to be good in order to survive the rigors of the competition which remains in spite of the many unwise and anticompetitive laws and practices which government has been dumping on the nation as a result of pressure-group politicking. The trade-union leaders boast today that they have the Congress in their pockets, and they intend to seek even further special privileges from it. But the duty of any Congress, regardless of party, is to the whole nation, and the interests of the whole nation require immediate revocation of the special privileges which, coming from the federal government, have created the conditions revealed by the McClellan investigation.

The truth about the big industry-wide trade unions is that they threaten the health, the well-being, and the survival of American society to a degree never before approached by either internal or external enemies. They are spreading corruption of every kind and at every level: corruption of truth and of ideas; moral corruption; corruption of business; and corruption of government. Freedom is the victim, freedom as an idea and freedom as a way of life. Trade unions, organizations which can exist only in a free society, continuously assault the very idea and practice which gives them existence, for the right of free and voluntary association is what creates trade unions, and it is the principal target of their attacks. They insist that no worker has an ironclad right not to join a union; that every employer who exercises his freedom to resist unionization by lawful means must be exterminated; that every politician or judge who protects these freedoms is incompetent to hold office.

*   *   *

The problem is now, I believe, in perfect focus. Freedom, the supreme value of Western civilization, is the supreme target of the trade-union attack. The question is whether America is willing to fight in defense of freedom.

Sperthias and Bulis—and Freedom

Men who have been born free and lived all their lives in freedom must make the same strenuous effort to value it as those who have never known freedom. Men who, once knowing liberty, have suffered tyranny, more readily assess the true worth of freedom. The victims of Teamster tyranny declared

themselves against the compulsory unionism which, with violence, had made serfs of them (1758, 1841). Karl A. Wittfogel
loves freedom, too, for he has suffered the worst tyranny, one of
Hitler's concentration camps, and out of this love, and this experience, and the resources of his learning, he has written a great
monument to freedom, the book *Oriental Despotism*.[7] He tells in
the preface how his belief in freedom put him behind "the
barbed wire of Hitler's concentration camps." And then he
continues:

> My final thoughts go to those who, like myself, were
> passing through that inferno of total terror.

Some asked him, he said,

> if ever opportunity offered, to explain to all who would
> listen the inhumanity of totalitarian rule in any form.
> Over the years and more than I can express, these men have
> inspired my search for a deeper understanding of the nature
> of total power.

Professor Wittfogel ends his book with the story of Sperthias
and Bulis, as recorded in The Seventh Book of Herodotus. Sperthias and Bulis were wealthy Spartans who had volunteered
to sacrifice themselves to Xerxes. Professor Wittfogel tells the
rest of the story:

> On their way to Suza, the Spartan envoys were met by
> Hydarnes, a high Persian official, who offered to make them
> mighty in their homeland, if only they would attach them-
> selves to the Great King, his despotic master. To the benefit
> of Greece—and to the benefit of all free men—Herodotus
> has preserved their answer:

> "Hydarnes," they answered, "thou art a one-sided coun-
> selor. Thou hast experience of half the matter; but the
> other half is beyond thy knowledge. A slave's life thou
> understandest; but, never having tasted liberty, thou canst
> not tell whether it be sweet or no. Ah! hadst thou known
> what freedom is, thou wouldst have bidden us fight for it,
> not with the spear only, but with the battle-axe!"

[7] (New Haven: Yale University Press, 1957).

Chapter 12

SUMMARY AND
RECOMMENDATIONS

*. . . the plain facts are that for anyone concerned with
the preservation of free institutions the power position
of labor has become truly ominous, that it has gone
largely unrecognized, and that it cries out for analysis
from a truly public, as distinct from a labor point of
view.*

—Edward H. Chamberlin

The industry-wide trade unions stand revealed by the Record as the greatest threat to its security and well-being that America has ever known. No nation can safely tolerate the multiple threats to its health and integrity which those unions pose here and now. It is not so much a matter of the peril from the Soviet dictatorship. The critical danger from that source lies mainly in the possibility that the more panicky in our population may turn us into the monster we are fighting; for they unceasingly induce us to accept the very policies of omnipotent government which account for the basic backwardness of Soviet Russia.

No, America has less cause to fear Russia than Russia has to fear us. Ours is the stronger and the more enduring system. If we fall, it will be from internal corruption. And the powers and privileges accorded to the industry-wide cartels which call themselves trade unions will be among the principal causes of the collapse.

But we need not fall. And we need not abandon the basic principles of personal freedom and the rule of law in order to remedy the illness which is now in course. On the contrary, those principles, the same ones which made this a great country, will restore its health. For it is their absence, in labor relations, which accounts for the disease. If they are maintained we will be free and strong, both economically and militarily, for military strength is but a by-product of economic power.

Facts, Consequences, and Causes

The Record shows that trade unions have been guilty of abusing union and nonunion workers alike; that they have been extorting from and shaking down employers; and that they have been weakening the basic institutions of society by spreading a subversive philosophy, by corrupting public officials in accordance with that philosophy, and by vituperative attacks and large-scale political action against public officials who resist their subversion. It shows finally that unions are destroying the competitive enterprise system by imposing upon it a rigid monopolistic structure, to the infinite abuse of the public, and to the great national peril. Our survival is at stake.

America's social philosophy, the sweet and pure refinement of the best thought and hardest experience of two thousand years of Western civilization, has created the political and economic institutions which account for its greatness. The political institutions have been: *first,* limited government, directed essentially to keeping the peace, to defending all against physical attack upon their persons, and to protecting the property rights necessary to freedom; and *second,* the rule of law, the principle which holds that the rules of society shall apply equally to everyone, that the courts of law shall ever be open to those who have been injured, to give them the best and swiftest remedies known to legal procedure.

These principles have put a premium on excellence and have discouraged aggression. They have encouraged the able and thus prevented stasis and stagnation. The result has been the most flexible, most powerful, and most productive economic and social system the world has ever known. America has been a land of opportunity for all. It has shown the world that the accident of humble birth need not be a bar to any of the kinds of success which men value, material or spiritual. For more than fifty years it has demonstrated an ability to arm itself more powerfully while at the same time providing greater personal freedom and a far higher standard of living than any other nation.

AMERICA AND RUSSIA

America, Western civilization's protagonist and the strongest nation the world has ever known, is now in a struggle with Communist Russia, the physical embodiment of the most corrupt social, political, and economic thought and action—Marxist socialism—the world has ever known. Lenin once said that it would not be necessary for Soviet Russia to conquer America by force of arms. Only patience was needed, he said, for the day would come when internal corruption would cause America to fall, like a ripe fruit, into the waiting hands of the Russian dictatorship.

America may fall like a ripe fruit, but not necessarily into the waiting hands of the Russian dictatorship, for the power and viability of that system have yet to be proved. The Soviet dictatorship has shown thus far a great capacity only for noise and propaganda. It has not yet shown that it could defeat any strong nation in an armed struggle, without overwhelming and critical outside assistance, mainly from us. The Germans alone were whipping the Communists, while holding off the rest of the world, till we came to the rescue with the arms provided by a supposedly decadent capitalism.

The Communists have not been able to raise the standard of living of the Russian people over that which prevailed under the relatively primitive and mediaeval economic system of the czars, despite substantial technological assistance from Americans before World War II and from captured Germans after the war, and despite the large-scale banditry it practiced upon nations, such as Germany, Austria, and Poland, conquered in World War II. To the Communist excuses of the brevity of their period of power and of wartime destruction, ready and definitive answers are available. They have been in power for more than forty years. America has, during *any* forty-year period of its history which may be chosen, dramatically increased its standard of living, without murdering and enslaving millions of its people in order to do so. Moreover, Western Germany suffered destruction at least the equal of Russia's, during World War II, and its standard of living has risen more during any twelve-month period since the war than Russia's has in the whole forty years since 1919.

The Soviet dictatorship has produced nuclear weapons and dramatic rocketry, thunder and lightning. Whether it could have produced even these without help from corrupted American traitors, on the one hand, and captured German scientists, on the other, will never be known. Let us suppose that it could; these would still be but a pitiful product for a nation of over two hundred million, especially when one considers that the Russian people themselves have for hundreds of years produced great geniuses in the arts and the sciences.

The Real Nature of the Threat to America

A free and therefore strong America has little to fear from other nations, Russia included. The threat to America is the threat of internal corruption, and the philosophy of some trade-union leaders and the action of all the big industry-wide trade unions are major components of that threat. That philosophy, when translated into the kind of action revealed in the Mc-Clellan Record, will, if unchecked, destroy the political and economic system which embodies America's freedom and produces its greatness. We are having difficulty competing in world markets now, solely because of our inflated labor costs in basic industries. The same costs, despite fantastic taxes, are putting adequate armament out of reach. The Soviet dictatorship will be a real threat to us when the big unions make arms so costly that we cannot afford them.

It makes no difference at all that some of the leaders of the American unions are vocally anti-Communist, for example, Walter Reuther. It does not make any real difference, either, that some are sincerely and dedicatedly anti-Communist, for example, George Meany. What counts is the real effect of present trade-union thinking and action upon the real events and real life of America.

Although Communists have no idea of how to build a great nation, never having had any experience in building or helping to build one, they do know a great deal about the processes which destroy nations, for that is the area of their greatest experience. Senator Goldwater performed a service for the American public, therefore, when he read into the McClellan Record the opinion of these experts as to the contribution of the trade-union leaders, both socialist and nonsocialist, to the hoped-for transformation of America from a free and strong nation to a rotten-apple, mediocre copy of the Soviet prototype. In this quotation from the United States Communist Party Convention, the reader must remember that Communist jargon uses the words "social democracy" to describe what we call "totalitarian dictatorship":

> To a degree the cooperation of labor reformists (trade union leaders who stand for capitalism and with no socialist background or traditions), social reformists (those labor leaders like Dubinsky, Reuther, Randolph, et cetera, who have a socialist background), and bourgeois reformists (liberal wing of the Democratic Party) in such organizations as Americans for Democratic Action is, in the absence of a mass social democratic party in the United States, and under the conditions prevailing in our country, performing the function of social democracy. (3706)

The language is characteristically devious, and the syntax characteristically tortured. Put simply, the Communists are saying that the big trade unions and their leaders, socialists and antisocialists alike, are helping to destroy America as a free nation. To repeat, this is expert testimony. Communists are professionals in destruction. Their time is spent exclusively in the fervid study and practice of the demolition of societies. When they say that the trade unions are performing the function of destroying the freedom and productivity of America, therefore, they are entitled to the most serious attention. On this subject, and on this alone, they know what they are talking about.

UNEMPLOYMENT, INFLATION, DESTRUCTION

Little need be added at this point on the kind of corruption at all levels which we have witnessed in the preceding chapters, especially Chapter 7. But we must bear in mind that moral and political corruption of the varieties recounted there rot integrity at all levels and thus weaken the fibre of society, making it prone to further corruption of a million kinds in a million ways, every day. Nonunion men treated brutally as outlaws and union members as serfs, the infiltration of unions by professional gangsters, extortion from businessmen, bribery and corruption of public officials, the theory that trade unions are *entitled* to special privileges from government—no society can survive much of that for very long.

All these put together, however, probably do not equal and certainly do not exceed the danger inherent in the necessary course of monopolistic unionism. As much as trade unions may protest their virtue and distort the truth, it is the opinion of the most competent economists in this country, and of the greatest economists in the world, that monopolistic trade unionism will destroy any free enterprise system if it is allowed to proceed unchecked. Many of America's ranking economists have come to more or less this same conclusion—Fritz Machlup, Milton Friedman, David McCord Wright, Edward H. Chamberlin, Philip Bradley, Henry C. Simons, and many others of equal ability and disinterested devotion to truth.[1] Their conclusions are shared by economists of unsurpassed international reputation, including Friedrich A. Hayek and Wilhelm Roepke, as well as

[1] For some of the books in which these men have expressed their conclusions and explained their reasoning, see: Henry C. Simons, *Economic Policy for a Free Society* (Chicago: The University of Chicago Press, 1948), pp. 121 ff.; Fritz Machlup, *The Political Economy of Monopoly* (Baltimore: The Johns Hopkins Press, 1952), pp. 333 ff.; David McCord Wright (ed.), *The Impact of the Union* (New York: Harcourt, Brace & Co., Inc., 1951) (containing a paper by Professor Friedman); *Labor Unions and Public Policy* (Washington, D.C.: American Enterprise Association, 1958) (which carries the articles by Professors Chamberlin and Bradley cited elsewhere in this book). See also Charles Lindblom, *Unions and Capitalism* (New Haven: Yale University Press, 1949).

the man who has in our time achieved the greatest stature of all in the social sciences, in my opinion, Professor Ludwig von Mises.[2]

All these men agree, not only as to the fact, but as to the process by means of which trade unions will, if unchecked, bring about the destruction of the free society. First, compulsory membership leading to dictatorial control of all workers; second, through the ensuing monopolistic regimentation of all industry, the securing of wage structures higher than the market will bear; third, in inevitable consequence, drastic and severe unemployment of great numbers of workers; fourth, clamorous insistence that government, through deficit spending, create jobs and other subsidies for the men thrown into unemployment by the union monopolies; fifth, loose money policies by the monetary arm of a government politically committed to "full employment" policies; sixth, a crack-up inflation; seventh, consequent mangling of the lives of all those who have attempted to save; eighth, increasing chaos and dislocation; ninth, the rise of vicious demagogues playing upon the confusion, chaos, and dissatisfaction of the populace to secure for themselves dictatorial powers which permit them to apply totalitarian remedies which the Constitution of the United States inhibits; tenth, dissolution into the jungle.[3]

The Record, as we have seen, bears out many steps in the process. But because it covers only a short span of time and because its scope did not extend to examination of intimately related governmental policies, it could not show the various steps together in respect to any of the unions under investigation. Besides, the Committee did not investigate at all the union and the industry which are most revealing in terms of this process of dissolution.

[2] One of the chapters of Professor Friedrich A. Hayek's forthcoming book, *The Constitution of Liberty*, is a masterful analysis and summation of the opinion of economists as to the consequences of unlimited union power. Professor Mises' great work is *Human Action* (New Haven: Yale University Press, 1949), although he deals with the destructive tendencies of monopolistic trade-unionism also in *Socialism* (New Haven: Yale University Press, 1951), pp. 457–84.

[3] See Mises, *Socialism*, pp. 457–500.

The most revealing example is that of the United Mine Workers and the soft-coal industry. The United Mine Workers —led, incidentally, by one of the most sincere, vigorous, and eloquent anti-Communists in the country, John L. Lewis—has already gone through many of the steps. A study of its history will reveal it guilty of organizing nonunion workers by a reign of terror, violence, and brutality easily the equal of those of the Teamsters and the UAW. It has imposed the equivalent of martial law in the territory of its sovereignty against all outlaws and rebels, whether workers or employers. It has totally regimented the industry and has thereby secured wage increases far beyond those which would otherwise have been forthcoming. The necessary consequences have been forthcoming, too—vast and permanent unemployment for hundreds of thousands of miners; poverty, sordidness, and misery for the small towns in the mining country; and anguished cries for government subsidies.

In 1958, the United Mine Workers secured another remarkable increase, and already the predictable results are occurring. An article by Homer Bigart [4] states that "mines have been shutting down at a steady pace"; that "more shutdowns are threatened by operators who said they could not meet the wage increases under the new agreement with the United Mine Workers"; that a state of emergency has been declared in some counties; that "13,056 persons were destitute" in Harlan County; that "miners hunted in vain for work in near-by towns"; that, according to local officials "people will be robbing and stealing for food"; and that, finally, with the exhaustion of existing doles and subsidies from federal, state, and local governments, cries for more governmental assistance were already being raised.

A savage war could scarcely cause more chaos. The United Mine Workers secured a two-dollar a day increase in 1958 for

[4] *The New York Times,* January 11, 1959, p. 1, cols. 2–3. The social demolitionists who call themselves socialists immediately seized upon Mr. Bigart's story as proof that *free enterprise* was failing. In a story captioned with the blaring headline, "A Preview of Capitalist Crisis," they attributed the desolation caused by the UMW in the mining towns to free enterprise. As usual, they could understand the destructiveness of the facts, but not the true causes. See *Weekly People,* January 24, 1959, p. 1, cols. 2–5.

some workers, bringing wages to about twenty-five dollars per day. But as a consequence, others earn nothing, the public pays more and ever more for coal and therefore buys less and ever less, so that fewer and fewer miners are employed while more and more become destitute. Mr. Bigart reports Jim Angel, father of seventeen children, as saying:

> I'll be starved to death in a year if I don't get work.
> I got young 'uns here so I don't want to work for nothing.
> But if a job paid twelve or fifteen dollars a day I'd grab
> that and run with it.[5]

At twelve or fifteen dollars a day, all the miners thrown out of employment by the United Mine Workers in the last thirty years would be able to get jobs again in the mines in the country where they were born and raised. The price of coal would drop sharply if the present twenty-five dollar per day wages were lowered. Moreover, the consuming public would be able to buy so much more coal, and so much more of the production which is based upon power and energy supplied by coal, if the price of coal were thus reduced, that there would be a shortage of workers in the coal field, instead of the calamitous surplus now existing.

The Causes

Violence, extortion, and widespread corruption are the facts disclosed by the Record. The probable consequences are destruction of the economic system and social deterioration, if these conditions are permitted to continue. To correct the conditions and to forestall their probable consequences, it is necessary to remove their causes; treating the superficialities will do no good.

There is no mystery as to the causes. No one can read the McClellan Record without having them leap to the mind. The causes lie in the special privileges which governments have given trade unions and which the public has tolerated. These

[5] *The New York Times,* January 11, 1959, p. 40.

special privileges are violence and monopolistic compulsion. No one in society has such privileges, except trade unions; and only trade unions are infected with the breadth and depth of corruption with which the McClellan Record reeks. Not even the blindest and most prejudiced person can deny the association thus exposed.

These special privileges draw *to* trade unions the worst kinds of men, and they drive *from* trade unions the best kinds of men. They make trade unions vehicles of money and power, without requiring in return any contribution to society. On the contrary, the money and the power become the greater the more society and all its working members are abused. The premium, then, is upon obstruction and destruction, not production. No wonder the results have been what they have been. If the power and the glory of the leaders of the industry-wide monopolies called trade unions depend upon the degree of their success in extorting from the public, they will continue in the future, as they have in the past, to exact as much money as they can for as little production as possible. The results will always be catastrophic unemployment. Government attempts to compensate with inflationary monetary policies can only bring about ultimate destruction. Our inflated labor costs are already pricing us out of world markets. Soon they will destroy us as a military power, for we shall not be able to pay the costs of adequate armament.

The causes must be removed if we are to survive as a good, free, and productive society. They must be removed, probably, if we are to survive at all.

The Argument Against Reform

In the face of the overwhelming and devastating dangers to the country posed by *all* industry-wide unions, their leaders contend that no case for basic reform has been made. They have not bothered to advance any serious argument in support of that contention. They apparently feel that they do not have to argue the point, and thus they apparently consider the nation so supine and so corrupt that its integrity is dissolved, its perceptions blunted, and even its will to self-preservation dead. Whether or not their opinion of the nation is accurate remains to be seen.

While the opponents of reform have made no serious argument in support of their position, upon occasion one or another has said something to the effect that "since the McClellen Committee investigated only six or seven of the international unions and only an infinitesimally small fraction of the 70,000 local unions, obviously it could not disclose accurately the conditions prevailing in all international and local unions."

The trouble with such observations is that no matter how often they are reiterated, they miss the point. In the first place, had the Committee examined all the nation's big unions there is the strongest reason to believe that it would have found exactly the same violent and monopolistic conduct in most that it found in the unions which it did investigate. The court records in the multitudes of reported cases involving practically all the big unions are as revealing as—*and even more reliable and authoritative than*—the McClellan Record. Those records show precisely the same kind of violent and monopolistic conduct on the part of practically all industry-wide unions as the McClellan Record shows on the part of the unions it covered.

In the second place, even if all the big unions were not guilty of violent and monopolistic conduct, it would not follow that such conduct should not be prohibited. For if prohibited, the innocent unions would not be affected at all, just as honest men are not hampered by the laws against robbery. Things have got pretty bad when it becomes necessary to point out, as Senator Ives had to point out to Mr. Reuther at the hearings, that all law aims to control the conduct of a lawless minority, "never the overwhelming group." (10044) The laws against murder, robbery, and fraud are not repealed merely because most people do not commit those crimes. Those laws are enforceable, as a matter of fact, to the degree that they are enforceable, only because the vast majority of people are decent and honest, or because they value decency and honesty in the abstract.

It would be wrong for Congress to pass punitive laws, placing greater burdens on union leaders than other citizens have, on the basis of the McClellan Record, or of any other record. But so long as the laws which Congress enacts only apply the same rules to unions which all others have to obey, then the fact that the McClellan Committee did not investigate all unions is of no significance whatsoever. Congress did not investigate all employers before enacting the Wagner Act, the Sherman Act, the Federal Trade Commission Act—or any other legislation designed to discourage them from conduct of which Congress and the public disapproved. The unions are only revealing here again their determination to get special favors and special privileges wherever they can.

The great contribution of the McClellan Record lies in its irrefutable demonstration that, of all citizens or entities, unions least of all deserve any special privileges or favors from society. They are infested with sneaks and cheats and robbers and thugs and subversives. They are, even the so-called legitimate unions, callously indifferent to the true welfare of the whole working population. All of them have shown at one time or another a vicious disregard for the interests of anyone but themselves. They may talk piously, but they have yet to show any consideration for others.

Unions are entitled to the right to strike, but they have abused that right to a degree unknown in any other segment of the population, calling strikes which should never have been called at all, and prolonging others disastrously beyond all reason. They would not even abide by an agreement to waive strikes during wartime. If the public had vividly before it the grim record of the vicious and subversive strikes called by unions during the war, it would make short shrift of the appeals of the unions for continuation of the special privilege to destroy the nation and its most precious institutions.

The normal American penchant for quick indignation and almost as rapid forgetfulness must be eschewed in the present case. The stakes are too high. Punitive legislation is always bad legislation. Passed in a huff, it is observed over the long run mainly in the breach. Even though unions have abused their basic rights as no other citizens have done, they must be allowed to keep them.

* * *

The job before us, as Americans, is to ponder carefully on the kind of country we want, and then to judge whether the violent and monopolistic conduct of trade unions is acceptable. If it is a jungle that we want, then let the present special privileges of trade unions prevail, for they will bring us to the jungle far more quickly than the Russians will. But if it is a good society that we want, then the special privileges must be removed.

* * *

I believe that Americans, including American legislators, wish to have a good society, and that they will therefore support the removal of the destructive special privileges which trade unions now possess. In affirmation of that belief, I offer the proposals which follow.

What Not To Do

Punitive laws enacted in a spirit of retaliation for the evils disclosed in the McClellan Record would be undesirable on all counts. They would be neither just nor effective nor practical. They would not serve the long-run public interest, either. The nation's true interest lies in re-instituting with vigor the rule of law. In order to do this, it is necessary only to withdraw the special privileges which unwise policy and administration have given trade unions: the policies and the administration of law which permit and encourage unions to engage in the violent and monopolistic regimentation allowed to no other person or entity in society.

ACCOUNTING FOR PERSONAL EXPENDITURES

Some thoroughly unsound proposals have already been advanced. It has been suggested, for example, that every union official be compelled to account for all personal expenditures, including those of his wife, if any, and of other members of his family. Not much need be said about this absurd idea. It would require an enormous number of persons to audit the accounts. More important, it is such a rank insult to the union officials who are fair and decent men that it would hasten the exodus of such men from unions. Finally, its absurdity and unfairness would mean, first, evasion, and, second, no enforcement. The problem of the thieving union official is best solved by enforcing present laws against robbery and embezzlement and those requiring union officials to act as the trustees and fiduciaries which their position makes them. Those laws have not so far been enforced, as shown in Chapters 9 and 10, because union members, whose cooperation is absolutely vital to enforcement, have hesitated to act owing to fear of their lives or their jobs. If unions are prevented from controlling jobs, they will not be so attractive to the thugs who are prone to use physical violence and to steal. Freed of such men and such fears, union members will no longer be virtual slaves accepting silently the abusive conduct of their leaders. More important, a healthy trend in the process of selection of union leaders will replace the present one —instead of the bad men driving out the good ones, decent and honest men will begin replacing the crooks, the thugs, and the prisoners of the power-lust.

POLITICAL CONTRIBUTIONS

The same is true of proposals to tighten the present law forbidding political contributions and expenditures by unions. The thing to do with that law is to repeal it. Existing decisions of the courts demonstrate that it is unenforceable, for all practical purposes. Moreover, it is the basic right of every voluntary organization to engage in political action, and the right of every man to spend his money for that purpose. The trouble with political expenditures by unions today is that they are not now voluntary associations; members may not quit paying dues to them without fear of loss of their jobs, even though they are deeply opposed to the union's political action. If the special privilege of compulsion which unions now possess is erased, unions will become voluntary associations, as corporations are, since stockholders are free to sell their stock at will. Then prohibition of political contributions, since it is both unsound in principle and unworkable in practice, may be repealed.

Voting by Replaced Strikers

The unions have long been seeking repeal of the present rule—found in Section 9 (c) (3) of the Taft-Hartley Act—which forbids voting by replaced strikers in representation elections. As pointed out in Chapters 8 and 9, this provision is not only manifestly just and fair, on the same theory that makes residents of New York City ineligible to vote in the municipal elections in Chicago; it also constitutes an indispensable check upon the arrogant abuse of the power of trade-union leaders to throw men out of work. The right to strike must be maintained, if we are to remain a free society. But the social interest manifestly requires that this right not be abused. Any provision which will discourage such abuse without transgressing upon the right to strike is an exceedingly valuable one. Section 9 (c) (3) is such a provision. It must therefore be maintained.

Supervisors

Not satisfied with their present powers to regiment industry and to share control of business with its owners, the unions have been seeking also to acquire dominion over supervisors. The present law does not forbid supervisors to organize. It merely provides that true supervisory personnel, who are agents of management, may be discharged if employers find them more interested in promoting unionization than in applying employer policies. If unions are permitted to dominate supervisors, there can be no doubt that existing evils will be magnified. The present law should be maintained.

The Closed Shop and State Law

The Taft-Hartley Act in Section 14 (b) specifically empowers the various states to prohibit all forms of compulsory unionism, including those forms permitted by federal law. Nineteen states have availed themselves of the power to do so.

A proper reading of the U.S. Constitution would suggest that the power of the states to prohibit all forms of compulsory unionism does not depend upon a specific grant by the federal legislature. That power is, rather, inherent in the sovereign power of the states to protect their citizens from corrupt and criminal abuse. The McClellan Record reveals to all who have clear vision that compulsory unionism is the principal cause of corruption and maladministration of unions; it draws into unions the kind of men who abuse union members, and takes from the members any real power to rid themselves of the looters. Therefore, every state has the constitutional power to prohibit compulsory unionism—under a fair and unprejudiced reading of the Constitution.

Chicago racketeers found Texas unions far less prone to their infiltration than they had found Illinois unions. Texas permits no form of compulsory unionism, while the most extreme forms prevail in Illinois. Senator Curtis did not miss the point. He associated the impenetrability to criminals of the Texas unions with the Texas Right-to-Work Law (12522). There is every reason to believe that he was correct in doing so. Therefore, all state right-to-work laws should be considered constitutionally valid police measures, quite apart from Section 14 (b). But until the Supreme Court abandons, or is compelled to abandon, its spurious pre-emption doctrine, the good of the nation requires the preservation of the section.

Union Democracy

A complete failure to understand the meaning of the Mc-Clellan Record is betrayed by those who would "correct" the evils there disclosed by making unions operate "democratically." Nothing emerges more clearly from a sober analysis of the Record than the conclusion that there is no future in that approach to reform. If the reader will refer to Chapter 6 of this book, where the relevant parts of the Record are covered, he will find that the true problem is, not how to secure democratic *forms,* but how to make honesty and democracy realities in all unions, as they are now in some. Senator Goldwater pointed out that the constitutions of most unions, like the constitution of Soviet Russia, are models of democratic form. Yet in both totalitarian despotism is found.

The causes of corruption in the badly run unions lie elsewhere. Summarized, they are: (1) the dragooning of vast numbers of workers into trade unions by violence and coercion; (2) the use of further violence and coercion in the form of job control to silence their complaints; (3) the consequent domination of national conventions by local henchmen of the top union dictators; and (4) the rubber-stamping, always pursuant to democratic *forms,* of the manipulations of the mighty. Attendance at local union meetings is as small as it is in many unions because dragooned workers have no real interest in attending, in the first place, and because it is safer to stay away, in the second place. The meetings, while satisfying the formal requirements of "democracy," are really designed to re-inforce the power plays of the looters and the despots. Those members who insist upon "putting in their two cents" soon learn better.

Statutory insistence upon democratic *forms* will not correct those conditions. Only excision of the special privileges which draw the looters and their bullies to trade unions will do the job. There is another very important side to the story. Some unions are well run. Why should they have to revise their procedures, as they would undoubtedly have to do should Congress pass a detailed statute regulating the internal affairs of trade unions? Such a statute would hit all unions alike, the ones which are decently operated internally, as well as the racketeering unions. The chances are very good that the well-run unions would be hurt more than the badly run unions would be corrected.

The well-run unions would in many instances be compelled to revise procedures which they have evolved naturally and which they have learned to handle smoothly. The badly run unions would probably evade the law. There are over 70,000 local unions in this country. At least 70,000 federal agents, and more probably a quarter of a million, would be required to police their activities daily in order to do any kind of a detailed job of supervision—so long as the basic causes of the drift to unions of thugs and racketeers remain. Naturally, such supervision is out of the question. It would never be forthcoming. A law imposing "union democracy" would therefore amount to a fraud upon the American public and upon the thousands of union members who have written letters to the Committee describing the hideous abuses and compulsions to which they have been subjected.

Such regulation would never work because it is bad in principle. Genuinely voluntary associations ought to be allowed to run their internal affairs in any manner they please. Social clubs, churches, business organizations, bar associations—none of these have any of the kind of trouble revealed in the McClellan Record. They do not have such trouble because they are genuinely voluntary associations which have practiced no violence or monopolistic compulsion either in securing members or in keeping them after they have become members. The "union democracy" proposal is bad in principle because it constitutes an implicit condonation of the compulsory character of trade unions; it amounts to an approval of their transmogrification from voluntary to compulsory associations. That is the root of the evil. The thing to do with the root of an evil of such magnitude is not to approve and build more evil upon it, but to extirpate it.

Unions can become genuinely voluntary associations if the law will but withdraw the special privileges of compulsion which they have enjoyed. That is the honest and effective thing to do —the only way in which unions now guilty of socially destructive abuses will become *and stay* clean. Union members will then be their own guardians and policemen, day in and day out, and they will have an effective shield with which to defend themselves against exploitation—the refusal to pay dues to those who abuse them.

When consumers do not like the goods they are getting from one businessman, they are not compelled to quit consuming; they are not even compelled to quit consuming the goods in question: they have the freedom to switch to a competitor's product. When stockholders do not like the way their company is being managed, they are not compelled to quit being stockholders; they are not even compelled to move their equities out of either the industry or the company in which their holdings lie: they may without fear of violence or monopolistic compulsion challenge their management or switch to a competing management.

Consumers and stockholders are in this good position because the area in which they operate is free of the special privileges of violence and monopolistic compulsion prevailing in trade unionism. If the conditions in trade unionism are to be brought up to the level of the conditions prevailing among the genuinely voluntary associations of this country, it is perfectly clear that the same principles and laws must apply to trade unions which apply to all voluntary associations. Trade unions must be changed from compulsory associations into voluntary associations. When that change is made, they will no longer be the happy hunting ground of the lustful despots which they now are. They will cease then to be, also, the threat to the future of America which they now are.

Remedies

Never has there been so powerful a case for the removal of special privilege as the one made by the McClellan Record. From every point of view, except that of those who would reduce civilization to a jungle, the case for the removal of the trade unions' special privileges is overwhelming. Workers, union and nonunion men alike; consumers; businessmen; good union leaders; men of politics; society—all would benefit. Again, the principles and institutions which have accounted for the growth of America into a good and great nation require it. The special privileges which trade unions have enjoyed cannot be squared with either the material welfare or the spiritual integrity of the nation. A strong case could be made for imposing tighter restrictions upon unions than apply to other private associations. The case for applying the same rules to them as apply to all others is imperative.

VIOLENCE

Strike Violence: Mass Picketing. As Senator Kennedy said during the Kohler hearings, "it does not seem [that] there is any defense of mass picketing." And no one can disagree with his refusal to concede that there is "any justification for a minority or even a majority to place themselves in such a position that others cannot do what they desire to do." (8673) Federal and state law should therefore provide that, during lawful strikes called by majority unions, not more than two observers are permitted to attend at the scene of a labor dispute.

The Job of the Police. The prohibition of mass picketing will, if enforced, considerably reduce the total job of the police—the job which is physically impossible to accomplish when great angry mobs are allowed to gather. The aid of the legal system is required, however, if the ban on mass picketing is to release the police to perform its other vital jobs during strikes.

The Job of the Law. The job of the law is to punish severely the unions and union leaders who defy the mass picketing ban. Unions and union leaders should be held responsible for any violence or obstruction of access to struck premises which occurs in connection with mass picketing, without requiring direct proof of instruction or authorization. That, incidentally, places no special burden upon unions. It is the rule of law, and always has been, in respect of all other members of society in the principal-agent relationship.

The Job of the Public. If the public prefers civilization to the jungle, it must begin to insist upon government's doing its basic job—the job of keeping the peace—rather than wasting the public's money and its own efforts on multitudes of activities which have nothing to do with keeping the peace but which, instead, are a vexation to, and an enormous burden, tax-wise, on good and honest citizens. It must ask governments to spend a greater share of their fantastic tax revenues upon the proper work of government and less upon wasteful interferences with peaceful and productive activity. There should be many more police, and much higher pay for all police. The men who perform the hazardous policing work necessary to preserve civilization should be among the higher paid, not among the lower paid, members of the society which they preserve and defend. It is sinful, in every sense of the word, that police officers are paid less than truck drivers. The public must remember that one gets what one pays for, here as elsewhere.

Furtive Crime and Violence. The kind of furtive crime and violence involved in the Kohler vandalism, in the Teamsters' organizing campaigns, and in connection with internal union affairs cannot be directly dealt with further than it is by present law. All such conduct is now unlawful. Existing law enforcement is not doing the job for three reasons: first, because there is so much in sheer quantity of that kind of violence; second, because the law-enforcement agencies have been less than vigorous in doing their jobs; and third, because the general climate of fear associated with unions makes the best witnesses unwilling to cooperate. Senator Curtis made the appropriate observation when he said that Congress cannot provide a special policeman for every citizen in every city (10417, 10442). There is an effective remedy, however, as has been pointed out in Chapters 9 and 10. While indirect, it will eliminate a great part of the problem, and reduce what remains to dimensions which the police can handle, if the public does its part. These indirect remedies are inherent in the removal of the special privileges of monopolistic compulsion which have done so much to attract thugs and racketeers to the trade unions. When unions are no longer so attractive the thugs will go elsewhere; maybe they will even go to work. Then there will be less violence in connection with trade unionism; the climate of fear will to a large extent disappear; and there will not be so much money available to the thugs and racketeers with which to corrupt the police and other law-enforcement officials. The best solution lies, therefore, in the remedies to which we now turn.

MONOPOLISTIC COMPULSION

The special monopolistic privileges which attract racketeers to trade unions and which make possible the regimentation of the economy by the legitimate unions are the varieties of stranger-picketing, secondary boycotts, and compulsory unionism described in Chapter 2 and analyzed in Chapter 10. Their role in compelling union membership, in shaking down employers, in cartelizing industries, and in enserfing union members has been made clear beyond all possibility of mistake or misapprehension. It has also been established that most of them were prohibited by provisions of the Taft-Hartley Act which an earlier majority of the National Labor Relations Board virtually repealed and which the current majority has refused to enforce. Not much new law is needed here. It is a matter mainly of Congress's doing once and for all now what it intended to do in the Taft-Hartley Act. That Act was passed by overwhelming majorities in both Houses of Congress. The evils at which the Taft-Hartley Act was aimed are greater now than they were in 1947, when the Act was passed. If they needed correction then, the need now is desperate.

Picketing by Strangers. Stranger-picketing has been condemned as a particularly vicious form of monopolistic coercion of employees by practically all courts which have considered it. Senator McClellan and the other members of the Committee, observing it repeatedly in operation, thought it had to be prohibited (e.g., 10709, 12707), since it not only violated the free choice of employees which national labor policy seeks to promote, but also led to extortion, shakedowns, and such perversions as sweetheart contracts. Stanley Lehrer, an attorney representing small businessmen in New York City, told the Committee how his clients were victimized and shaken down by so-called organizational picketing. "The biggest weapon," he said, "is the picket." His small clients "could not get deliveries by truckdrivers who would refuse to cross the picket line." (3885) Senators Ives, Curtis, Mundt, and Goldwater all concluded from Mr. Lehrer's testimony that such picketing cannot be tolerated

(3890-3900). When pressed by Chief Counsel Kennedy to describe how he felt about the impositions forced upon his clients by the organizational picketing, Mr. Lehrer replied: "I would say it was the penalty for lack of proper legislation to avoid this very situation." (3904)

If the NLRB would do its sworn duty to apply the Taft-Hartley Act as it was intended, no legislation at all would be needed. But in the absence of such fidelity to their oath of office by the members of the NLRB, the Congress must make its intention unmistakable by an express provision, outlawing all picketing by strangers. The law should be amended to provide that picketing is permissible only to employees of the picketed employer, and then only in connection with a lawful strike called by a union representing a majority of employees in the bargaining unit.

Secondary Boycotts. The incomprehensible and labyrinthine complexities in which the NLRB has shrouded the law on secondary boycotts have been discussed in Chapter 10. It is necessary only to summarize here what was said there: the complexity is not the responsibility of the Taft-Hartley Act, which yields a perfectly clear set of rules upon a careful reading. The Circuit Courts of Appeals had no trouble understanding and applying the Act's boycott proscriptions until the NLRB fouled them up, as demonstrated in the monograph, *How the NLRB Repealed Taft-Hartley,* of whose existence the NLRB Solicitor was unaware when testifying before the Committee.

Most members of the Committee were stunned when they saw the kinds of regimentation which unions could exert through the various kinds of secondary boycotts which the NLRB has held privileged under the doctrines it has legislated—the hot-cargo privilege, the allies privilege, the common-situs privilege, the roving-situs privilege, and others. Senator Ervin observed, the reader will remember, that the Teamsters' boycotts made Attila the Hun seem benevolent. Senator McClellan could see no excuse for the secondary union pressures so long as employers may not impose secondary pressures upon strikers or employees generally (9810; see also 9680). Senators Curtis,

Mundt, and Goldwater took a firm stand against all secondary boycotts throughout the hearings.

As in the case of organizational picketing, so too here. Congress must re-legislate because of the failure of the NLRB to do its duty. A provision which will reach all forms of secondary pressure must be passed. This is not an easy task. In spite of the complaints of many so-called labor law experts, the present Taft-Hartley provision is phrased clearly, precisely, and unambiguously—exceptionally so, considering the complexity of the conduct with which it deals. There is nothing vague or contradictory in it at all. Of course it does not read as easily as a comic strip, but then labor law experts are supposed to be able to cope with precisely formulated legislation. For whatever it may be worth, the following provision is offered in substitution of present Section 8 (b) (4) of the Taft-Hartley Act. Readily understandable even to experts, it will, I believe, fairly prevent all forms of monopolistic union compulsion, while clearly safeguarding the right to strike.

> It shall be an unfair labor practice for a labor organization or its agents to induce or encourage any interruption or termination of an economic relationship or any refusal by any person to enter into such a relationship, whether by means of a work-stoppage, contractual arrangement, rule, picketing, or any other method or threat: *Provided* that nothing herein shall be construed as prohibiting a peaceful, primary strike concerning the wages and working conditions in an appropriate bargaining unit, called or ratified by the labor organization representing a majority of the employees in that bargaining unit: *Provided further* that nothing herein shall be construed as prohibiting appeals by a labor organization or its agents to the general consuming public, if such appeals contain no threat of reprisal or force and are not combined with activities violative of this or any other law.

Compulsory Unionism Agreements and Free Riders. Paul Bradshaw, a former union agent who told the Committee that he loved unions and that they were "just like a religion" to him (1758), said all there is to say about compulsory unionism agreements: that they are not acceptable in a free country. No employer should ever agree to one, and no legislature should ever

permit one. Senator Ives tried his best to shake Bradshaw, using
the spurious "free rider" argument, but Bradshaw would not
be shaken. He said that no man should be compelled to join a
union, even if the union's efforts benefited him. (1759) Unlike Senator Ives, he had had some real experience in the "labor
movement."

Unions and their apologists would be well advised to be very
quiet about the free-rider argument, for the big unions are the
real free riders, and the public will soon begin to appreciate that
fact.[6] They have not increased wages generally; they have,
rather, assumed more and more control over the disposition of
employee wages by the various forms of fringe benefits they have
imposed. The union leaders have had a long free ride on the
backs of the workers, consumers, and investors of the country: A
free ride which has permitted Walter Reuther to spend $10
million in an attempt to break the Kohler Company, the Carpen-
ter bosses to spend over $300,000 on a book about a past Car-
penter president, Hoffa to spread money around in local union
elections in which the contributing members have no interest,
Dave Beck, Ray Cohen, James Cross, and thousands of others to
live off the fat of the land.

If the unions do not keep very quiet about their fraudulent
free-rider argument, someone might even suggest that the
premise upon which it rests be erased; and that premise is one
which unions want very badly. The unions' free-rider argument rests on the premise that unions are compelled by law to
bargain nondiscriminatorily on behalf of *all* employees in the
bargaining unit, even though only a majority of those employees
choose freely to pay dues. Three points should be noted about
this requirement. *First,* it places no burden on the union whatsoever. One may be sure that unions expend no special efforts
upon securing benefits for the nonunion men in a bargaining
unit. If the nonunion men get anything, it is only an incidental
result of the union's efforts to get something for its own members. *Second,* the fact is that unions never produce anything at

[5] See the first-rate editorial, "Labor's Free Ride," in *Fortune,* Dec., 1955,
p. 97.

all; they cannot exact more than fair market wages without engaging in socially abusive conduct. Workers who do not wish to participate in and finance such conduct ought not to be forced to do so. *Third,* the exclusive bargaining principle is not something which the law has forced upon unions; it is something which the unions have sought and wish to retain, for it gives them almost the power over employees which compulsory unionism agreements provide—and may, indeed, be viewed as a species of compulsory unionism. In shrieking so much about free riders, the unions have managed to cover up the fact that they have been battening on *forced riders.*

If unions persist in complaining about free riders, the proper thing to do is to repeal the provision which makes them bargaining representatives for employees who do not want them. That provision is bad on principle, anyway, and if it were repealed there would be no need of an NLRB at all, for representation elections would no longer be necessary if unions were bargaining agents for only those employees who voluntarily designated them as such.

There is every reason in the world to prohibit all forms of compulsory unionism, and not a single valid reason to perpetuate it in any form. The Taft-Hartley Act should be amended to prohibit all devices which tie employment to union membership. Indeed, not a single word has to be added to the act in order to extirpate this incubus, and in that fact lies a very interesting point. The fundamental principle of the Taft-Hartley Act is the principle of free employee choice. Those portions of the act from which unions derive the power to compel dues-payments by unwilling employees are all in the form of exceptions or qualifications to basic principles and provisions of the act. These qualifications, to be found in Sections 7 and 8 (a) (3), need only be removed. When they are, the principle of free employee choice will emerge cleanly and coherently, and one of the worst evils America has ever known will disappear.

One final point must be emphasized. The compulsory membership contracts allowed by the Taft-Hartley Act are a special privilege. Every form of economic coercion is prohibited to employers. They may in no manner or form whatsoever make employment hinge upon *non*membership in a labor organization. They may not condition hiring on a promise by an employee to stay away from unions. They may not fire, threaten to fire, or in any other way put pressure on an employee for his taking up union membership. All these prohibitions rest upon the theory that an employee's choice of union membership should be completely free. That is the principle of free employee choice. Equally applied to unions, it would forbid compulsory union membership of every kind. Viewed in this light, the precise nature of the union's complaint about free riders may accurately be judged. It is the tireless and insatiable lust for power and special privilege expressed in still another form.

THE RIGHT TO A DAY IN COURT

The best laws in the world are not worth a tinker's damn if persons hurt by unlawful conduct cannot count upon immediate and direct access to the courts, and immediate relief from the courts. No person can measure the intolerable conditions prevailing in labor law until he realizes that most employers and employees in the country today have no access to the courts at all for injunctive relief against even the most coercive, destructive, and monopolistic trade-union conduct. They must bring their complaints to the National Labor Relations Board, and that agency has the power and discretion, it holds, to refuse to prosecute or to adjudicate virtually at will. Moreover, even if it decides to take a case, and if it decides to apply the law as written to the abusive union conduct, the NLRB's relief is too little and too late. Employers and nonunion employees may not go to the federal courts for immediate relief because the Norris-LaGuardia Act bars the way. They may not go to the state courts because the Supreme Court's pre-emption doctrine bars the way. Some employers and employees are completely without hope, of any kind. These are the small employers whose businesses affect interstate commerce, but who do too little interstate business to come within the NLRB's jurisdictional standards. As to them, also, the Supreme Court has held, access to state courts for relief is pre-empted.

These matters are explained in detail in Chapter 10, where the responsibility for the current conditions is allocated specifically, and where the supporting legal authorities are cited. Here we need emphasize only that if the unacceptable conditions in labor relations are to be remedied effectively, it is not enough to correct the deficiencies in the law. It is equally necessary to provide direct access to all courts, so that the remedies may be secured dependably and immediately. Law and law enforcement must go together or they do not go at all. Citations to this or that page of the McClellan Record would be supererogatory. *Every page* of the forty-odd volumes of the Record carries the story of victimization immunized by the failure of the legal system to provide immediate relief to the victims.

The Norris-LaGuardia Act. This law should be repealed. There is no excuse for a law which denies injunctive relief to persons suffering irreparable injury from clearly and plainly unlawful conduct. Injunctive relief against harmful conduct pending decisions on the merits is as important as the decisions themselves, even in the case of harmful conduct the legality of which is only dubious. When the conduct is clearly unlawful, and when, if continued during the process of decision it will ruin the victim, to withhold interim relief is shocking. It is the same as making conduct lawful procedurally when it is clearly unlawful substantively.

An age-old rule of equity holds that if more harm will be done to the injured party by withholding injunctive relief than to the party doing the injuring by granting it, the relief should be granted pending trial. In every single case of stranger-picketing and secondary boycotting, the injured employer and his employees are exposed to destruction if injunctive relief is withheld, while no harm at all accrues to the aggressor union if it is granted. If it turns out that the union's conduct is not unlawful, which will of course rarely be the case, the union action may be resumed without the slightest harm having been done. Conversely, if it turns out that the union action is unlawful, as will usually be the case, the greatest possible harm will have been done in the interim. As Tom Coffey pointed out to the Committee, he never lost a case before the courts or an election before the NLRB. But he lost his business. He lost his business because the Teamsters' vicious boycott was privileged to continue throughout the tortuous, long-drawn-out election procedures of the NLRB (Tr. 663).

The Norris-LaGuardia Act must be repealed if any decent labor policy is to be effective.

The NLRB. The NLRB should have its power to adjudicate in unfair practice cases withdrawn. The case for abolishing the NLRB totally, election procedures and all, is a strong one. But it is not immediately exigent and should therefore be postponed until Congress has had a chance to examine as coolly and deliberately the NLRB's performance in election cases as it has the NLRB's emasculation of the substantive provisions of the Taft-Hartley Act.

But no delay is needed in regard to the unfair practice cases. Self-respect requires Congress to take away from the Board the powers which it has so blatantly abused. But there are other, more powerful reasons for doing so. The Board is not now and never will be capable of doing the judicial job which has to be done. Its short-term political appointees can never be entrusted with the enforcement of *law.* That is a job for legal experts, the kind of job that only true judges can perform. They bring to legal decisions legal expertise, while the Board brings to them political considerations. Moreover, under the Constitution, such administrative agencies as the NLRB can never be given true judicial powers; those are reserved for true constitutional courts. Hence the Board can never afford to injured employers and employees the immediate relief which most cases of trade-union aggression require.

As long as the NLRB has the primary responsibility of enforcing the nation's labor laws, those laws will go unenforced, employees will continue to be victimized, extortion from employers will continue to flourish, and the nation will continue to pay grievously for the moral and material corruption which the McClellan Record discloses. The NLRB's judicial powers in unfair practice cases should be immediately revoked, and the Board should be continued temporarily as a purely administrative agency for the conducting of elections, with immediate access provided to the courts on legal issues in election cases as well as in unfair practice cases.

Pre-emption. In providing direct access to the courts in unfair practice cases, Congress should specifically declare that the injured parties may go to state and federal courts indiscriminately, subject to the rules of federal jurisdiction which have prevailed now for almost two hundred years. If the defending party feels that he will not get as fair treatment in the state court as he will in the federal court which has jurisdiction, he should be allowed to request removal—if the complaint is brought under federal law. If the complaint is brought under state law, then the procedure should be confined to the state court system, subject always to ultimate appeal to the U.S. Supreme Court for those who feel that the law applied by the state court conflicts with federal law.

The foregoing is the only sound and effective way to remedy the difficulties created by the Supreme Court's pre-emption doctrine. Some proposals designed to that end have already been submitted to Congress. However, they are defective because they still depend upon Supreme Court cooperation. They provide that the Court must not hold state jurisdiction pre-empted unless Congress expressly provides for exclusion of the states, or unless state laws conflict with federal laws. The trouble with such proposals is that they do no more than restate the legal theory which prevailed when the Supreme Court set forth on its pre-emption course. There is no reason to believe that the Court will change that course as a result of the proposals now under consideration. This point becomes clear when one realizes that the Court considers differences in procedures and remedies between the state courts and the NLRB to be conflicts of the same kind as conflicting substantive law. If the Congress does not abolish the NLRB as a judicial agency, and if it does not provide for direct access to state and federal courts for immediate injunctive relief, the Court will remain in a position to hold the state courts pre-empted. The leading pre-emption case, *Garner v. Teamsters*,[7] sounds the warning clearly. It ex-

[7] Garner v. Teamsters, 346 U.S. 485 (1953).

pressly states that differences in remedies provide as ample a base for pre-emption as conflicts in substantive law.

Congress must overrule the pre-emption doctrine. There is no question about that. But if it wishes to do so effectively it must abolish the NLRB as a judicial agency. It must do this because it is impossible to give the NLRB the kinds of judicial powers which the state and federal courts may exercise. And so long as that is true, there will always be conflicts between the remedies available from the NLRB and those available in the state courts, in the Supreme Court's sense. That conflict will be sufficient for the Supreme Court to continue the pre-emption doctrine, even under the defectively conceived antipre-emption laws now before Congress.

Ridding the nation of the pre-emption doctrine therefore requires ridding the nation of the NLRB as a judicial agency. From the point of view of the public interest, indeed from the point of view of the national integrity, perhaps even from the point of view of national survival—it will be good riddance to both.

In Conclusion: Some Questions and a Plea

The McClellan Investigation established the facts and dangers in labor relations. It also raised issues which go far beyond labor relations. The victimization of employees, employers, and society revealed by the Record constitutes a serious threat to the nation. But with that threat we have already dealt in the preceding pages. There is another kind of peril lurking behind the rank growth of corruption which we have been viewing: the threat to representative government. The plain fact is that the NLRB, with an assist from the Supreme Court, has been making a monkey of Congress, and that Congress has been taking this ignominious treatment for ten years without giving much of a sign that it even resents what is going on, much less doing something about it.

During the boycott hearings, the members of the Committee, including such astute men as Senator Curtis and Senator Ervin repeatedly expressed their confusion about the meaning of the Taft-Hartley Act. I have the greatest respect for the ability and integrity of these men, and do not by any means intend to condemn them. Nevertheless, the fact is that they petitioned the NLRB witnesses to explain the Taft-Hartley Act to them, although the NLRB has spent the last ten years emasculating the Act, and then seemed to accept at face value the contention of the NLRB personnel to the effect that their confusing explanation merely reflected the allegedly ambiguous and overly complicated language of the Act itself.

The allegedly confusing language of the Taft-Hartley boycott prohibition can be explained satisfactorily to any person of reasonable intelligence in not more than one hour. Its full meaning can be explored and understood in not more than five hours. I am in a position to testify on this issue with perfect certainty and authority. I have been explaining the Act to students for ten years, and I have had more than a thousand students in that period, all of whom have managed to master the Act's boycott proscriptions in less than five classroom hours. I am on the whole satisfied with the ability of my students, I should add, but only a small proportion reveal more than normal native ability and not many more work hard.

The confusion does not arise out of the Taft-Hartley Act. It arises out of the almost incomprehensible vagaries of the politically motivated NLRB decisions. Senator Ervin is an able man and a conscientious member of Congress. The Taft-Hartley Act is a product of the Congress of which he is a part. Is there not something seriously wrong in a country in which the ablest and best legislators do not understand their own laws? The gravity expands when one considers that the Taft-Hartley Act is one of the most significant internal measures ever passed in the history of this country.

Can representative government work if the time of legislators is so absorbed by the eternal quest of pressure groups for special privileges that they have neither time nor energy to understand what the existing, necessary laws provide and whether or not they are being faithfully administered?

The McClellan Record demonstrates the fundamental culpability of the Federal Government for the intolerable conditions which exist in labor relations. Attacks on thugs, racketeers, and power-hungry union leaders miss the real point. The real problem, the real fault, lies in a theory of government which insures an awful paradox: a virtual anarchy within a plethora of laws. We have thousands upon thousands of rules and statutes, millions upon millions of government employees. Yet we have no *law*.

The ultimate responsibility falls to the public. But this fact does not absolve the members of the government from all responsibility. It is their job to inform the public that they cannot deal with all the things which the special privilege groups are seeking and still run a decent government in the *general* welfare. Then it is the job of the public to understand that government, like all other human institutions, has very narrow limits. It may be able to do a fair job of providing for the national defense, of keeping the peace, of enforcing the laws, and of administering justice in the courts—if it devotes all its time and energy to those difficult tasks. But it cannot do those things at all, as the McClellan Record so vividly demonstrates, if its energies are expended on every pet project upon which every pressure group from the National Education Association to the National Committee for the Protection of Tropical Fish comes running to Washington for help.

I do not know of any short way to bring about limited and therefore effective government in this country; that will come only when large numbers of people appreciate its value and insist upon it. Yet I am convinced that the jungle, retrogression, and decay are the necessary result of unlimited government, just as they are the necessary result of unlimited power in trade unions. No civilization can long survive unlimited power in any hands. The greatest contribution of the McClellan Committee lies in its overwhelming documentation of that truth.

DOCUMENTARY NOTE

The source of the facts recounted in this book, with a few exceptions, is the Record of the McClellan Committee, a record which ran to 15,000 consecutively numbered pages, published in 39 volumes (called "Parts"), as of the time this book was completed, early in January, 1959. The vast preponderance of the numerical references found in the text of this book are to that printed Record. A few are to the McClellan Committee's Interim Report, published in March, 1958, and are in each instance identified as such. Another few are to the mimeographed Transcript of the McClellan Record, involving matters disclosed at the November 13–20, 1958, Hearings, and not yet published in printed form, as of January, 1959. These references are in each instance identified as "Tr." or "Transcript." Ultimately, the mimeographed materials will become a part of the printed Record, probably Parts 40–42, depending on how much space they require in print. In one or two cases, involving matters revealed very late in the Hearings, references are to *The New York Times* news reports, normally a dependable source.

The full name of the McClellan Committee is: The (Senate) Select Committee on Improper Activities in the Labor or Management Field. Its hearings began on February 26, 1957 and are continuing during 1959. The members were, when hearings opened, Senators John L. McClellan, Chairman; Irving M. Ives, Vice Chairman; John F. Kennedy; Sam J. Ervin, Jr.; Pat McNamara; Joseph R. McCarthy; Karl E. Mundt; and Barry Goldwater. Senator Frank Church took Senator McNamara's place and Senator Carl T. Curtis took the place left vacant by Senator McCarthy's death. Robert F. Kennedy has been Chief Counsel to the Committee since its inception. Ruth Young Watt has been its Chief Clerk.

The official title of the Record is: *Hearings Before the Select Committee on Improper Activities in the Labor or Management Field* (85th Congress, 2d Session).

The Interim Report is officially identified as: *Interim Report of the Select Committee on Improper Activities in the Labor or Management Field*, United States Senate, Report No. 1417, 85th Congress, 2d Session (March 24, 1958).

Other sources are fully identified as and where cited.

NAME INDEX

This index contains references to witnesses and other individuals mentioned in the McClellan Committee Hearings.

SUBJECT INDEX

This index includes references to unions, companies and other organizations, and authors quoted.